Aunt Phil's Trunk

Volume Three

Bringing Alaska's history alive!

By
Phyllis Downing Carlson
Laurel Downing Bill

Aunt Phil's Trunk LLC
Anchorage, Alaska

www.auntphilstrunk.com

Front cover redesigned by Laurel Downing Bill in 2013. Photo credits from top left: salmon pickers, Anchorage Museum of History and Art, Ward W. Wells Collection, AMRC-wws-156-R23; Wiley Post, University of Alaska Fairbanks, Wiley Post-Flat Alaska Collection, 1933, UAF-1998-129-3; Native voter, University of Alaska Fairbanks, Mary Cox Collection, UAF-2001-129-111; car and train on tracks, Alaska State Library, President Harding's Trip to Alaska, ASL-P418-7; bi-plane, University of Alaska Fairbanks, Frederick B. Drane Collection, UAF-1991-46-759; baseball team, University of Alaska Anchorage, Marie Silverman Collection, UAA-hmc-0778-5-14; little girls in parkas, Alaska State Library, Dr. Daniel S. Neuman Collection, ASL-P307-0104; and swimmers, University of Alaska Anchorage, Marie Silverman Collection, UAA-hmc-0778-4-99.

Back cover photo credits, from left: Dogs on tracks, Seward Community Library, Sylvia Sexton Collection, SCL-1-688; Skagway streetcar, Anchorage Museum of History and Art, General Photograph File, AMRC-b88-3-67; and first U.S. Mail plane, University of Alaska Fairbanks, Edward Lewis Bartlett, UAF-1969-95-464.

International Standard Book Number 978-1-940479-24-8
Library of Congress Control Number 2008908361

Printed and bound in the United States of America.

First Printing 2008
Second Printing 2010
First Printing Second Edition 2015
First Printing Third Edition 2018

DEDICATION

I dedicate this first revision of *Aunt Phil's Trunk* Volume Three to the memory of my paternal aunt, Phyllis Downing Carlson. She was one of Alaska's most respected historians, and without her lifelong interest, and then researching and writing about Alaska, this series would never exist.

I also want to dedicate the work to Aunt Phil's stepchildren, grandchildren, great-grandchildren and their families; to my brothers and sisters, their families and all our cousins. And I dedicate the work to my husband, Donald; daughter Kim and her husband, Bruce Sherry; son Ryan Bill and his wife, Kaboo; and daughter Amie and her husband, Toby Barnes. Thank you so much for believing in me.

Lastly, I dedicate this collection of historical stories to my grandchildren, Sophia Isobel and Maya Josephine Sherry; Aiden Kou and Fischer Nhia Bill; and Toben Alexander, Connor Vincent and Zachary Victor Barnes. They remind me how important it is to preserve our past for their future.

ACKNOWLEDGMENTS

I owe an infinite debt of gratitude to the University of Alaska Anchorage, the University of Alaska Fairbanks, the Anchorage Museum of History and Art, the Alaska State Library in Juneau, the Z.J. Loussac Public Library in Anchorage, the Seward Community Library and the University of Washington for helping me collect the photographs for this book. Without the patient and capable staffs at these institutions, the following pages may not have been filled.

I want to extend a heart-felt thank you to Robert DeBerry of Wasilla for his excellent attention to detail as he readied for publication the historical photographs that appear in Volume Three of *Aunt Phil's Trunk*. I also am extremely grateful to Nancy Pounds of Anchorage for slaving away with her eagle eyes to carefully proofread the pages. And special thanks to Joe Koczan of Harlingen, Texas, for keeping me on track to finish the book when I sometimes just wanted to bask in the warm sunshine of Southern Texas.

My family deserves medals, as well, for putting up with me as I chased down just the right photographs to go with Aunt Phil's stories, pored over notes and the collection of rare books that make up Aunt Phil's library and sat hunched over my computer for hours blending selections of Aunt Phil's work with stories from my own research.

Aunt Phil's Files

Aunt Phil's Trunk Volume Three is filled with stories about the birth of Anchorage and the Matanuska Valley, the early days of daredevil flyboys and other tales of courage and fortitude shown by Alaska's early pioneers.

T A B L E   O F   C O N T E N T S

TABLE OF CONTENTS

Early Cook Inlet

1

Cook Inlet Timeline

As late as 1914, there was no town at the head of Cook Inlet. There was only a spot called Ship Creek, where small ships entered because the water was deep enough to transport cargo to trading posts scattered in the area.

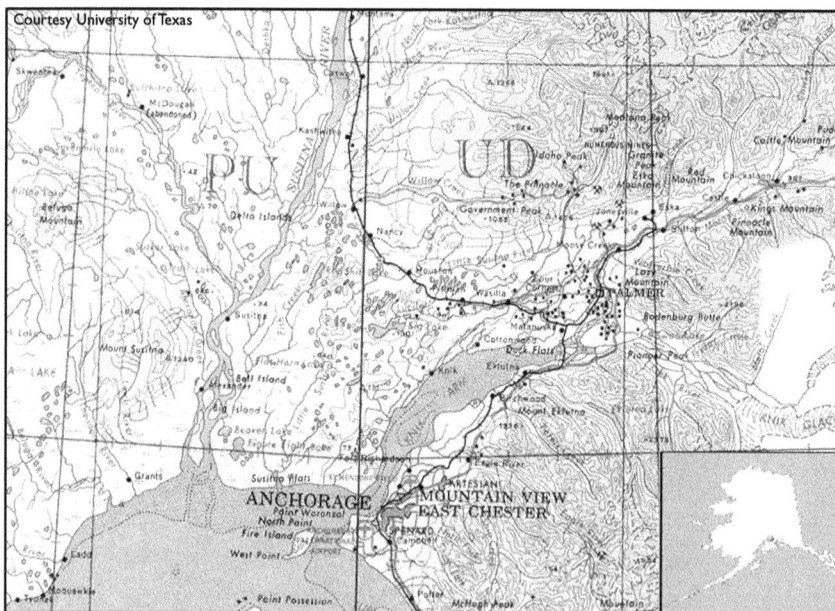

Large ships anchored off Fire Island, lower center left, and freight then was transferred to smaller ships that carried cargo to settlements up Knik Arm.

Based on anthropological data from the Beluga Point area near Anchorage, the earliest-known human habitation of the Cook Inlet area was by Eskimo people about 3000 B.C.

But long before white settlers plied the waters of Cook Inlet, Native Alaskans roamed the territory living a subsistence lifestyle in the bountiful country.

Early human habitation

According to anthropological research around Beluga Point in Southcentral Alaska, human occupation of Cook Inlet occurred in three waves: the first wave of Alutiiq Eskimos around 3000 B.C., the second in 2000 B.C. and the third at the start of the new millennium.

Athabaskan Dena'ina Indians entered Cook Inlet through mountain passes to the west as early as 500 A.D. and as late as 1650 A.D., displacing the Eskimos.

It is estimated that more than 5,000 Dena'ina inhabited the Southcentral area at first contact with Europeans in 1756.

The Dena'ina, also called Tanaina, adapted the Alutiiq peoples' knowledge of living in a coastal region, such as using kayaks for saltwater fishing, and subsisted entirely on the fisheries and wildlife.

They migrated with the seasons, fishing inlet streams and hunting goat and sheep along the upper reaches of Ship Creek in the summer.

Natives made summer shelters from willows bent into shape and covered with skins.

In the fall, they hunted caribou in the foothills and moose and beaver in the basin. The Indians spent winters at trading route junctions, where they traded with the Ahtna Indians of the Copper River and Dena'ina who lived on the lower inlet at Point McKenzie.

1778: Capt. Cook enters Southcentral

Recent research indicates that it was Dena'ina Indians that met Capt. James Cook in May 1778 when he entered what is now known as Cook Inlet. Cook did not name the inlet – instead he called it "River Turnagain." British Lord Sandwich later ordered that it be called "Cook's River." Explorer George Vancouver changed "River" to "Inlet" in 1792.

During his exploration of the coast, Cook noted that "there is not the least doubt that a very beneficial fur trade might be carried on with the inhabitants of this vast coast. But unless a Northern passage should be found practicable, it seems rather too remote for Great Britain to receive any emolument from it."

While on his third voyage of discovery in 1778, English explorer Capt. James Cook mistook one of the arms of Cook Inlet for a river and named it River Turnagain.

1786: Russians build trading posts

The Russian Shelekhov-Golikov Company established a trading post at English Bay near the mouth of Cook Inlet in 1786. Farther up the inlet, rival Lebedev-Lastochkin Company founded Fort St. George at Kasilof, and in 1791, built Nikolaevsk Redoubt at Kenai above Kasilof.

The only Russian trading post on the upper Cook Inlet was at Niteh, on the delta between the Knik and Matanuska rivers. And Russian Orthodox missionaries established a mission at Knik, on the western shore of Knik Arm, in 1835.

By 1845, the Dena'ina population in villages like Tyonek, pictured here around 1900, was decimated by smallpox.

1839: Russians bring disease

But along with their language and religion, the Russians brought smallpox and tuberculosis. The population of the Dena'ina in the upper inlet plummeted to 816 by 1845, half of what the Russians had counted when they'd arrived 10 years earlier.

By 1850, after Czar Paul I granted a monopoly to the Shelekhov-Golikov group, former Russian workers established small agricultural settlements along Cook Inlet at Seldovia, Ninilchik and Eklutna.

Russian-American Company employee Petr Doroshin was sent to look for minerals along the Kenai River area in 1849. During two seasons, he found gold in almost all the valleys, streams and canyons he covered and coal deposits at Port Graham.

1867: America purchases Alaska

Due to mounting diplomatic problems in Europe and Asia, the Russians sold Alaska to the United States for $7.2 million in 1867.

The fur trade continued to be an important economic activity as Americans streamed into the former Russian colony, and although the sea otter continued to be the most valuable fur, other furbearers like mink, marten, land otter, fox, beaver, muskrat, bear, lynx and wolverine brought good prices as well.

Fishing and fish processing also grew in importance for the Cook Inlet economy. Hundreds of fishing boats harvested salmon, herring, halibut, crab and clams.

Prospectors looking for gold entered the region, too. Some crossed the Portage Pass from Prince William Sound to Turnagain Arm, while others traveled up the Susitna River.

Large ships stopped at Tyonek, a Dena'ina village on the northwest shore of Cook Inlet, where travelers transferred to smaller boats that could enter Knik and Turnagain arms on high tide.

Prospectors, trappers and Alaska Natives soon were trading at Alaska Commercial Company stores established at Tyonek, Knik and Susitna Station. By 1900, AC was operating a dozen trading stations in Cook Inlet, from Cape Douglas in the south to the head of Knik Arm in the north.

Over time, Americans hacked out primitive trails connecting scattered camps and eventually unified the region between Cook Inlet on the south and the Talkeetna Mountains on the north, and the Matanuska River in the east and the Susitna River in the west.

1888: Turnagain gold discovered

When Alexander King discovered gold around Kenai in 1888 and Resurrection Creek in 1893, thousands of hopeful miners streamed into Cook Inlet. Towns like Sunrise, Hope and Girdwood grew up out of the timbers in the Turnagain District between 1895-1897.

Alaska State Library, Maynard C. Dahlstrom Collection, ASL-P414-372

Col. James Girdwood staked a placer claim at Crow Creek in 1896. He named the community Glacier City, but it later was renamed Girdwood.

When Al King discovered gold in Southcentral Alaska in 1888, many prospectors, like the man pictured here, headed up the creeks and valleys in search of their fortunes.

1897-98: Klondike gold rush

The captain of the schooner *L.J. Perry* brought news that emptied the boomtown settlements in Southcentral Alaska. Capt. Austin E. Lathrop, an entrepreneur who hauled supplies and prospectors to and from Tyonek, told the miners about the Klondike Gold Rush.

Stampeders, who had to travel to St. Michael or Skagway to get to the rich diggings in the Yukon or the gold fields at Rampart and Circle City, began demanding an all-American route be blazed.

The U.S. government sent expeditions to study possible routes through Alaska's wilderness. U.S. Army Capt. William Abercrombie started at Valdez, where stampeders were scaling the Valdez Glacier to reach the Klutina River, a tributary of the Copper River.

Another Army officer, Capt. Edwin Forbes Glenn, set out to find a glacier-free route from Portage Bay on Prince William Sound to Turnagain Arm, as well as to find a way to Interior Alaska by going up the Matanuska and Susitna rivers.

Among the resulting recommendations, Glenn said he thought a military base could be located "at or near Palmer's cache [George W. Palmer opened a store at Knik around 1880] which is the head of navigation, and where good anchorage can be obtained for seagoing vessels."

He also wrote that he had "no doubt that a railroad could be readily constructed from Tyoonok [sic] up the Sushitna [sic] River Valley and thence via the trail followed by the Van Schoonhoven party to the Tanana," but it probably was not warranted since there was little agricultural or mineral resource development in the Cook Inlet area.

A little more than a decade later, the government deemed that a railroad was indeed warranted.

University of Alaska Anchorage, Edwin Forbes Glenn Papers, 1889-1917, UAA-hmc-0116-series3a-25-1

Capt. Edwin Forbes Glenn and Capt. Culp navigated on snowshoes around Portage Bay, located in Prince William Sound, while they searched for a suitable route to the gold fields.

Mr. and Mrs. Bud Whitney, pioneers in the Ship Creek area in 1911, were among the first homesteaders in Cook Inlet. Whitney Road in Anchorage was named after them.

1898: Alaska Homestead Law

Congress extended homesteading to Alaska under the Alaska Homestead Law in 1898. It differed from the original provisions of the 1862 law, which covered the rest of the United States, in that a homesteader was limited to 80 acres and limited entry to surveyed land.

Since little Alaska land had been surveyed at the time, and surveys were expensive and the land remote, the law was amended in 1903. The amendment expanded the acreage to a maximum of 320 acres.

The act again was revised in 1912, when Congress passed the Three Year Homestead Law. It reduced the length of residence required, specified the amount of land to be cultivated and changed the requirements for absences from the property.

1912: Alaska becomes a U.S. territory

Congress passed the Territorial Organic Act of 1912 that made Alaska a U.S. territory.

1914: Congress passes Alaska Railroad Act

The Alaska Railroad Bill, which overwhelmingly passed in both the U.S. House and Senate, authorized the president to locate, construct and operate a railroad that would unite the Pacific Ocean with the navigable waters of Interior Alaska.

points as the General Superintendent of the Life-Saving Service may recommend.

Sec. 2. That the Secretary of the Treasury be, and he is hereby, authorized and directed to provide increased quarantine facilities at the port of Portland, Maine, to cost not exceeding forty-three thousand eight hundred and eighty dollars.

Approved, August 24, 1912.

Portland, Me.
Quarantine facilities to be increased.
Post, p. 597.

August 24, 1912.
[H. R. 26414.]
[Public, No. 333.]

CHAP. 386.—An Act To authorize the Government of Porto Rico to construct a bridge across the Cano de Martin Pena, an estuary of the harbor of San Juan, Porto Rico.

Be it enacted by the Senate and House of Representatives of the United States of America in Congress assembled, That the government of Porto Rico be, and is hereby, authorized to construct, maintain, and operate a bridge and approaches thereto across the Cano de Martin Pena, an estuary of San Juan Bay, Porto Rico, in accordance with the provisions of the Act entitled "An Act to regulate the construction of bridges over navigable waters," approved March twenty-third, nineteen hundred and six.

Sec. 2. That the right to alter, amend, or repeal this Act is hereby expressly reserved.

Approved, August 24, 1912.

Cano de Martin Pena.
Porto Rico, may construct bridge.
Vol. 34, p. 84.

Amendment.

August 24, 1912.
[H. R. 38.]
[Public, No. 334.]

CHAP. 387.—An Act To create a legislative assembly in the Territory of Alaska, to confer legislative power thereon, and for other purposes.

Be it enacted by the Senate and House of Representatives of the United States of America in Congress assembled,

ALASKA TERRITORY ORGANIZED.—That the territory ceded to the United States by Russia by the treaty of March thirtieth, eighteen hundred and sixty-seven, and known as Alaska, shall be and constitute the Territory of Alaska under the laws of the United States, the government of which shall be organized and administered as provided by said laws.

Sec. 2. CAPITAL AT JUNEAU.—That the capital of the Territory of Alaska shall be at the city of Juneau, Alaska, and the seat of government shall be maintained there.

Sec. 3. CONSTITUTION AND LAWS OF UNITED STATES EXTENDED.—That the Constitution of the United States, and all the laws thereof which are not locally inapplicable, shall have the same force and effect within the said Territory as elsewhere in the United States; that all the laws of the United States heretofore passed establishing the executive and judicial departments in Alaska shall continue in full force and effect until amended or repealed by Act of Congress; that except as herein provided all laws now in force in Alaska shall continue in full force and effect until altered, amended, or repealed by Congress or by the legislature: *Provided,* That the authority herein granted to the legislature to alter, amend, modify, and repeal laws in force in Alaska shall not extend to the customs, internal-revenue, postal, or other general laws of the United States or to the game, fish, and fur-seal laws and laws relating to fur-bearing animals of the United States applicable to Alaska, or to the laws of the United States providing for taxes on business and trade, or to the Act entitled "An Act to provide for the construction and maintenance of roads, the establishment and maintenance of schools, and the care and support of insane persons in the District of Alaska, and for other purposes," approved January twenty-seventh, nineteen hun-

Alaska.
Territorial organization for.
Vol. 15, p. 534.

Capital at Juneau.

Constitution and laws extended.

Provisos.
Restriction on altering, etc., specified laws in force.

Vol. 33, p. 616.

From the text of the document that made Alaska a U.S. territory: "Be it enacted by the Senate and House of Representatives of the United States of America in Congress assembled,

– That the territory ceded to the United States by Russia by the treaty of March thirtieth, eighteen hundred and sixty seven, and known as Alaska, shall be and constitute the Territory of Alaska under the laws of the United States, the government of which shall be organized and administered as provided by said laws.

– That the capital of the Territory of Alaska shall be at the city of Juneau, Alaska, and the seat of government shall be maintained there."

2

RAILROAD MAKES HEADLINES

EXTRA! EXTRA! Read all about it! Banner headlines shouted across America that Germany had invaded Belgium in August 1914. World War I was officially under way.

But something else was under way in the nation's northernmost territory. Congress had authorized construction of an Alaska railroad, and the Seward newspaper's headline proclaimed that its little port city would become the terminus for the project.

Late one afternoon that August, according to an article by Clark Dinsmore in the *Alaska Sportsman*, a "few loafers were hanging around the half-empty saloons, housewives were shopping for their Sunday dinners, children played in the streets and on the wharves a few boatmen were idly passing their time.

"Suddenly out of the printing office of the *Seward Gateway* burst a group of newsboys shouting 'EXTRA! EXTRA!'

"An extra in a small town like Seward is a sensation, but more sensational was the news. The United States Government had chosen Seward as the saltwater terminus for its proposed Government Railroad!"

That was welcome news to the residents of Seward, who had seen two railroads go bust in the past decade – railroads that had offered the promise of delivering Alaska's rich resources to tidewater and jobs to those in the picturesque little town in Prince William Sound.

Before the announcement that the federal government was going to build a railroad to the Matanuska coalfields and beyond, it was a common sight to see dog teams pulling handcars along the tracks that already had been laid in Seward.

Seward, which started as a railroad camp in 1903 on the west shore of Resurrection Bay, had been awaiting a resurrection of its own – and the stunning news report suggested this was it. Seward was to be the headquarters for the new railroad.

Houses, which the owners practically would have given away earlier in the day, were selling at boom prices by the afternoon. Speculators swallowed up choice lots. New stores opened and stores already there worked feverishly to expand and enlarge. Building went on around the clock.

Boatloads of men arrived from the states seeking work on the new railroad, which was to be built from the deepwater port of Seward to Alaska's Interior where abundant resources like Matanuska coal and Fairbanks gold awaited transportation to the coast.

It looked like Seward was on its way to fulfilling the prophesy of the man who thought it would become the most important city in Alaska, perhaps boasting a population of 500,000.

John F. Ballaine, the city's founder, was convinced the new town would one day be the metropolis of a great territory and should fittingly bear the name of the man who foresaw the primacy of the Pacific Ocean in the world's future.

Seward Community Library, Sylvia Sexton Collection, SCL-1-598

Above: Seward's deepwater port in Resurrection Bay, seen here around 1908, made it an ideal spot for a railroad terminus.

Below: By 1909, several businesses lined Fourth Avenue in Seward. Seen here are Brown & Hawkins, Northern Hotel, Palace Saloon and Ellsworth Chemist.

Seward Community Library, Sylvia Sexton Collection, SCL-1-603

Alaska Central Railway formed and began construction in Seward in 1902. Its first engine is seen here arriving by steamship in 1904.

President Theodore Roosevelt agreed that the town on the Kenai Peninsula should be named for U.S. Secretary of State William H. Seward.

"You are quite right," Roosevelt said to Ballaine when he broached him with his choice for the town's name. "This railroad should give rise to an important city at the ocean terminus. The city deserves to be named in honor of the man who is responsible for making Alaska an American territory."

The formation of what later became the Alaska Railroad actually started in 1902 with the creation of the Alaska Central Railway, Ballaine's brainchild. The real estate and newspaperman from Seattle saw an opportunity to open a trans-Alaska route to the Yukon and chose Resurrection Bay as his terminus. The route he started building from Seward in 1903 was close to what the Alaska Engineering Commission would study 11 years later.

But Ballaine never realized his dream. Due to rough terrain, lack of capital and closure of coalfields by the federal government in 1906, his Alaska Central Railroad went bankrupt in 1908. It reorganized as the Alaska Northern in 1910.

The new company continued to push single-track standard gauge line, and about 20 more miles were added to the old Alaska Central right of way that brought it to Kern Creek at the upper end of Turnagain Arm. From this railhead the tracks met boats that came up the arm and freight that went out over the Iditarod Trail from this point, 71 miles from Seward.

At no time was the railroad even able to earn out-of-pocket expenses. Its "tracks, bridges and docks were not adequately maintained, and by 1914 it was hardly in operating condition except for light gasoline-driven equipment used from Seward to Mile 16 when snow slides didn't interfere," wrote Edwin M. Fitch, in his book, "The Alaska Railroad."

By 1912, Judge James Wickersham, then Alaska's delegate to Congress, urged both houses to pass legislation enabling the government to build a railroad in Alaska along a route to be determined by the president.

President Woodrow Wilson signed the Alaska Railroad Act into law in 1914 and Secretary of Interior Franklin Lane appointed three men, geologist Thomas Riggs and experienced railroad builders

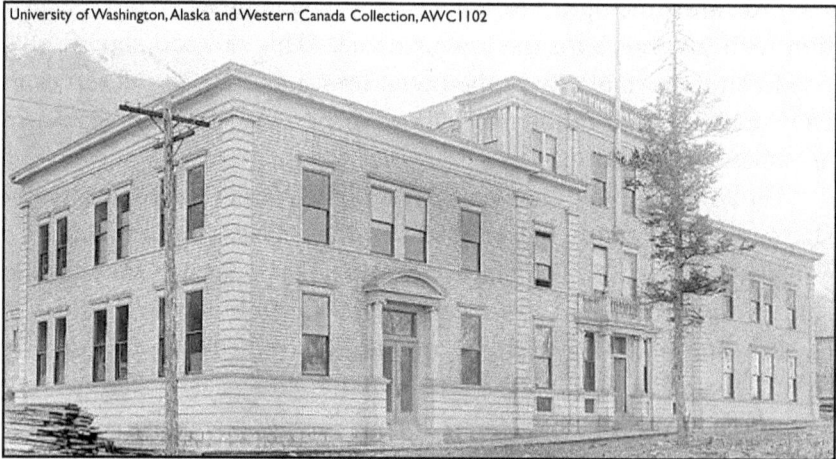

University of Washington, Alaska and Western Canada Collection, AWC1102

The Alaska Engineering Commission occupied this building in 1914 after Seward was chosen as the headquarters for the government's new railroad to Interior Alaska. The building, which had been constructed in 1906, previously housed the Alaska Central Railway.

William C. Edes and Lt. Frederick Mears, to the Alaska Engineering Commission.

Eleven survey parties spent the summer of 1914 examining possible routes for the proposed railroad. Edes and Mears determined a site located on Ship Creek in Cook Inlet provided easy access to the Matanuska coalfields and Fairbanks gold deposits. It also had ample land for a large construction camp, coal bunkers and railroad yards, and offered a port that was ice-free for about six months of the year.

On April 10, 1915, President Woodrow Wilson selected the "Susitna Route," running from Seward through the Kenai Peninsula, the Matanuska Valley and to the Nenana lignite coalfields.

Officials hoped that the Nenana coalfields might end the Fairbanks fuel famine and revive the declining gold mining industry. They also hoped that coal from the Matanuska fields could be carried from Ship Creek to Seward and on to markets outside Alaska.

And so the government's choice of Seward as the terminus for its railroad, estimated to cost $35 million, breathed new life into Ballaine's dream. It appeared that the town's destiny might be fulfilled after all.

But as land prices in Seward ballooned and Ship Creek's central location to the entire project became more evident, officials decided to move operations from Seward.

By early 1915, Ship Creek, which was originally foreseen only as a construction camp, was chosen as the headquarters for the government's large-scale project.

Residents of Seward weren't happy when the railroad headquarters was established at Anchorage instead of their town. The reason for the change, officials said, was because the government was confronted with legal obstructions and high prices in its purchase of the Alaska Northern and surrounding property.

The decision angered one man who thought he'd make a killing from selling his Seward property. Pat P. Cotter blamed his losses on AEC commissioners Edes and Mears, as well as Andrew Christensen, superintendent of lot sales in the new townsite at Ship Creek. Cotter wrote a poem, which was widely distributed, to express his feelings.

"The Unholy Trinity"
By Pat P. Cotter
(From Legends & Legacies by John P. Bagoy)

A little group of willful men,
Edes and Mears and Christensen,
Are running a scheme of common cause,
And barely keeping within the laws,
Wrecking a country they were sent to save
And this will follow them to the grave,
This self-same group of little men,
Edes and Mears and Christensen.

The first is a relic of bygone days,
Too old to curse, to poor to praise,
The dean of the willful Trinity
Is a relic of scrap from the old S.P.,
Doddering, old, decrepit and all,
He could only hear "his country's call"
When they told him the wages paid this mob,
He tottered North on his farewell job.

And Mears, the ward of the Grape Juice King,
A political pet from the Panama Ring,
Sulky and silent and fearing a fall,
Though raised to a Captain, he hears no call,
Clings like grim death and obsessed by fear
Lest someone might steal his ten thousand a year,
Wanting to go and fearing to flee,
The first and the last of the Trinity.

And Andy, the Czar of official greed,
Cunning and crafty, a red tape Swede,
Staking his all on a side track spur,
Sneaking his scraps like an alien cur;
Selling townsites and missing the pen
By rating as one of "Our Government men."
Shall we stand for this Swede in the north country,
The brains and the boss of the Trinity.

Tell us ye group of little men,
Edes and Mears and Christensen;
Tell us the money you've spent and lost
Give us the Anchorage townsite cost,
The money you spent on graded roads,
Thrice built bungalows for your abodes;
Ships that your incompetence lost,
Oh! Tell us, Trinity, what was the cost?

Christ cleared the temple in olden days
And drove the grafters and thieves away.
Won't Congress do what Christ has done,
And give this Trinity gang the run,
And send us one man to build the road,
Forgetting townsites and his own abode;
And there is only one thing we want him to do
It's open the country and put the road through,
And tie the can to three little men,
Edes and Mears and Christensen.

3

KNIK WITHERS

Railroad officials didn't make the people of Knik happy, either. Located a few miles south of Big Lake on Cook Inlet, the town suffered a significant loss of its population when the government planned the railroad route north.

The residents of Knik, which had become a thriving supply center during the late 1890s, first started trading with white men when the Russians established a mission there in 1834.

Anchorage Museum of History and Art, General Photograph File, AMRC-b63-16-34x

This view of Knik was taken looking back from the beach. Businesses shown include Knik Trading Company, Knik Roadhouse and Knik Bend Hotel.

INSPECTING
PALMERS LAUNCH
KNIK APRIL 16/07

A crowd gathered on the beach in Knik to see George W. Palmer's launch in 1907.

The Russians converted the Dena'ina Indians to Christianity and began trading with them and through them with the Indians of Interior Alaska.

After the American purchase of Alaska, George W. Palmer opened a store there in the 1880s called Palmer's Cache. It relied upon the local fur trade.

Knik, an Indian name meaning "fire," also supplied the Willow Creek Mining District, which organized in 1898. However, the combined efforts of the various mining enterprises only came to $30,000 in that district between 1897 and 1914.

But activities in other parts of Alaska breathed life into the little settlement.

Gold found in the Interior in 1903 brought prospectors and supplies to Knik, where they then disembarked and headed north. Construction of the Iditarod Trail brought mail bound for Nome, and shipments of gold by dog team came back down the trail to meet boats at Knik.

Then gold was found in the Talkeetna Mountains to the north and coal discovered in the Matanuska Valley.

Knik soon became the major trading center for the gold and coal mines, as well as the supplier for various sawmills in the Matanuska Valley, Susitna River Basin and Willow mining area.

Mining in the Willow Creek district during the summer and travel to and from the Iditarod District in the winter promoted growth in the tiny village, which by 1910 boasted 118 residents.

One of the town's highlights happened on Jan. 10, 1912, when 33 dogs pulled two freight sleds loaded with 2,600 pounds of gold into Knik from Iditarod on the Kuskokwim River.

Knik prospered for several years and men like the Bartholf brothers and Robert Hatcher built wagon roads to handle heavy machinery needed for lode mining operations.

By 1913, the town was home to 500 people during the summer and 1,000 during the winter. It had a post office, four docks, a grade school and a four-page weekly newspaper called the *Knik News*.

It also featured several businesses, including two trading posts, three roadhouses, a restaurant, a hardware store, a saloon, a barbershop and two physicians.

Anchorage Museum of History and Art, General Photograph File, AMRC-b67-1-123

Small ships sailed up Knik Arm to load and off-load goods at Knik.

But the Alaska Railroad Act of 1914 spelled the end of Knik.

At first, Knik's residents welcomed the announcement. They expected their town to be an important stop on the railroad.

But surveying crews defined the railroad right of way a few miles to the northeast of Knik and located a construction camp where the railroad route intersected the wagon road from Knik to the Hatcher Pass mines. That camp was named Wasilla, after Athabaskan Chief Vasilie.

So the route chosen to connect Seward to the Matanuska coalfields and on to Fairbanks bypassed the community on Knik Arm, and its residents eventually moved to either Wasilla or the railroad camp on Ship Creek called Anchorage. Knik became a ghost town.

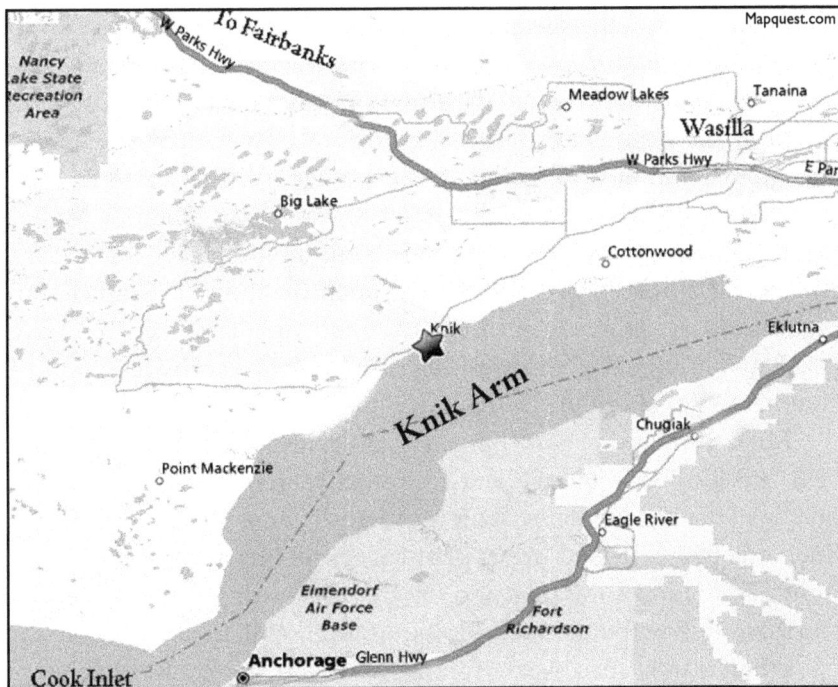

The Alaska Railroad planners charted a course that bypassed Knik.

EARLY RAILROAD DAYS

4

RAILROAD BIRTHS ANCHORAGE

The history of Anchorage is firmly tied to the history of the Alaska Railroad. At first the Alaska Engineering Commission, which was created in 1914 and developed the railroad, only saw the site at Ship Creek as a major construction camp and terminal point along a route to link Seward with Interior Alaska.

But its central location to the entire railway, and skyrocketing land prices in the deepwater port of Seward, caused the commission to change its mind in 1915 and make Anchorage its headquarters.

In 1911, President Howard Taft's Secretary of the Interior, Walter L. Fisher, urged the federal government to purchase the Alaska Northern Railroad out of Seward to open up the rich Southcentral region of the territory. And in 1912, under the same act that gave Alaskans "home rule," the president was given authority to appoint a commission to study the railroad question.

Taft's commission was charged with reporting what routes would best "develop the country and resources thereof for the use of the people of the United States." A few months later, it recommended two lines: one that extended the Copper River and Northwestern Railway from Cordova to Fairbanks and another that would link the Alaska Northern line with the Innoko-Iditarod mining district.

When Taft's successor, Woodrow Wilson, took office, he was reluctant to move on recommendations made by his predecessor.

But Wilson strongly supported the idea of a railroad in the nation's northernmost territory and made a speech that foretold the role his administration would play in developing the Alaska Railroad.

"Alaska, as a storehouse, should be unlocked. One key to it is a system of railways. ... These the government should itself build and administer, and the ports and terminals it should itself control in the interest of all who wish to use them for the service and development of the country and its people."

In 1914, Congress created the Alaska Engineering Commission, and in 1915, President Woodrow Wilson, seen here, authorized funds for the construction of the Alaska Railroad.

Determined to carry out his desire to have the federal government develop a railway system in Alaska, President Wilson pushed for legislation to support the project. With help from Interior Secretary Franklin K. Lane, Alaska's delegate James Wickersham and several congressmen, support for the railroad grew.

The Alaska Railroad Bill, which overwhelmingly passed in both the U.S. House and Senate, authorized the president to locate, construct and operate a railroad that would unite the Pacific with the navigable waters of Interior Alaska. The railroad could not exceed 1,000 miles in length and could not cost more than $35 million.

Following the bill's passage in 1914, Wilson created the Alaska Engineering Commission. He appointed William C. Edes, a renowned locating engineer, as chairman, as well as Frederick Mears, who'd been the chief engineer on the Panama Railroad relocation project. The third member, Thomas Riggs, had broad experience in Alaska as a geologist, mining engineer and surveyor. Riggs later served as Alaska's territorial governor from 1918 to 1921.

The team studied two primary routes: The Cordova-based route that had been examined earlier by the 1912 Alaska Railroad Commission, and the "Susitna Route," which was basically aligned like the present Seward to Fairbanks route. It also checked out auxiliary links, including Portage Bay to Turnagain Arm and a branch to the Matanuska Valley.

The AEC members were impressed with the potential for development along the western route. They felt that farming in the Matanuska Valley, mining in the Kenai and Willow Creek areas and mining and grazing in the Interior would bode well for Alaska's future. Not to mention the Matanuska coalfields, which easily could be tied by rail to Ship Creek, 75 miles away.

The commission submitted its report to President Wilson on Feb. 11, 1915, but a final decision on his choice for the route wasn't announced until April 10.

Within a week of the commission's report, Alaska's Gov. John Franklin Alexander Strong wrote a friend: "I am unofficially advised that work will begin this spring on a line between Ship Creek in Cook Inlet to the Matanuska coal fields."

By the time the AEC approved the route, more than $5.2 million had been spent developing the railway. The government finally

The government's decision to make Seward the terminus for its railroad was welcome news to the residents of the little town in Prince William Sound, pictured here in 1910.

A train chugs across a trestle at Mile 1 of the Alaska Northern Railroad in Seward in 1910. Resurrection Bay is in the background.

purchased the Alaska Northern Railroad for $1.2 million, and then rehabilitated it, for the act of March 12, 1914, required that the government railroad terminate in an ice-free harbor on the south coast of Alaska.

Except for the few miles of railroad already built, construction continued in a wilderness where every agency had to be developed and carried along with the actual road construction, according to a report made in 1921 to the Secretary of Interior. Ocean docks, building materials and supplies of every description had to be transported 1,500 miles from Seattle, the nearest Pacific Coast port. It cost about $80,240 per mile, including terminals, to build the railroad, the report said.

While new towns sprang up along the right of way, officials decided to establish the commission's headquarters at Seward, the ocean terminus. The chairman would be located there and have active charge of the Alaska Northern Railroad when it was taken over by the government.

Another member of the commission was placed in charge of new line construction, with a base at the head of ocean navigation on Cook Inlet, now known as Anchorage.

The third member of the commission was sent to Fairbanks to make the final location of the railroad line at that section.

The office of the purchasing agent was established at Seattle, and a representative was sent to the Isthmus of Panama in March 1915 to arrange for the assembling and shipment of available machinery, equipment and other material for the railway construction.

Upon hearing of the new construction camp in Cook Inlet, hoards of men and women poured into Ship Creek hoping to snag jobs building Alaska's railroad. When Mears stepped off the steamer *Mariposa* in late April 1915, he saw hundreds of tents and temporary shelters housing those awaiting work.

Anchorage Museum of History and Art, Alaska Engineering Commission Collection, AMRC-aec-g469

Equipment used in construction of the Panama Canal was sent to Alaska to help build the railroad. In this photograph, an Alaska Engineering Commission crane is unloading canal cargo from the *S.S. Turret Crown*.

5

SHIP CREEK BLOSSOMS

U nlike other settlements in Alaska's past, Anchorage didn't evolve as a result of major gold discoveries, lucrative fur trading or rich fisheries. It developed because the federal government strove to link Alaska's vast resources to tidewater.

In order to access the massive coalfields in the Matanuska Valley, the government decided to lay hundreds of miles of railroad track. Those tracks eventually would connect Seward with Fairbanks, where abundant supplies of gold also awaited transport to the coast.

University of Alaska Anchorage, Marie Silverman (APU) Collection, UAAhmc-0778-11-10

This June 1915 view, looking south from Government Hill, shows the mouth of Ship Creek and newly laid railroad tracks.

While studying routes to get those resources to tidewater, the Alaska Engineering Commission came upon Ship Creek, which was centrally located between Seward and Fairbanks. It had a protected anchorage that could be dredged and a large amount of flat land on which a construction camp could be built.

Other than Dena'ina Indians establishing fish sites and smokehouses in the area, there were few settlers around the mouth of Ship Creek during the Alaska Engineering Commission's 1914 summer reconnaissance.

Jack and Nellie Brown and Keith McCullough, employees of the Chugach National Forest, had built rustic cabins, and the J.D. Whitneys had a homestead about four miles up the creek, according to an inventory of historical sites listed in "Patterns of the Past," by Michael Carberry and Donna Lane. A squatter named Thomas Jeter also had a cabin.

By the spring of 1915, Ship Creek was teeming with boatloads of men who heard about work on the new railroad. They streamed in from dwindling gold discoveries in the north and from many of the states.

Anchorage Museum of History and Art, General Photograph File, AMRC-b80-194-13

Jack and Nellie Brown came to Ship Creek on their honeymoon in 1910 and built the first cabin in the area. This photo shows their home on Government Hill in 1922.

University of Washington, John E. Thwaites Collection, THW247

The Alaska Engineering Commission chose Ship Creek Landing as the main camp for the new government railroad. A tent city filled with job seekers sprang up in the wilderness at the mouth of Ship Creek, seen here in April 1915.

Soon a "tent city" sprang up on the north bank, and the population of Ship Creek swelled to 2,000. Many entrepreneurial squatters built tents and frame buildings on skids so they could be moved when a permanent townsite was laid out.

One observer gave the Cordova Daily Times an account of what he had seen on a trip to the railroad camp.

"I found the largest tent town I ever saw," said George C. Hazelet in an interview on June 29, 1915. "From 2,000 to 2,500 people are fed, housed, and their wants, in a way, taken care of in tents, all located on the government railway terminal ground.

"There are from 25 to 30 restaurants and as many lodging houses, ranging from 8x10 to 16x34 feet. There are from 13 to 16 places where groceries are sold, running from peanut stands with sugar, coffee and the staples up to fair stocks of groceries, including fresh vegetables and fruits, and more are coming in with each boat. There are two or three places where men's furnishings goods are sold in conjunction with hardware, etc., and as many dry goods and ladies' furnishings places. The town has 15 or 20 barber shops and one bath tent, six

Above: The Alaska Engineering Commission set up camp near Ship Creek during the spring of 1915.

Below: Hundreds of job seekers and businessmen staked tents on the flats at Ship Creek in early 1915. Businesses shown include The Crest House, Anchorage Fish Market, The Panhandle, Montana Pool Room, White Road House and Riverside Hotel.

laundries, two watch and clock repair shops, three tin shops, five transfer outfits, two drug stores, one sawmill, one picture show, one newspaper, several lawyers, no saloons – but plenty of booze, 10 cigar stores, several real estate and brokerage firms. Numerous other small businesses are represented.

"There are 600 to 700 men out of work. The railway officials tell me they employ 1,000 men in all capacities. The work is strung along 20 miles from Anchorage towards the Matanuska River let out in station work. The right of way is cleared beyond that for some distance. Common labor is 37.5 cents an hour for eight hours work, with a shut down on Sunday. Carpenters receive 40 to 60 cents per hour. ...

"Dissatisfaction on all sides is rife at Anchorage. This, however, is common to all big new enterprises. There seem to be several bones of contention between the people and the government officials, such as low wages, short hours, employment of foreigners, discrimination against Americans, etc. ..."

Living conditions were less than ideal as more and more job seekers arrived along the creek. With no sewers, and Cook Inlet tides

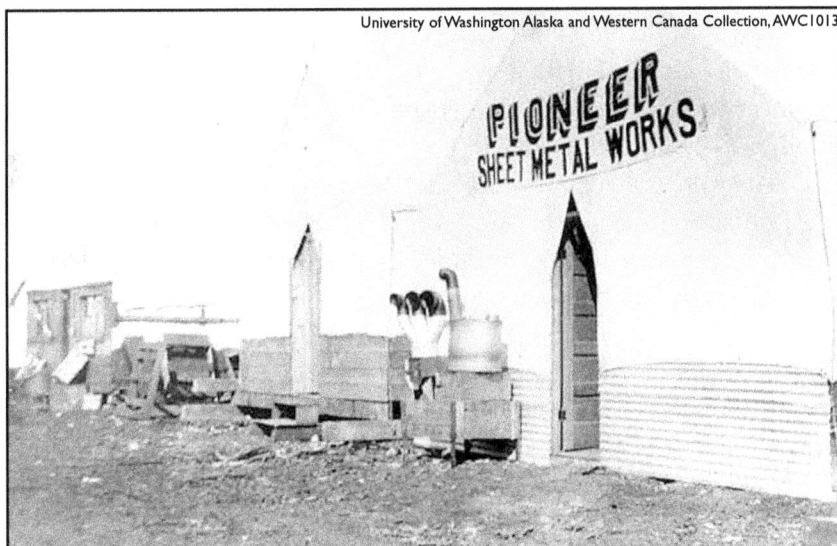

Pioneer Sheet Metal Works was typical of a tent-and-frame business in early Anchorage.

Anchorage Museum of History and Art, General Photograph File, AMRC-b83-146-6

Dirt streets in Ship Creek's tent city turned to mud in the rain. Sanitation quickly became a major problem. Businesses and buildings along this street include Two Girls Waffle House and Young American Lodging House.

providing the only means of waste disposal, the Alaska Engineering Commission surgeon warned that the new settlement's water supply soon would become contaminated.

In an effort to move the settlers from the tent city, the commission, which was charged with governing the populace, had its railroad engineers quickly lay out a townsite on 350 acres of higher ground south of Ship Creek.

"The Anchorage plan was typical of railroad town planning in the western states and territories," wrote Elizabeth Tower in her book, "Anchorage," which is part of the City History Series.

"All roads and lots were at right angles – the only exception being Christensen Road, appropriately named for Andrew (the Land Office chief of field division in charge of the surveys) – which ascended a bluff too steep for a T-square road. East-west streets were named numerically and north-south streets alphabetically."

One Land Office commissioner said the only excuse for such lack of imagination in the naming of the streets was the urgent need for the town – and that railroad engineers designed it, Tower wrote.

The first town lot auction was scheduled for early July. And according to an article in the *Cook Inlet Pioneer*, businessmen were encouraged "to visit the townsite and to go over the ground as thoroughly as possible so as to become informed" before the auction began.

President Wilson issued Alaska Railroad Townsite Regulations for the auction on June 19 that included a minimum price of $25 per lot. The winning bid had to be paid in full, or one-third down and the balance paid in five equal installments.

In an effort to stem vice in the new townsite, the regulations also stated the lots and payments thereof would be forfeited if the land was "used for the purpose of manufacturing, selling, or otherwise disposing of intoxicating liquors as a beverage, or for gambling, prostitution, or any unlawful purpose. ..."

The regulations stated that successful bidders would receive patent to the land after five years if conditions were fulfilled.

Anchorage's founding fathers designated a reserve district outside of the town's boundaries for prostitution – they thought it would be easier to control there. They also withheld two blocks from public sale that constituted the Federal Reserve and the Municipal Reserve.

University of Washington, Alaska and Western Canada Collection, AWC1258

Workers placed a temporary track for the Alaska Railroad in Ship Creek in spring 1915.

Above: Horses pulled sleds through mud as the first rails were laid for the Alaska Railroad in Ship Creek on April 29, 1915.

Below: A woman identified as Miss White drove the first spike in the track for the government's Alaska Railroad in Ship Creek on April 29, 1915.

They also allocated a large portion of Fourth Avenue, with an 80-foot-wide street, for the commercial district.

The area that was to become the main street of the new railroad town was the obvious choice for commercial establishments, because it was the closest land to the terminal yards that offered many lots for sale on level ground. While First, Second and Third avenues were actually nearer to the terminal yards, major portions already had been set aside for government purposes.

The first land auction on July 10 opened with enthusiastic bidding. At its conclusion, the Land Office had auctioned 655 lots for about $150,000.

Local merchants had paid more for lots along Fourth Avenue than anywhere else in town. Those first bids on Fourth Avenue property averaged $548 per lot, whereas the average price for other townsite lots ran about $225. Corner lots along the center of the avenue, between C and F streets, sold for between $800-$1,000, twice the appraised value.

A headline in *The Seward Weekly Gateway* on July 10, 1915, proclaimed, "Highest Anchorage Lot Goes for $1,150."

Two days later, the *Cook Inlet Pioneer* reported:

"While perhaps local residents did not anticipate the fancy prices that were paid for lots, it is better that there should have been an eager

Anchorage Museum of History and Art, General Photograph File, AMRC-b80-194-11

Workers built a dirt road that would later become C Street.

Land Office chief Andrew Christensen auctioned lots in the new townsite near Ship Creek on July 10, 1915.

demand than a lack of interest and consequent cheap prices. The one means faith and optimism and the other doubt and pessimism. And confidence is a large contributing factor that builds a center of population."

Among those buying lots were Swedish-born Oscar Anderson, the town's first butcher, and Della and Irving Kimball, who bought lots at the corner of Fifth Avenue and E Street and started a dry goods business.

Once lots had been purchased, the Alaska Engineering Commission ordered all tents to be moved from the Ship Creek flats to the new townsite by mid-August. While some lot owners hauled their tent-covered frames up to their property, others hastily chopped down trees and constructed frame buildings. Some businessmen had stockpiled construction supplies and had permanent commercial enterprises up and running in no time. Others built substantial

Many merchants constructed their buildings and businesses on skids in the Ship Creek area, which allowed them to drag the structures up to the new townsite once lots were auctioned. This photograph shows the Kootenay Inn, Murray's Lodging, Cosy Inn, Crescent Hotel and White House Restaurant.

structures, including the Wendler and Lathrop buildings, Brown & Hawkins and the Carroll Building.

During the mad dash to develop the townsite, settlers also decided their new city needed a name.

Monikers considered included Matanuska, Terminal, New Knik, Alaska City, Ship Creek, Woodrow City, Gateway, Winalaska, Homestead and Lane – then U.S. Secretary of the Interior. The new residents also tossed in Whitney and Brownsville – in honor of the original settlers.

It's widely believed that Anchorage, submitted by Ray McDonald, won in an election held on Aug. 2, 1915. But according to records of the Alaska Engineering Commission, discovered by M. Diane Brenner, past archivist for the Anchorage Museum of History and Art, the vote went to Alaska City. The second-highest vote was for Lane. Anchorage came in third.

However, the settlers later learned that the U.S. Post Office had already arbitrarily named the new Alaska settlement Anchorage.

Above: Early residents gathered to play baseball amid the tents along Ship Creek on July 4, 1915.

Below: Oscar Anderson snapped this picture of Anchorage looking north along the mud flats from Third Avenue. Only one pier stood in the port area, and it wasn't used that summer because of the extreme tide.

EARLY RAILROAD DAYS

Anchorage Museum of History and Art, General Photograph File, AMRC-b83-146-36

Above: This photograph of Fourth Avenue from H Street, looking west, shows businesses like the partially constructed Northern Drug Company on Aug. 26, 1915.

Below: What would become Alaska's largest city started blossoming in the wilderness along Fourth Avenue, seen here on Aug. 28, 1915, looking west from F Street.

Anchorage Museum of History and Art, General Photograph File, AMRC-b73-43-2

Fourth St. From F. Looking West Anchorage Alaska
Aug 28d 1915

Above: By the fall of 1915, Ship Creek's tent city had been replaced by an Alaska Engineering Commission depot, commissary, warehouses, shops, offices and power plant.

Below: The railroad town's first snowfall found Fourth Avenue taking shape.

Above: Sternwheelers, including the *Matanuska*, brought passengers ashore at Anchorage.

Below: Once they disembarked, people coming into the Ship Creek area had to walk across a boardwalk built on the mud flats to get to town.

As Anchorage boomed with the construction of the railroad, the Land Office continued to sell lots and lease business sites, but some infrastructure problems popped up.

Secretary Lane didn't authorize the installation of a water system in the new townsite until Sept. 1, 1915, just before winter set in. The commission then began pumping water up to the townsite from a sand-filter bed in Ship Creek.

Kenneth Gideon, who took a job in a hand laundry that winter, gave an account of the water situation in his book, "Wandering Boy."

"The usual government bungling was to be seen in about everything that was done. They didn't start to lay the water mains till the freezing weather started and the frozen earth was dumped in the trenches on top of the mains. They all froze solid and all that winter they were driving steam into them trying to get them open. Probably the local officials were capable enough, but someone in a position of authority the length and breadth of a continent away insisted in displaying his authority by refusing to be hurried and as a result Anchorage hauled water on sleds."

When Land Office chief Andrew Christensen opened the auction

University of Washington, Alaska and Western Canada Collection, AWC 1257

In May 1915, the Alaska Engineering Commission began building a hospital, seen here under construction with the tent city in the background.

Passengers arriving at Ship Creek walked up to the business district of Anchorage on the boardwalk on the left side of the photograph. Alaska Railroad buildings are pictured in the distance, looking north toward Government Hill across the Ship Creek area.

for sites above Ship Creek on July 10, bidding became so brisk that prospective lot owners couldn't hold down prices. Christensen claimed the sale had "injected confidence in the people of the town" and that he could sell lots in Anchorage every day because demand never ceased.

But confidence in the growing community may have been tempered somewhat when the residents realized the Alaska Engineering Commission had overlooked a vital component in the new town.

The commission had sold the parcels of land with the understanding that the lots could be assessed to finance such public services as water and sewer utilities, fire protection and garbage pickup, but it had neglected to provide for financing a school.

It took months to solve the dilemma. In summer 1915, the editor of the *Cook Inlet Pioneer* wrote:

"If we are to retain the families, and they compose the backbone of any community, we must provide the children with adequate school facilities. It is highly important that this should be done without undue delay. ..."

The federal government finally solved the predicament in late September after Alaska Engineering Commissioners William C. Edes and Frederick Mears convinced the Comptroller General to issue funds for construction of a public school.

Completed in November 1915, the public school was constructed to serve about 90 students. From the beginning, residents labeled the school "entirely inadequate," "unsanitary" and "of an order of the early eighteenth century." The school lacked a solid foundation, paint and a satisfactory heating system, and its unheated outdoor toilets didn't meet townsite standards.

Alaska Engineering Commission Chairman William C. Edes ordered Christensen to take over the responsibility of "school

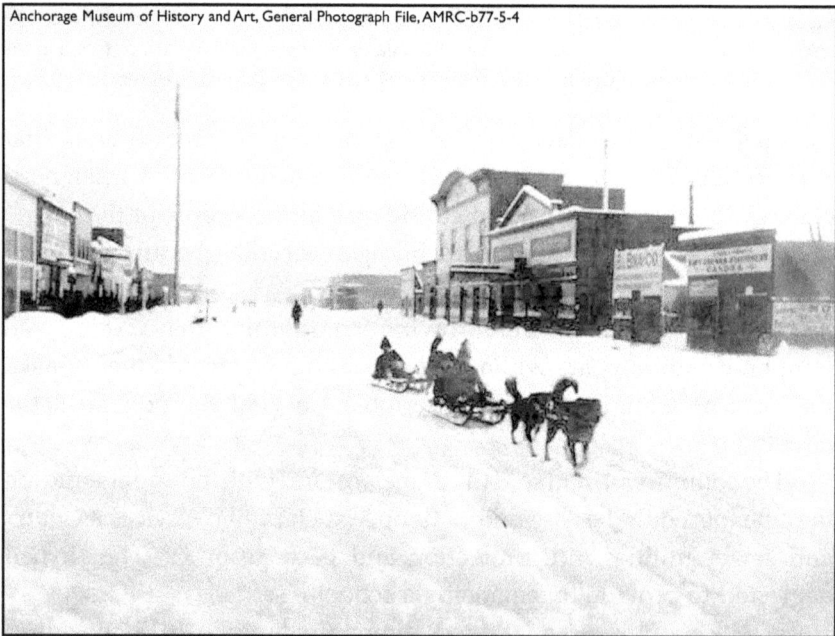

Anchorage Museum of History and Art, General Photograph File, AMRC-b77-5-4

By November 1915, a patch of forest along Ship Creek had transformed into Fourth Avenue in the new Cook Inlet townsite. Businesses in this photograph include the Montana Pool Room, B&B Navigation Company and The Model Tailor Photographer, C.F. Peterson.

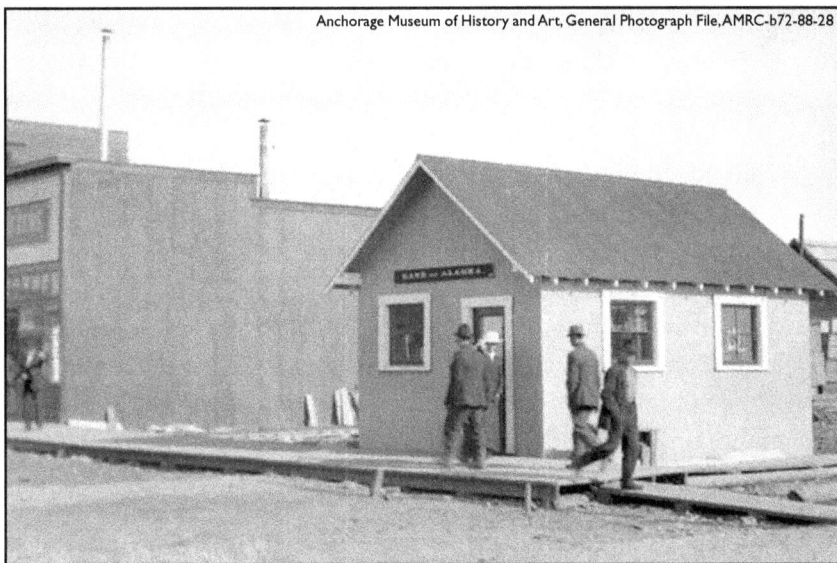

Early Anchorage residents could do business with the Bank of Alaska in 1915.

director in addition to your other duties," in 1917. Although school board members A.J. Wendler, Mrs. W.T. Normile and M. Finkelstein had handled the first year of operation admirably, enrollment had doubled to more than 200 pupils by early fall 1917. The school also had management problems. One teacher taught 70 primary students in half-day shifts.

Christensen told the principal he "must quit going to the pool halls and must get down to business," and he advised one teacher "to stop gossiping, complaining and criticizing, and to bring her work up to standard."

The first public school was only used for overflow after a second school, finished in December 1917, opened on the School Reserve. Named Pioneer School, it served both elementary and high school students until the mid-1930s.

By September 1916, Christensen had sold 1,108 lots and Anchorage's population had reached about 4,000. By 1917, it boasted a hospital, a school, a telephone/telegraph/electric office, concrete sidewalks and graded streets for an estimated 5,000 residents.

Four physicians, six dentists, seven lawyers, two engineers and two architects practiced their professions, and along with fraternal organizations like the Elks, Moose, Masons and Odd-fellows, five churches dotted the landscape.

While the town took shape, laborers continued to lay track. Those hardy souls who built the railroad with their hammers and drills, their axes and mattocks, their mauls and gauges found it took muscle, hardihood and endurance.

Most of the country over which the railroad was built had a top covering of undrained tundra, varying from a depth of 2 to 6 feet, extending not only over the level and flat areas, but also over foothills and mountain slopes.

The work done by these hardy men with hand tools – and under indescribable living conditions – hardly can be exaggerated. Anton Anderson, an early railroader, wrote a vivid description.

"Tents without floors, pole bunks covered with wild hay for mattresses and no bedding [you packed your own] were the accommodations then available. There was no smiling assistant camp steward to direct the new arrivals to their quarters. The new arrivals generally had to provide and build their own.

Anchorage Museum of History and Art, General Photograph File, AMRC-b72-88-28

The Pioneer School, built in 1917, was a three-story structure. Anchorage's population had outgrown the school before it even opened its doors, so seven teachers taught about 300 students during the day, and 10 teachers taught around 200 students at night.

Above: Sydney Laurence climbed a tripod to snap a picture of Fourth Avenue near C Street in 1916. Businesses pictured include Lennon's Bakery and Coffee House, H & W Grill, Shonbeck General Merchandise, Union Cafe, Merchant Tailors, The Fairbanks, Polley Bros. and Carstens Packing Company.

Below: This sign on the trail from Seward to Anchorage may be the first billboard of its time.

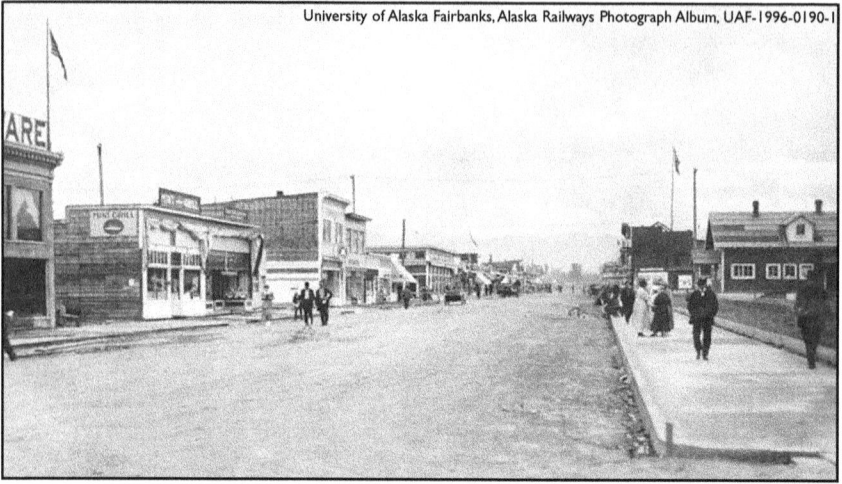

The government built concrete sidewalks along Fourth Avenue between E and F streets during the summer of 1917. The new railroad town soon boasted 18 blocks of 12-foot concrete sidewalks and two blocks of 6-foot concrete walks. It also had about 20 blocks of gravel walks, 80 blocks of plank walks and more than 150 blocks of graded streets.

"At some locations along the access winter trails or tote roads, crude log houses chinked with moss were hastily constructed. Roofs on such houses were made of strong poles laid with very little pitch, then covered with bark, hay and moss and capped with an overall covering of two or three feet deep of top soil or earth.

"Door hinges were ingeniously made out of bent nails, or leather from old boot tops and homemade wooden latches held the doors shut [Alaska was then a land without locks or policemen]. Flour sacks covered the opening where windows should have been.

"Such trail accommodations were a combination cook house, storeroom, social hall and bunkhouse. The bunks were built out of poles in tiers across both ends of the room, similar arrangement to post office boxes. They usually were four feet square and eight feet in depth and were known as "muzzle loaders" [the extra two feet were for duffle storage].

"It was no uncommon sight to find four tiers of such bunks, six bunks wide at each end of the room. Two coal oil lamps suspended from the ceiling provided illumination to the group that gathered

Above: Supplies to build the Alaska Railroad arrived in Seward from Seattle onboard steamers like the *Santa Clara*. Here a worker loads packages onto a flatcar on rail tracks in 1915.

Below: Timber for the construction of the Alaska Railroad was turned into lumber at a sawmill just outside of Seward.

around the central heating stove, or climbed up and down the crude ladders to and from their muzzle-loading bunks. One should not claim to be a real sourdough unless he has spent at least one night in an Alaska muzzle-loading bunkhouse."

World War I pulled many railroad workers away from Anchorage.

As a devastating war raged across Western Europe in 1916, President Woodrow Wilson recognized that the United States could be drawn into the war at any moment by the act of some obscure German submarine commander. Hence, while he advocated continued neutrality, he also called for a prepared military.

The resulting preparedness boom drew unskilled labor away from the Alaska Railroad project, which hampered construction after 1917. The commission's work force went from more than 5,600 to an average of 2,800 by 1918.

The commission itself dwindled, too.

When offered a position as colonel in the 31st Engineer Regiment

Anchorage Museum of History and Art, Alaska Engineering Commission, AMRC-aec-h1

Workers milled about the Turnagain Arm camp in 1917.

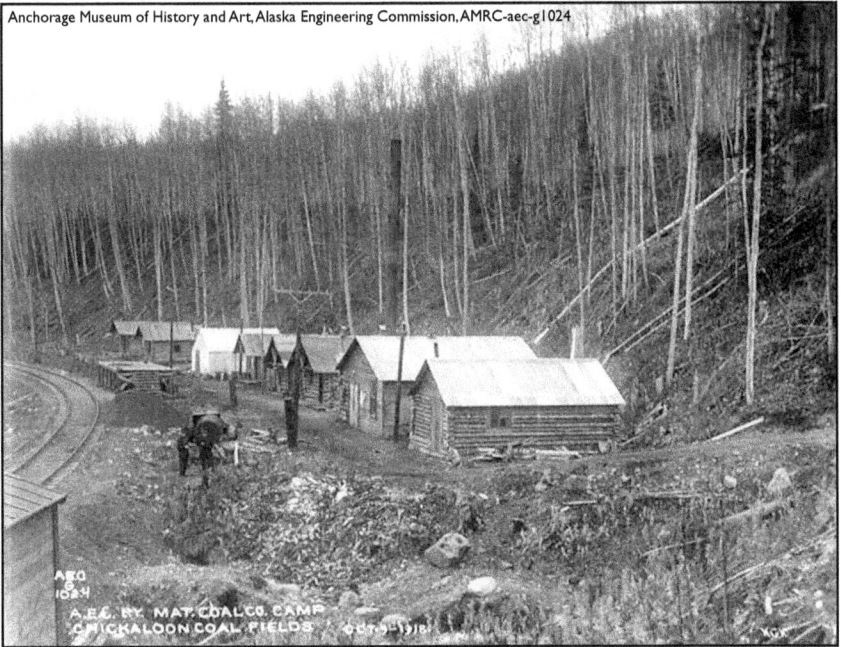

Tents and hastily constructed log cabins lined the newly laid railroad tracks at Matanuska Coal Company camp in Chickaloon in 1918.

in January 1918, Mears resigned from the commission, taking many AEC employees with him.

Edes, who relocated his headquarters to Anchorage in October 1918, after the Seward to Anchorage railroad construction was completed, was one of the first to catch the devastating flu sweeping the world in 1919 and resigned on Aug. 29.

Mears later returned at the request of Secretary Lane and assumed the dual role of chief engineer and chairman of the commission. He then centralized all railroad administration in Anchorage.

Alaska Pacific University, Anchorage Historic Photographs, APU-AHP-f10-18

Above: The track-laying gang placed the last ties to complete the railroad between Seward and the coalfields on Sept. 11, 1918.

Below: The first passenger coach arrived at Matanuska Junction on Sept. 27, 1916.

Anchorage Museum of History and Art, Alaska Engineering Commission, AMRCaec-g127

Both of these photographs show the first train leaving from Anchorage's new depot on Nov. 1, 1916.

The people of Anchorage turned out to honor recruits about to leave for training stations during World War I. Above, City Hall is to the left and the *Anchorage Daily Times* is in the background. Eckmann's Furniture Store, Empress Theatre, The Bon Marche and Club 25 can be seen in the photograph below.

Anchorage Museum of History and Art, Alaska Engineering Commission, AMRC-aec-g552

Above: AEC employees prepare to leave for military service with the 31st Engineers Regiment during World War I.

Below: The Alaska Railroad terminal, pictured here, was left with few workers after World War I recruits left for training.

Anchorage Museum of History and Art, Alaska Engineering Commission, AMRC-aec-g863

6

GOLDEN SPIKE MYSTERY

A missing golden spike. Corrupt government officials. Tainted shellfish. Were any of these factors involved in the mysterious death of U.S. President Warren G. Harding shortly after his visit to celebrate the completion of the Alaska Railroad in 1923?

Following World War I, construction continued on the Alaska Railroad as workers displaced enormous amounts of earth and rock to lay track. While railroad gangs encountered many obstacles along the way, including unstable ground caused by permafrost, avalanches that buried the track and landslides, the railroad was completed in July 1923.

To commemorate the end of the 470-plus-mile project, President Harding traveled to Alaska to drive in the last spike. He was the first U.S. president to visit the territory, and the Fairbanks Daily News-Miner called it "the Glory of the Coming."

Traveling with the President were

Library of Congress

In 1923, Warren G. Harding became the first U.S. president to visit Alaska.

Secretary of the Interior Hubert Work, Secretary of Commerce Herbert C. Hoover and Secretary of Agriculture Henry Wallace, along with their wives.

Hoover later said Harding was thrilled about coming to Alaska and his enthusiasm was like that of "a school boy entering on a holiday," according to "Warren G. Harding" by John W. Dean. Harding spent hours on the deck of the U.S. transport *Henderson* watching in awe as the ship swept past the territory's majestic landscapes.

The ship first stopped in Metlakatla, where Alaska Natives entertained the President with traditional music and dancing.

Hoover was quite interested in this port of call, because his uncle, John Minthron, who had raised him, lived in Metlakatla for a time to study the famous Anglican missionary William Duncan's methods with the Tsimshian people. The uncle also had married a woman from that village.

Alaska State Library, President Harding's Trip to Alaska, ASL-P418-4

Alaska Territorial Gov. Scott Bone, President and Mrs. Harding and Secretary Wallace sit on the porch of the schoolhouse in Metlakatla during their 1923 stopover.

The people along Market Street in Ketchikan welcomed the presidential party. A brass band, located on the wooden street amid automobiles and a large assembly of people, played to mark the occassion. People gathered in upper-story windows and on rooftops to catch a glimpse of President Harding.

The people of Ketchikan bestowed gold and ivory jewelry on their distinguished guests when the party arrived in that Southeastern town. And while in port on July 8, the President, a Free Mason himself, laid the cornerstone of the Masonic Temple along Main Street.

Ketchikan was described by the press as notable for "hillsides of wooden homes decorated with Independence Day bunting and misspelled signs," according to a story written by June Allen titled "A President's Ill-Fated Trek to Alaska" that appeared in the July 23, 2003, issue of *Ketchikan's Stories in the News*.

After leaving Ketchikan, the procession moved on to Wrangell where Natives clad in colorful blankets paddled canoes out to the President's ship to greet him. Then, after three hours ashore, the

Alaska State Library, President Harding's Trip to Alaska, ASL #418-7

Above: A specially ordered steel-wheeled Dodge roadster modified to run on tracks carried President Harding on some of the rails north.

Below: President Harding climbed into the cab of engine No. 618 at Wasilla and took the throttle for the 26-mile run to Willow.

Alaska State Library, Marguerite Bone Wilcox Collection, ASL-P70-35

group traveled to Juneau, where Alaska's Territorial Gov. Scott C. Bone showed them the sights.

The *USS Henderson* pulled into Seward on July 13, and the presidential party boarded a Pullman car for the long trip to Nenana on the new railroad.

On a hot and sunny July 15 in Nenana, Gov. Bone placed a specially made golden spike into the rail at the northern end of the 702-foot Mears Memorial truss bridge, which crossed the Tanana River at Milepost 413.7. It was the last piece of track connecting the new Alaska Railroad between Seward in the south and Fairbanks in the north.

Harding raised the maul and missed the spike twice before smacking it to officially complete the construction of the Alaska Railroad. The $600 golden spike then was replaced with an iron one to finish the track.

The President and his entourage then continued on the railroad

Alaska State Library, Marguerite Bone Wilcox Collection, ASL-P70-85

President Warren G. Harding drove a golden spike into the rail in Nenana.

Destroyers hovered in Resurrection Bay as President Harding and his party climbed onboard the *USS Henderson* for the return trip to the Lower 48 on July 17, 1923.

to Fairbanks, where he visited the Alaska Agricultural College and School of Mines that opened on Sept. 13, 1922, with six students.

Harding spoke to a crowd at Week's Field and said, "... I wonder if you know what has most impressed us on our ... trip to Alaska. You have a sample of it here in Fairbanks. ... While Alaska is majestic and boundless and mighty ... it is also strikingly a homeland, and that is the finest thing that may be said of any section of any nation in the world."

The President returned to Seward and boarded the *Henderson* on July 17 for the return trip home. He made a brief stop in Cordova and then was greeted by the residents of Sitka on July 23.

Two days out of Sitka, Harding began experiencing severe abdominal pain after eating crab drenched in butter. Tainted shellfish was suspected, as the group had been eating seafood the entire trip. But no one else on the voyage showed any symptoms of ptomaine poisoning.

Upon reaching Seattle, a very ill Harding predicted eventual statehood for part of Alaska.

"Alaska is designed for ultimate statehood," he said. "In a very few years we can well set off the Panhandle and a large block of the connecting Southeastern part as a state. The region now easily contains 90 percent of the white population and of the developed resources. As to the remainder of the territory, I would leave the Alaskans of the future to decide."

The President became more ill as he traveled by train to San Francisco. Harding, 57, died on Aug. 2, less than three weeks after he drove the golden spike into the last piece of track for the Alaska Railroad.

For years some people claimed the president had been murdered by his wife for his unfaithfulness. According to several sources, Harding had an eye for the ladies, and his escapades made presidents John F. Kennedy and Bill Clinton look like choirboys.

Other theories surrounding Harding's demise suggested members of his cabinet killed the President to keep him from investigating their wrongdoings, while others said he committed suicide because he'd learned his friends were crooks and he was weighed down by their bad deeds.

Library of Congress

Some people suspected that Florence Harding, shown here, murdered her husband because she couldn't deal with his string of mistresses and illegitimate children.

Famous journalist William Allen White said the President told him that what kept him awake at night was not the actions of his political foes, but those of his friends.

Almost from the outset of his election in 1920, Harding's administration was plagued with scandal. He installed several of his old Ohio friends in important positions within his cabinet, and his White House was known more for its poker games, philandering and evening burlesques than for any actual legislation.

University of Washington, Museum of History & Industry Collection, SHS12098

President Warren G. Harding, pictured here with his wife, was ill while riding in this motorcade in Seattle on July 27, 1923. He died seven days later in San Francisco.

Also, shortly before he left for Alaska, the President received information that someone in the Justice Department was receiving kickbacks from Chicago gangster Al Capone's organization in order to protect Capone's monopoly on bootlegging.

Hoover wrote that Harding, on the fateful trip, asked Hoover what he should do if it was revealed that scandal might engulf his administration. Hoover's advice was to "get it out in the open" so the President could remain above the wrongdoings.

But while rumors ran rampant, there is no evidence to support either the murder or suicide theories.

Recent investigations reveal that Harding had a history of heart problems due to an unhealthy diet and his fun-loving lifestyle. He often was short of breath and slept propped up on pillows in order to breathe. His physician's records indicate that Harding suffered from

A solemn procession left the White House as a horse-drawn carriage carried the body of President Warren G. Harding on Aug. 8, 1923.

high blood pressure and an enlarged heart, and that a heart attack caused his death.

The mystery about the golden spike that he drove into the track in Nenana remains, however.

No one seems to know what happed to the spike.

There may have been two official golden spikes, according to Howard Clifford, author of "Rails North, the Railroads of Alaska and the Yukon."

One spike, which was presented to Col. Frederick Mears by the city of Anchorage for his work as chairman of the Alaska Engineering Commission, is now owned by the Southern California Arms Collectors Association. This spike was driven on the last rail laid between Bird Creek and Girdwood at Milepost 78 to connect Anchorage and Seward on Sept. 10, 1918.

The second golden spike, driven by President Harding at Nenana upon completion of the railroad, was thought to have been on display at the Harding Home Museum in Marion, Ohio. However,

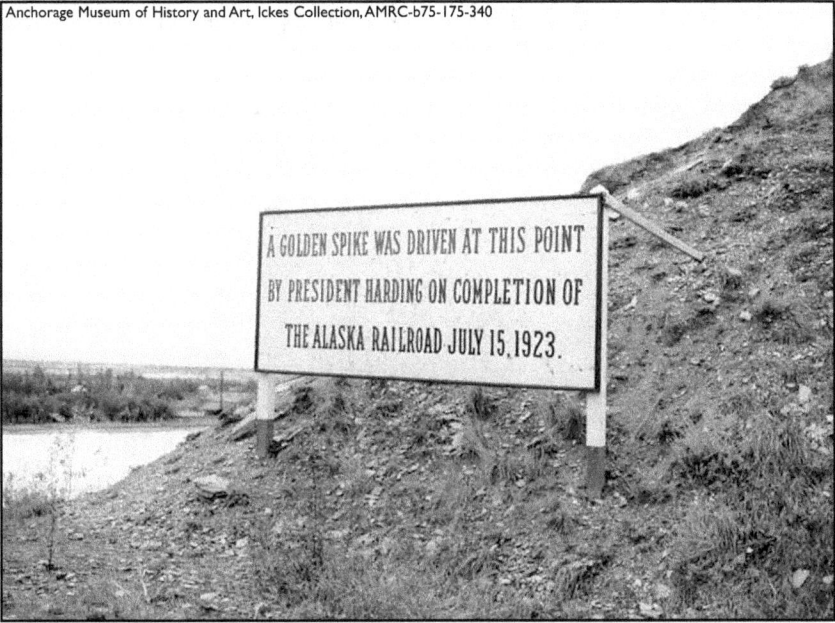

The golden spike that President Harding struck to commemorate the completion of the Alaska Railroad may be missing, but a sign signifying that the event took place on July 15, 1923, stands in Nenana.

the museum's curator, Phillip Payne, told John Combs of Alaskarails. org – who has been researching this mystery for years – that it was at the Smithsonian Institute in Washington, D.C.

But Sharon Tolbert of the Smithsonian told Combs it is not part of the Institute's inventory.

As of this printing, that golden spike still is missing.

* **UPDATE:** It appears that the golden spike has been found. Ben Nysewander contacted John Combs of AlaskaRails.org in 2010 and informed him that he had purchased the spike from the estate of Fred Johnson of the California Arms Collectors Association in 1983. It is engraved: "Presented to Col. Fredrick Mears by the City of Anchorage in commemoration of the building of the Alaska Railroad 1915-1923" and the reverse side is stamped "Jos. Mayer Inc. Makers Seattle USA 14K." Further research verified this is the long-lost golden spike.

BIG CITY CONCERNS

7

VOTERS CHOOSE SELF-RULE

Anchorage had become an established railroad town within five years of the land auction. And while many of its residents seemed content to have the Alaska Engineering Commission continue to govern the day to day affairs, others thought it was time the citizens took over management of the town.

And some government officials, including Land Office chief Andrew Christensen, seemed willing to wean themselves from city management.

"Personally, I should think it would be a good idea to always have in mind the withdrawal from the management of these towns, so that it can be done gracefully and with dignity," he said in December 1915.

So, technically speaking, Anchorage was born in November 1920. According to information gleaned by the League of Women Voters many years ago, it was eligible to become a first-class city because its population surpassed 400 – provided that two-thirds of the voters were ready to assume responsibilities of city government for its 2,500 residents.

A group of interested citizens filed a petition with the U.S. District Court at Valdez, which was the headquarters of the Third Judicial Division. The petition requested that a special election be held to determine the wish of the majority in the former tent city.

Although there was some organized protest during a hearing on

Early Anchorage residents enjoyed baseball games, and spectators crowded onto railcars and headed to Potter Marsh to support their teams.

the matter, Judge Frederick Brown ordered an election. That ruling wasn't to be the last that Judge Brown would render on the issue, however. He would be called upon again to decide the question after the citizens of Anchorage cast their ballots.

The election returns showed a count of 328 votes for incorporation and 130 votes against. Another 85 blank ballots had been stuffed into the ballot box. If all 543 ballots were considered cast, then the percentage of those for incorporation would miss the two-thirds mark necessary.

After careful consideration, Judge Brown ruled the 85 blank votes were to be ignored. He decided it was as if those voters had not been to the polls at all and that Anchorage had voted itself into incorporation.

Anchorage became a city on Nov. 23, 1920.

Its boundaries stretched from one-half mile off shore in Cook Inlet to East G Street (now Gambell Street) and from 11th Avenue to

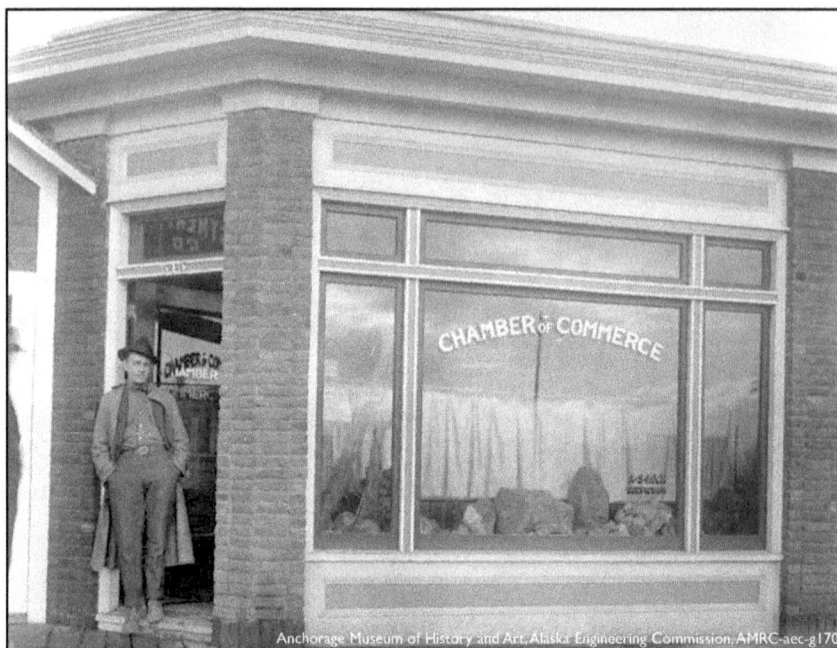

The Chamber of Commerce office supported businesses in early Anchorage.

Government Hill, including a small section that is now inside Fort Richardson.

The city received restricted patents for some properties reserved for recreation or municipal purposes, including the City Hall block, a school block between Fifth and Sixth avenues and E and G streets, the cemetery, the baseball park, the playground on M Street between Ninth and 10th avenues and the fire break between Ninth and 10th avenues from Gambell Street to the inlet.

The residents of the new city chose the mayor-council system, and their first mayor, Leopold David, faced some weighty issues in the year that followed.

Above: Anchorage residents could shop for food at Larson and Wendler Groceries.

Below: The business of the new city was handled at City Hall, seen here. The *Anchorage Daily Times* building sits in the background to the left.

8

FIRST MAYOR TACKLES VICE

Anchorage's first mayor, elected on Nov. 29, 1920, bore the responsibility of governing a railroad town of about 2,500 people five years after Alaska Engineering Commission management ended.

When Judge Leopold David became Anchorage's mayor, he helped the new city council develop ordinances to provide law and order. They included establishing a 9 p.m. to 5 a.m. curfew for youth younger than 16, setting a speed limit of 8 mph in town and outlawing spitting in public places.

University of Alaska, regents

Mayor Leopold David

Judge David, an immigrant from Germany, came to Alaska in 1904 with the U.S. Army and served as a pharmacist's assistant in the Hospital Corps at Fort Egbert. After his discharge a year later, the 24-year-old settled in Seward, married Anna Karasek and managed the Seward Drug Company. Like many pharmacists of the time, his basic medical knowledge earned him the title "Dr. David" among the townspeople.

Ever public-service minded, he served as the U.S. marshal at

Susitna Station in 1909 and also as a U.S. commissioner at Knik when he moved there in 1910. It's believed he studied law while living in Knik and served as ex-officio probate judge.

David continued his role as commissioner and district recorder after he arrived at Ship Creek in 1915 and signed almost every land transaction in the new community.

When he became mayor in 1920, he faced a few issues of the illegal nature.

Documents for land use for Anchorage's 1915 townsite stated the property was not to be used for any unlawful purpose.

But vice flourished. Thirty or 40 women "entertained" construction workers in tents and shacks southeast of town, but they were forbidden to mingle on the main street with the townspeople.

Anchorage also had 11 billiard and pool halls, which inevitably drew a gambling crowd.

Anchorage's curtain ordinance was enacted to stymie gambling. Pool halls, like the California seen to the left, often were associated with illegal gambling.

During the prohibition years, some Alaskans drank moonshine made in clandestine homemade whiskey distilleries, like the one shown here hidden in the woods near Anchorage.

Mayor David and the city council tried to curtail gambling by adopting a "curtain ordinance," which required an unobstructed view from the street into "pool halls, cigar stores, soft-drink emporiums, and other businesses of a similar character."

That ordinance helped somewhat, but the problem of alcohol and bootlegging proved more difficult to address.

From the time the U. S. Army took over responsibility for governing Alaska in 1867, law enforcement found it had its hands full trying to stem the flow of liquor into the territory. Up until alcohol possession was legalized in 1899, smugglers brought their illegal brew into Alaska via whalers, fishing vessels, American and foreign ships and Indian canoes from both British Columbia and U.S. ports.

Enforcement also had problems controlling the manufacture of "hootch," a name taken from the Tlingit village of Hootchenoo or Hootznahoo. The distillers of "this vile stuff" had learned their trade from soldiers stationed at Sitka.

Since the opportunity to make a bundle of cash in the illegal trade of spirits encouraged dishonesty, many early government officials looked the other way. Some even assisted the smugglers. Evidence that law enforcement was ineffective in rooting out "the demon rum" was evident in Southeast Alaska where 27 saloons operated openly in Juneau in 1895, and just about as many flourished in Sitka and Wrangell.

However, the tide turned against the smugglers in 1898 when a grand jury in Juneau indicted seven customs officers: four who helped smuggle liquor into the territory and three who sold impounded liquor to thirsty prospectors.

Dry laws were enacted in Alaska in the early 1900s and not repealed until 1934. But that didn't stop smugglers from getting alcohol into the railroad town growing along Ship Creek, even though the Alaska Engineering Commission had banned spirits on its property.

On June 19, 1915, President Woodrow Wilson issued regulations pertaining to the Alaska Railroad townsite. The detailed rules for the conditional sale of lots at public auction contained one clause that reflected hopes for high standards of sobriety. The lots and payments for them would be forfeited if the property were "used for the purpose of manufacturing, selling, or otherwise deposing of intoxicating liquors as a beverage, or for gambling, prostitution, or any unlawful purpose. ..."

Anchorage Museum of History and Art, General Photograph File, AMRC-b70-19-342

Bootleggers' cabins, like this one shown near Chester Creek, filled the needs of those in search of alcoholic refreshment.

As a child, Frank M. Reed, who later became a banker and whose mother owned the Hotel Anchorage, sold bottles to bootleggers. The family's hotel also offered housing for travelers' four-legged friends.

Government officials, law enforcement and teetotalers kept a wary eye out for liquid contraband. But bootleggers managed to supply those thirsty for their product by coming ashore near Anchorage in what's still known as "Bootleggers Cove," an area hidden by a bend in the shoreline along Cook Inlet.

Bootlegging continued to be an underground industry during the 1920s, and Anchorage children were paid a $5 reward for telling officials about the locations of illegal stills.

Even respectable families dabbled in the "devil's drink." Some made their own homebrew, while others, like Frank M. Reed, made a few bucks off the thirst of their neighbors. Reed, who later became an Anchorage banker and community leader, started his entrepreneurial career collecting bottles discarded by guests at his mother's Hotel Anchorage and selling them to bootleggers for 35 cents a dozen.

Since bootlegging provided a revenue stream for so many of Anchorage's citizens, Mayor David, who died of heart disease in 1924 at 43, found it virtually impossible to keep alcohol from flowing in the frontier town.

So in an effort to control the criminal element in Anchorage, he and the city council authorized the establishment of the city's first police department soon after the city became incorporated.

But tragedy soon hit that new department. The first police chief was murdered shortly after taking his post.

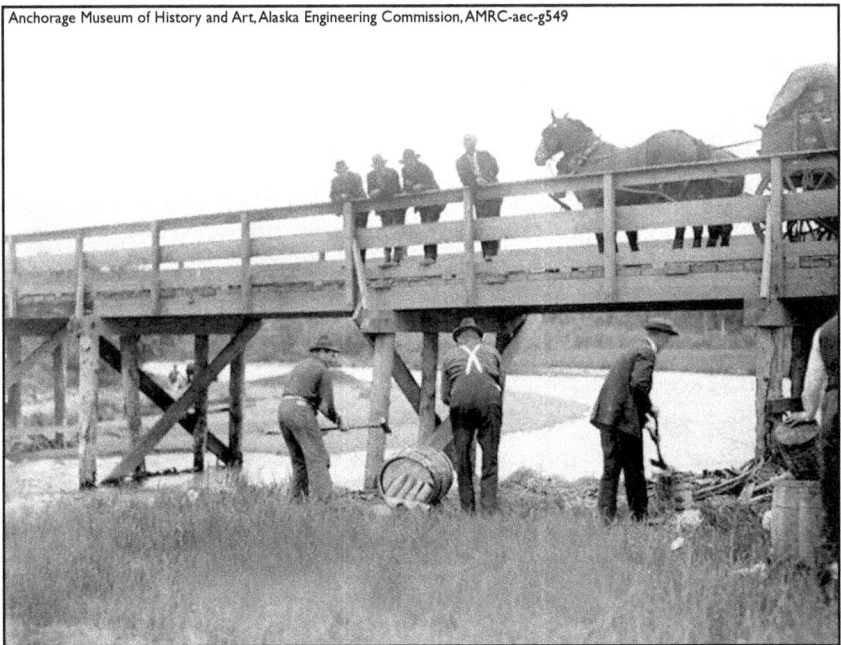

Before Anchorage became a city, it was up to U.S. deputy marshals to destroy confiscated liquor. This photo shows the marshals smashing kegs and bottles of illegal brew near Ship Creek on June 30, 1917.

Voters strongly supported prohibition in the 1916 election, and the Women's Christian Temperance Union was organized in October 1917 to help keep Anchorage dry.

Anyone caught with liquor faced one year in jail and a heavy fine.

9

FIRST POLICE CHIEF MURDERED

Although the government tried to monitor illegal activities in its new railroad town, prostitution, gambling and bootlegging flourished. According to "Anchorage, A Pictorial History," by Claus M. Naske and Ludwig J. Rowinski, those who were looking didn't have to go far to find the vice of his choice.

"The licensed saloon at Knik, 30 miles from Anchorage, supplied much of the 'booze.' There were wide-open gambling games, and characters with nicknames such as 'Dago Jim,' 'Creampuff Bill,' and 'The Pale-Faced Kid' brought a certain professionalism to the games," the authors wrote.

"In shacks and tents southeast of the town, some 30 or 40 prostitutes 'entertained' the construction workers."

An eyewitness account of Anchorage's early days where vice ran rampant comes from Kenneth Gideon, author of "Wandering Boy," who visited the town in late 1915.

"The government had decreed that there was to be no liquor sold in Anchorage nor in a five-mile strip on either side of the railroad right of way. The effect was to make bootlegging a science in Anchorage. In the winter liquor came in over the trail, on hand sleds and by dog team. In the summer when navigation opened up it might be found in five-gallon cans inside bales of hay. Cases of canned tomatoes would prove other than tomatoes."

Ladies, similar to these damsels from Dawson, worked "the line" in Anchorage. Since their cribs were located on the outskirts of town, the girls had to get camping permits from Chugach National Forest officials.

Gideon also experienced firsthand what life was like on "the line," located on land within the Chugach National Forest on the outskirts of town. Foresters often complained about having to issue camping permits to prostitutes.

"There was quite a gap between the main town and the block of houses where these women were, but a person could have found the place in a London fog. There must have been fifteen or twenty phonographs going at once, old-time phonographs of the scratch and screech variety, and the evening air was shuddering under the impact of sound. ..."

The young man had heard of the "fancy joints" that housed women of the night, but the reality of the Anchorage establishments did not meet his expectations.

"... I looked around. No rose petals. No silk curtains. The wallpaper didn't match, and the divan was an iron bedstead in the back room, with a patchwork quilt instead of a leopard skin. The bedstead had the paint knocked off in spots."

In an effort to combat increasing crime in the five-year-old railroad community, the newly formed Anchorage City Council officially established its police department in December 1920. After sifting through several applications, it appointed John "Jack" Sturgus as its first chief of police. The 60-year-old peace officer assumed his duties in January.

On Feb. 3, 1921, the *Anchorage Daily Times* reported that the council urged the chief to crack down on gambling:

"The police and jail committee reported that there were several complaints made in regard to open gambling in pool rooms, cigar stores and other places in town. The chief of police was in attendance at the council meeting and was called on for his views on the matter. After a thorough discussion, the council instructed the chief of police to rigidly enforce the provisions of the ordinance relative to gambling."

University of Alaska Fairbanks, George & Lilly Clark, UAF-1986-109-20

These four men appear to be playing cards with stacks of chips. The notice on the right reminded players that gambling for money was strictly forbidden.

Armed with his marching orders, the one-man police department spent the next few weeks patrolling the streets of Anchorage. But somewhere along the way, Sturgus may have stepped on the wrong toes. Someone shot the chief in the chest with his own gun less than three weeks after that news article appeared.

Oscar Anderson, Anchorage's first butcher, passed Sturgus on Fourth Avenue around 9 p.m. on Feb. 20, 1921, according to inquest transcripts and news articles of the time. Anderson noted that the chief was heading up E Street.

A few moments later, the chief lay dying at the bottom of a flight of stairs behind the Kyvig Building, which housed the Anchorage Drug store and now is an alley next to the Hotel Anchorage.

Night watchman John McNutt, who patrolled the downtown area and stoked fires for local businesses, saw what he thought was a drunken man lying in the snow in an alley off E Street at 9:15 p.m. McNutt called out, but only heard groans.

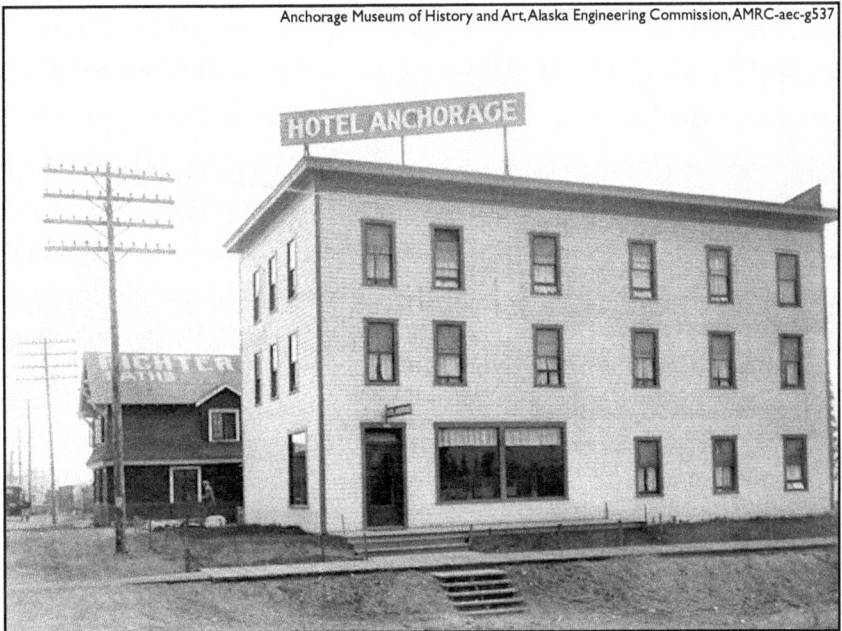

Anchorage Museum of History and Art, Alaska Engineering Commission, AMRC-aec-g537

Chief of Police John "Jack" Sturgus was gunned down in an alley off E Street in 1921.

Instead of investigating, McNutt decided to inform the chief. He turned and walked to a nearby newsstand that Sturgus often frequented during his rounds. Along the way, McNutt met a Mrs. Baxter, who lived in an apartment above the drugstore. He told her about the fallen man.

Baxter went to have a look and immediately recognized her longtime friend. She later testified that she knelt beside Sturgus, and while he drifted in and out of consciousness, he called out her nickname, "Ma." She then rushed to the Baxter's cigar store and cried for help.

When rescuers reached Sturgus, they found his Mackinaw coat and vest were thrown open. He was cold and in pain. The chief's .32 caliber Colt revolver was lying in the snow next to him and a bullet hole had pierced through the left pocket of his woolen shirt.

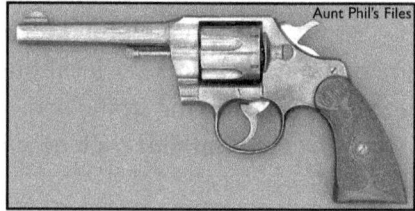

Anchorage's first chief of police was killed with his own .32 caliber Colt revolver.

They carried the gravely injured man to nearby Richter's Hotel and Bathhouse. One of the rescuers, William C. Hunt, later testified that he heard Sturgus groan and say "Oh, my head," and "Oh, Bobby, Bobby."

After a brief examination, firefighters rushed Sturgus to the hospital in their new hose wagon. As doctors Romig, Spalding and Cannon prepared for surgery to stem the bleeding from the bullet that had entered his chest and lodged near his spine, Sturgus complained about the bright lights and his hands being cold. But he remained silent on repeated questions from U.S. deputy marshals Clarence Mossman and Frank Hoffman about the identity of his attacker.

Sturgus died at 10:50 p.m. "with his lips sealed and a mystery remaining to be unraveled by the arm of the law."

Articles appearing in the *Anchorage Daily Times* revealed that during the official inquest people said they either "saw the flash of a gun" or "heard the report of a gun" the night of the shooting. But no one saw any suspicious characters.

The bullet taken from the body during the autopsy matched the gun found at the scene. The coroner's inquest, conducted by Judge Leopold David on Feb. 23, concluded that Sturgus died by the hands of unknown parties.

The *Anchorage Daily Times* offered several motives for the murder of Sturgus.

One suggested the chief was killed "while endeavoring to make an arrest or while watching in the rear of the drugstore for some man under suspicion."

Other theories suggested that Sturgus had been "murdered by members of an illicit liquor gang," "in revenge" because of the "activity of the marshal's office during the past week," and while "watching for someone conveying moonshine liquor through the alley, and when attempting to halt them, met his death."

The Alaska Dispatch also suggested Sturgus' death was connected to Anchorage's thriving illegal bootlegging business when it reported that the chief may have been killed in revenge for the "capture of 12 moonshine outfits last week by United States marshals."

Although the city offered a reward of $1,000 for information about its chief's death, and council members pledged another $950, the murder has never been solved.

Sturgus is buried along the iron fence that faces Cordova Street in the Anchorage Memorial Park Cemetery.

A FEW CITY FOREFATHERS

10

PIONEER PHILANTHROPIST ARRIVES

"**D**own but never out" could well be the biographical title for one of Anchorage's first philanthropists. Z.J. Loussac's is a tale that could have been written by Horatio Alger, for it has all the ingredients of one of that author's success stories. Three times Loussac came to Alaska to make his fortune. The third time was the charm, for twice he returned to the Lower 48, not only broke, but deeply in debt.

He was broke, too, when he arrived in the United States from his native Russia in 1901. The 18-year-old boy, a refugee from the tsar's secret police, landed in New York and found a job running errands for a drugstore in a Russian neighborhood. He worked there long enough to learn basic English – enough to understand the glowing tales he heard of Klondike gold.

When a man emptied large nuggets from his pockets to prove his stories of Yukon wealth, it was enough for the wide-eyed youth. Since the streets of New York weren't paved with gold, as so many immigrants had been led to believe, Loussac decided to go where he thought he could pick up gold by the handful.

His first attempts to reach the Klondike gold fields landed him broke in Great Falls, Montana, where he had to work as a drugstore clerk until he could save enough money to return to New York. He again worked and decided to get a pharmacist's degree so he could get into the drugstore business. He attended the New York College of Pharmacy and graduated in 1903.

The thoughts of gold nuggets weren't far from his mind, however, and in 1907 he tried again to make it to the North Country. This time he made it as far as Seattle. Although the Klondike fever had subsided by this time, people still were picking up gold from the beaches of Nome.

Three months passed before Loussac landed on a boat bound for Nome, his savings depleted to the point that he ate on 10 cents a day. Later he recalled:

"My diet wasn't healthy or balanced."

In Nome, Loussac met with the first of his Alaska failures. The sluice box he and his partners built was not constructed properly and the whole mine washed down the creek when the snow melted and the water rose. In later years, he told how he had to hock his fur coat and shirt studs to buy a ticket back to Seattle.

After making another bankroll by working at drugstores in

Z.J. Loussac probably shopped in the Nome Alaska Mercantile, pictured here, while he was there in 1907 trying his hand as a gold miner.

Dentist F.W. Herms and Z.J. Loussac, right, traveled along the Iditarod-Flat Creek Trail in 1912.

Seattle, as well as San Francisco, he headed to the gold fields that had opened up the Iditarod region. Loussac began a drugstore in a new 10x12-foot tent.

When a fire destroyed a whole business block and wiped him out, his credit was good enough to borrow money from a local bank to rebuild. However, the gold fever in the district had burned out, as well, and the miner left for a new gold strike at Ruby. Loussac lost his building and his stock when the bank and Northern Commercial Company took them over.

By this time he was close to $5,000 in debt. He found no work in Seattle when he returned, so he again traveled to San Francisco and hired on at the Owl Drugstore, where he lived frugally as he paid off his debt.

Twice he'd sought riches in Alaska and failed. But the North drew him back again, and by 1916 he had made his way to the new tent city on Cook Inlet. The third time proved to be the charm for Zachariah J. Loussac, for he got in on the ground floor of the town that would grow to be Alaska's largest city.

He soon made a reputation for himself as an up-and-coming merchant – wide-awake and progressive. He advertised his drugstore

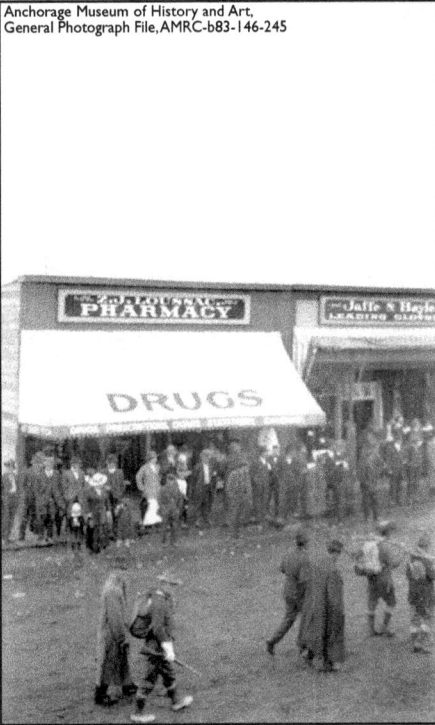

Z.J. Loussac built a drugstore in fledgling 1916 Anchorage.

as having "what you want when you want it."

Loussac put in a writing desk and supplied it with paper and envelopes free to anyone who wanted to write a letter. He offered a phonograph with all the latest records, and customers were invited to play them without charge. Long before airlines, he imported fresh flowers – since they were a week in transit and often either frozen or dried up, he gave most of them away rather than let them dry up in the store.

His daily newspaper advertisement, titled "Loussac's Daily Gossip," had a subhead, "Cents and Sense." At the beginning of a New Year, he titled his column, "Full Steam Ahead," and told how the past year was wonderful and the New Year would be even better.

And each succeeding year did prove better than the last for Loussac. By 1939, he was out of debt for the first time since 1909. The mushroom growth of Anchorage during World War II was the turning point for his business. Not only was he able to pay off all his debts, but he found money "rolling in by the bushel baskets!"

"I had to fill up the showcases and get out more stock every night after the store closed," he said later. "I couldn't hire enough people to keep up with the job. Every morning, when I opened the store, I was swamped with customers … they picked out what they wanted and handed me the money. All I had to do was to take the money, ring up the cash register and wrap some packages."

Anchorage had spread out toward Ninth Avenue by 1918, where new-fangled automobiles mixed with pedestrians and horse-drawn wagons on its wide streets. Businesses included the New Method Cleaners, Empress Theatre, Pioneer Steam Laundry and Mrs. T.D. Corlew Dry Goods.

He'd acquired another drugstore by this time and was one of the organizers of the Evan Jones Company, one of Alaska's major coal producers. He owned various Anchorage buildings, too, but he gradually began phasing out his business interests.

"It's no fun to run a business when the money comes in bushel baskets," he said. "That's no fun, just work."

A fire rages in the business district on Fourth Avenue Anchorage on Feb. 7, 1922.

Manley & Mayer Architects designed the Z.J. Loussac Public Library in the early 1950s.

The entrepreneur evidently didn't consider the next phase of his life to be work. He threw himself into a civic career. He accepted all the jobs others turned down – every sticky community drive and chore that no one else wanted. Chairmanship became, for him, a fulltime operation. He then progressed to the presidency of every organization to which he belonged and was elected to three terms as mayor of Anchorage.

Ben Boeke, who was city clerk during Loussac's terms, said he was a "progressive mayor, who pressed for street paving and utility expansion. He was one of the founders of the League of Alaskan Cities."

In 1946, Loussac set up the Loussac Foundation, which he dedicated to the recreational, cultural, scientific or educational activities in the Anchorage area. The year before, he'd become seriously ill and hospitalized in Seattle.

While convalescing, he had time to consider the ups and downs of his life – his struggles, failures and final success. He wanted to do something for Anchorage – the city had been so good to him – and decided to give it half his wealth.

His gift was hailed as the "most generous gesture ever made by a living Alaskan toward his fellow Alaskans."

"I hope it will set an example for others who came here to

Z.J. Loussac established a foundation for the city he loved that allowed it to build a grand library.

Alaska and accumulated some wealth," Loussac said. "I hope it will encourage them to keep the wealth here and make Alaska a better place to live."

The city's Z.J. Loussac Pubic Library was built by the foundation and given to the city. The foundation also made grants to different Alaska universities and the Anchorage Community Theatre. Several gifts were given to the King's Lake Corp., and a two-year grant was given to study Alaska Native music.

In 1962, Loussac celebrated his 80th birthday, and the whole city celebrated with him. Gov. William A. Egan proclaimed it Zack Loussac Day, a day of celebration for all Alaska, and he and the other state officials joined with Loussac's Anchorage friends in observance. Even President John F. Kennedy sent birthday greetings.

Plaques from the Pioneers, Rotary Club, the YMCA and the city of Anchorage, as well as gifts from other organizations were bestowed upon him. As a climax, a tape recording was played of a speech made by the late Anthony J. Dimond, who said:

"He's one of the best public officials I've ever known in my lifetime, and I've known quite a few of them."

In return, Loussac replied, "You've been hearing some awful good things about someone called Z.J. Loussac. I would like to be the one described ... in all the things I've done for Alaska, I have to ask the people of Anchorage to share this achievement ... some of the finest people in the world are here in Alaska."

He also paid tribute to his wife, Ada, whom he'd married in 1949. He claimed that the "greatest thing that has happened to me here (in Anchorage) was that here is where I met my wife."

The Loussacs had moved to Seattle in 1953, but they made frequent trips back to Alaska. Loussac was in Anchorage during the 1964 Good Friday Earthquake and someone who met him then said, "He was very calm, walking around with his hands in his pockets and helping keep up morale."

Loussac died in Seattle in March 1965 at 82. On Zack Loussac Day, the honored guest had said, "If any man or any person has as happy a life as I've had throughout the years here, I couldn't ask any more for him. In the years I've lived in Anchorage, I've found all the happiness a man could hope to achieve."

Philanthropist Z.J. Loussac

Anchorage Museum of History and Art, General Photograph File. AMRC-b75-134-151

11

"Cap" Lathrop Gambles on Alaska

One of Alaska's greatest industrialists began his long and distinguished career by operating a contracting business out of a tent he'd pitched in Seattle in 1889. Austin E. "Cap" Lathrop, then 24, offered his services to raze and clean up burned buildings from a fire that had roared through the city shortly before his arrival. He also excavated for new structures and soon became known as the "boy contractor."

The young go-getter continued in the building industry until his prosperity dissolved during the depression of 1893. Broke and in debt, he became intrigued when he heard about the discovery of gold in the Turnagain Arm area of Cook Inlet in Alaska.

The news interested the Michigan native, not due to the lure of gold, but because the rush offered opportunities in shipping and freighting. Through a loan from A.E. Barton of the Fry Meat Packing House, Lathrop and his friends, a Capt. Kelly and John O'Neill, bought a small two-mast schooner, the *L.J. Perry*.

Alaska's rivers have provided its rugged pioneers a means for transportation and exploration from the time the Natives first crossed the land bridge from Siberia. Canoes, kayaks and other small craft were the usual mode of passage in the river systems until after the United States purchased Alaska in 1867.

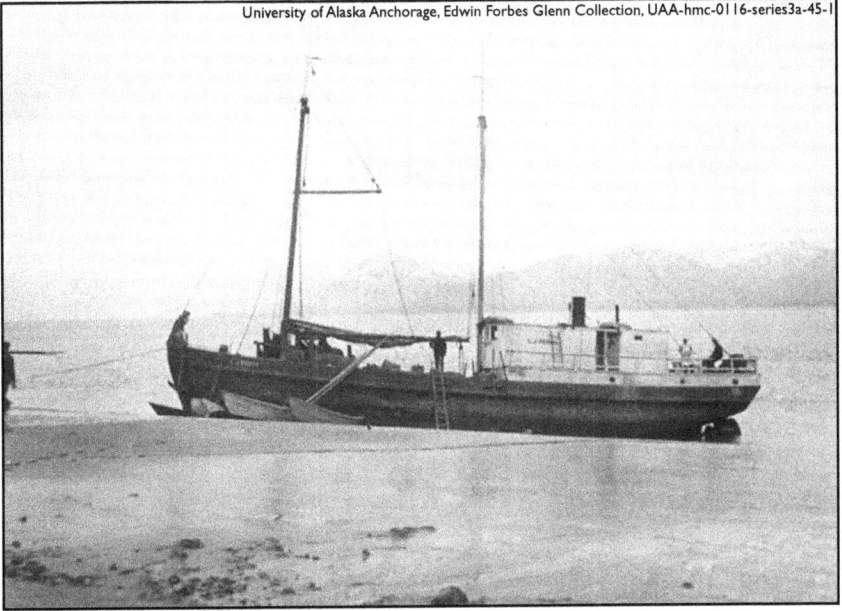

Capt. Austin Lathrop plied the waters of Cook Inlet during the 1890s, transporting people and supplies to mining camps along the way.

On July 4, 1869, the Alaska Commercial Company's sternwheeler *Yukon* made its first voyage up the Yukon River. It pushed two boats with supplies and carried a government surveying party. After 1,000 miles and 23 days, it successfully arrived at Fort Yukon, according to Alaska History and Cultural Studies.

The *Yukon* paddled along the river between May and September carrying supplies to trading posts, taking furs to market and moving freight, fur traders and prospectors up and down the river.

Its first competitor showed up in 1878, with others following, but Alaska Commercial always bought them out.

After gold was discovered in the Klondike in 1896, 30 steamboat companies formed to operate around 300 boats on the Yukon. The route from St. Michael to the gold fields proved to be a liquid gold mine, as a boat could pay for itself on a single trip upriver. On its first trip from St. Michael to Dawson, the *Leah* carried 300 passengers and 600 tons of freight and made a $41,000 profit.

The steamboat crews worked hard for that money, however, since the boats burned wood. A two-boiler boat needed around two cords of wood an hour, around the clock, so the vessels had to stop every 10 to 12 hours for fuel.

Boat crews cut wood in the beginning, but soon wood camps were established that provided work for Natives and unsuccessful miners. The steamboats, which only traveled about 7 mph on the lower Yukon, also had to stop frequently to have their boilers cleaned. This operation took about 10 hours because the fire had to be put out, the boiler cooled and washed, and then river water flushed through to remove mud and debris.

The steamboat companies often hired local Natives as firemen and deckhands, and those who knew the channels and bends in the rivers, were recruited as pilots to guide the boats through stretches of the upper river.

Lathrop and his partners sailed out of Seattle aboard the *L.J. Perry* in 1896 loaded with supplies for Alaska Commercial. The venture proved successful, and within a year, Lathrop bought out his partners and obtained his master's ticket. The seagoing captain, "Cap" Lathrop, was on his way to years of steady success.

Anchorage Museum of History and Art, General Photograph File, AMRC-b84-75-4

Sternwheelers tied up at Capt. Austin Lathrop's dock at Ship Creek in 1915.

Lathrop plied the waters of Cook Inlet carrying freight and passengers for several years. He also dabbled in coal, oil and copper until the federal government set aside millions of acres of public land for reserves.

It's reported that he, like other Cordova residents, was embittered about the closing of the coalfields, which forced Alaskans to import coal when they had more than enough of the fuel close by.

And some say Lathrop had a big hand in dumping tons of imported coal into Cordova Bay during a "coal party" in 1911. The message hit its mark; within three years the government opened the coal lands.

Around 1910, he started the Alaska Transfer Company in Seward. He moved the business to Anchorage in 1915 when he learned the Alaska Railroad needed men to handle moves from the tent city to the new townsite. By 1919, he had sold Alaska Transfer and built the Empress Theater and an apartment house on the corner of Fourth Avenue and H Street.

Movies provided a social outlet for people struggling to survive in

Austin Lathrop saw opportunity knocking when he realized that the Alaska Railroad would need a moving service for its labor force.

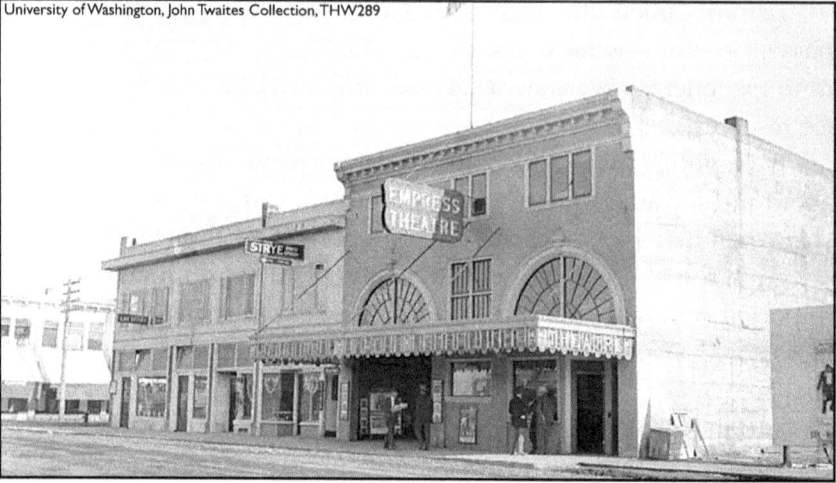

Above: The railroad workers in the new Ship Creek community of Anchorage needed entertainment and Capt. Austin Lathrop was happy to oblige. He built the Empress Theatre between 1916-1917 and soon went into the movie-making business, too.

Below: Lathrop moved on to Fairbanks and built another Empress Theatre in 1927.

the Last Frontier. Lathrop, who delighted in providing motion picture entertainment to adults and children alike, decided to get involved in film production, as well.

Movies about Alaska, mostly based on books by Jack London and Rex Beach, thrilled audiences during the early 1900s. But all motion pictures were filmed outside of Alaska. So when a group of Oregon promoters planning a travelogue and feature film about the territory toured Alaska's towns in 1922, several Anchorage residents decided to go into the filmmaking business themselves.

They formed the Alaska Motion Picture Corporation and elected Lathrop, who owned theaters in Anchorage, Fairbanks, Seward, Valdez and Cordova, as president. The businessmen raised $75,000 to produce a 12-reel picture titled "The Cheechakos," which included a three-reel travelogue followed by a nine-reel drama.

The group built a 7,000-square-foot studio in downtown Anchorage

Many Anchorage residents dressed up in gold-rush clothes and took small parts in the movie "The Cheechakos." This is a dancehall scene.

with an eye to becoming the "Hollywood of the North." About 1,000 Anchorage residents hosted a "free dance and jollification at the moviedome" to welcome the cast of actors recruited from Oregon, New York and Hollywood when they arrived in 1923.

Shortly thereafter, the cast and production crew traveled by train to McKinley National Park, now called Denali National Park and Preserve, to film winter scenes with dog teams to show the drama of the gold-rush days. They also traveled to Girdwood where they recreated the days of 1898 when miners climbed the Chilkoot Pass.

The *Anchorage Daily Times* reported on the production of the silent film in its April 4, 1923, edition:

"The struggles of former years will once again be fought by real veterans of the early days, many of them still retaining and wearing the identical garments and packs, such as jackets, parkas, fur hats and pack boards used by their owners during the stampede days over the great Chilkoot Pass. Tandem dog teams will once again hit the trail with the Yukon sled in prominence. The vast illumination will portray sled loads of supplies of flour, bacon, salt, beans, sugar, coffee, tobacco and other bare necessities used by the prospectors."

Alaska State Library, Winter and Pond, ASL-P87-0707

Gold-seekers braved the elements to climb the Chilkoot Trail in Southeast Alaska during the late 1890s. For the movie, "The Cheechakos," actors simulated the climb on a mountain at Girdwood.

A FEW CITY FOREFATHERS

The script of the only movie made by the Alaska Motion Picture Corporation tells the story of two good-hearted gold prospectors who take in a young girl who was left motherless after a ship explosion. When the sourdoughs strike it rich, the younger miner falls in love with the girl. Through tough experiences, they all learn that disreputable gamblers can be as dangerous as the frozen north.

When released in New York in 1924, Variety dismissed the plot as "hokey," and expressed doubt that a film with such an unpronounceable title could succeed. Indeed, "The Cheechakos" failed in the Lower 48 and dropped from movie history.

Although Lathrop and his group had hoped to make more movies in their Anchorage studio, they soon modified it into an exhibition center for the Western Alaska Fair over the 1924 Labor Day weekend. It later served as the Anchorage community center for years.

After the commercial flop of his silent movie, Lathrop turned his attention to other pursuits.

He pushed north to Fairbanks in 1927, where he built a new theater

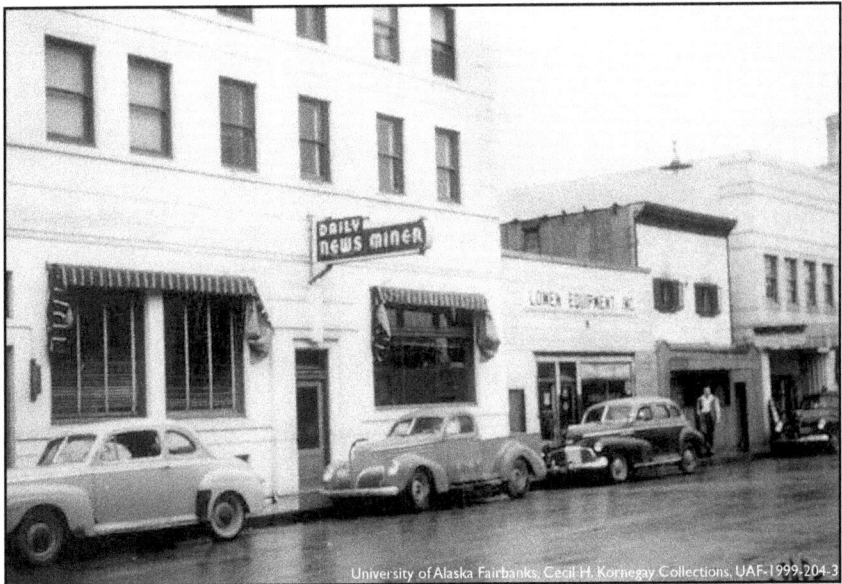

Austin Lathrop built a four-story concrete building in Fairbanks that housed the Daily News Miner.

from reinforced concrete, a first in Fairbanks. He also purchased an interest in the Healy River Coal Corporation, operating in Suntrana, 117 miles south of Fairbanks.

Lathrop later built a four-story concrete apartment building, which housed his newly acquired *Fairbanks Daily News-Miner* newspaper on its first floor.

In 1939, he brought radio to the community when he went on the air with KFAR. His station was the first to hear about the attack on Pearl Harbor the morning of Dec. 7, 1941, and relayed the message to Gen. Simon Bolivar Buckner in Anchorage.

The sea-captain-turned-broadcast pioneer began construction of the 4th Avenue Theatre in Anchorage in 1941, but the war diverted raw materials to the war efforts. The modern art deco building finally opened its doors in 1947 with "The Jolson Story" flashing on its marquee.

"The theatre is a landmark in the transition of Anchorage from a frontier community to a city of permanence," an *Anchorage Daily Times* editorial proclaimed.

Anchorage Museum of History and Art, Ward W. Wells Collection, AMRC-wws-3292

Austin Lathrop was the main pioneer who brought radio to Alaska. He located KENI's offices above the 4th Avenue Theatre in Anchorage.

Capt. Austin E. Lathrop, seen here looking over a set of blueprints, was one of Alaska's greatest entrepreneurs.

After the war, Lathrop built the KENI radio transmitter at the mouth of Chester Creek in Anchorage. He located its studios and offices over the 4th Avenue Theatre in the new Lathrop Building. KENI and KFAR were the forerunners of what later became Midnight Sun Broadcasting Company.

"He was very colorful and had a lot of charm," general manager Al Bramstedt once said of his boss. "He was very popular with the wives of his employees, as with every employee. He could be the most cantankerous man on Earth, and then turn around half an hour later and be the most charming, gallant and the most courtly individual you ever knew. He was a man of different moods, and I think he used his temper at the right time in business for emphasis. A lot of people never learned to be comfortable with him because they were afraid – they didn't know him that well."

Lathrop's political philosophy, tempered during his bitter experiences in resource development and the consequent resource withdrawals, leaned toward Alaska independence.

The News, a weekly started by Norman Brown in 1946, received assistance from Lathrop to start publishing the *Anchorage Daily News* in May 1948. For the next decade it tried to neutralize the pro-statehood editorial policy of the *Anchorage Daily Times*.

Lathrop remained active well into his 80s. But on June 26, 1950, he died when a railroad car accidentally ran over him at his Healy River coal mine at Suntrana. He's buried in Forest Lawn Cemetery in Seattle, Washington.

12

MR. BASEBALL HITS TOWN

The infant town of Anchorage, only a few years old, had always been interested in baseball when "Mr. Baseball" blew into the lusty, young railroad town in 1922. Everyone turned out to watch the games played evenings after supper and weekends. As far back as 1916, Anchorage had a regulation baseball diamond, built by the Bridge Engineers, located in what was known as Recreation Park in the railroad yards north of Ship Creek.

A press box, with private telephone communication to the

Railroad workers enjoy a game of baseball on a roughed-out ball field in Ship Creek's tent city on July 4, 1915.

University of Alaska Anchorage, Marie Silverman Collection, UAA-hmc-0778-5-14

Baseball players lined up to play ball on July 4, 1915. Spectators eagerly looked on amidst tents near Ship Creek.

newspaper office, provided avid fans with a play-by-play account of the games. And competition was keen, not only in Anchorage, but also with nearby communities like Knik and Seward. Fans who loved the game traveled by boat to Kern Creek, and then pumped themselves to Seward by handcars to catch a glimpse of the action.

For a short time, baseball was eclipsed by the clouds of World War I, when Anchorage lost most of its able-bodied men. Seventy-five percent of the town's male population was eligible for the draft.

The town did rally enough fellows for a special benefit game in 1918, however. The game between the Elks and the Masons turned out a little lopsided, with the Masons taking it 19-9, but the townspeople had a great time and netted $57.60 for the American Red Cross.

When the war ended, Anchorage's fortune took an upward turn. Ample funds were available, for the first time since building of the railroad started, and construction went full steam ahead.

In September 1922, William F. Mulcahy hired on from the New York, New Heaven and Hartford Railway to take the position of station auditor assistant – he retired as general auditor. Before that he had never traveled farther from his native Connecticut than Boston or New York to watch the Yankees and Red Sox play ball.

A FEW CITY FOREFATHERS

Alaska Pacific University, Anchorage Historic Photograph Collection, APUAHP-f10-53

The Elks, on the right, and Masons, on the left, challenged each other to a baseball game to benefit the American Red Cross on May 25, 1918.

The new land must have seemed strange and different from his former home. The days were getting short and cold in September and the winter nights long and dark. But sitting around the bunkhouse at night, he found the talk was all about the previous season's baseball games, and predictions were rife about what the next summer would bring.

Alaska State Library, Ray W. Moss Collection, ASL-P11-102

Workers liked to talk about baseball while hanging out in the railroad bunkhouses.

Baseball teams met at the Alaska Engineering Commission camp at Potter Creek for some of their games. Note all the spectators who arrived by train cars from Anchorage to watch.

Mulcahy, who loved baseball, began to feel that maybe Alaska wasn't so strange and different after all.

In 1923, Mulcahy became president of the baseball league, as well as its treasurer, secretary, groundskeeper and ticket seller. He traveled to Fairbanks with an all-star team to play in the Midnite Sun Celebration, and told his wife, Gertrude, his team "was phenomenal."

The Alaska Railroad supported Mulcahy's involvement with the growing baseball program. His employers not only gave him time off to arrange games, they helped in other ways, too. Mulcahy's wife remembered one time sitting in the railroad's personnel office waiting for him.

"It was summertime," she said during an interview in the early 1970s," and a dozen or so husky young men came in from the states looking for jobs. Most of the work was for unskilled labor, and the employment manager, after reading their applications, would say, 'and what position do you play in baseball?' "

The fellows who knew what position they could play were the first ones hired, and they came back each summer during school vacation.

There was always a shortage of money for equipment, and because all transportation was by boat, it took at least three weeks to get baseball equipment. The league's finances were so precarious that to order a large amount of baseballs in advance was unheard of, so baseballs were treated like gem stones.

"Bill had kids posted outside the park to retrieve the balls – collecting 10 cents for every one brought back," Gertrude Mulcahy remembered.

She, herself, was up in the stands the minute a ball left the bat – foul, out or fly, in order to rescue the precious horsehides. Called "Bill's Bat Boy," Gertrude carried the equipment, balls, tickets and extra wraps to protect the players from the winds that invariably came off the inlet every afternoon.

During those first 10 years that Mulcahy ran the league, teams were sponsored by the Moose Lodge and the railroad; a team with real uniforms was sponsored by a prominent plumbing company. Most uniforms, donated by various merchants, had the

William Mulcahy encouraged children to try baseball. This young man, glove in hand, appears ready to play a game.

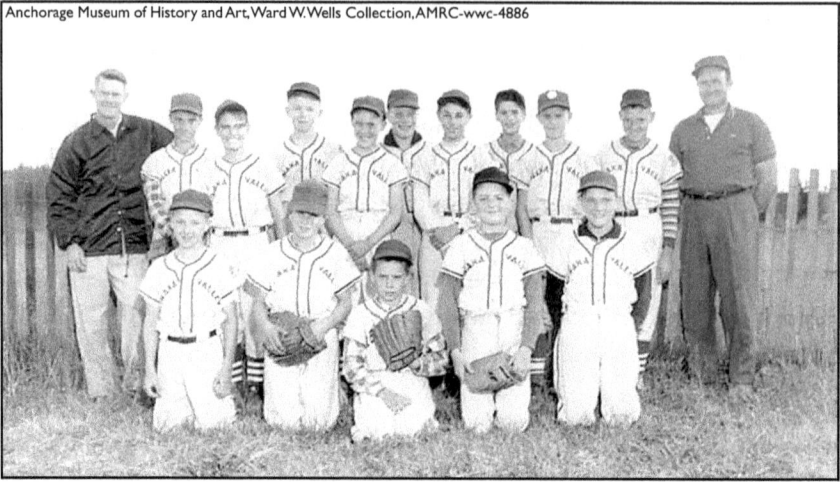

William Mulcahy promoted sports for youth as a way to keep children out of trouble. This is a Little League team from the Nunaka Valley area of Anchorage on July 7, 1961.

names of the donors blazoned across their backs, making the players walking advertisements.

Besides his work with adult baseball, Mulcahy became deeply involved in recreation for the youth of Anchorage. He believed sports to be an answer to the problem of juvenile delinquency and devoted countless hours to promoting sports and facilities for the boys and girls of the city. He interested civic leaders and clubs in providing facilities for basketball and hockey, as well as baseball.

Anchorage had five teams by the time World War II rolled around. With construction of military bases, and necessary personnel increases, many more teams entered the mix. Competition was hot and heavy. Special Services and chaplains were anxious to have recreation for their men, and buses were run between the bases and Anchorage.

"I'd like to bet many thousands of boys who served in Alaska remember those wonderful games and the 'Old Man' or 'Pop' as Bill was affectionately called," said Gertrude Mulcahy during an interview in the early 1970s.

In 1947, Mulcahy was named Alaska's first National Baseball Congress Commissioner, which was the beginning of a program that was to carry Anchorage's Glacier Pilots and Bucs to several national championships. In 1948, he organized a team of all-stars to go to Wichita, Kansas, and the team unanimously voted that he should go with them. Appointed as a scout for the St. Louis Browns, Mulcahy produced players that made their mark in the big leagues.

Mulcahy also assisted in getting youth in the community interested in the game. He had his own boys' teams – the Bear Cats and the City Slickers – for boys ages 9-11. They played on the regular diamond before the main games, and they played exhibition games at the Matanuska fairs.

He served as chairman of the City Parks and Playgrounds in his continuing service to the youth of Anchorage. That service was recognized in 1948 with a salute from Red Barber's "Club House" over the Columbia Broadcasting System. He was cited for "promoting good citizenship through sports," and he turned the check for $100 that accompanied the citation over to junior ice hockey.

Mulcahy always found time for a worthy cause. He helped establish the YMCA, serving on its first board of directors; he was

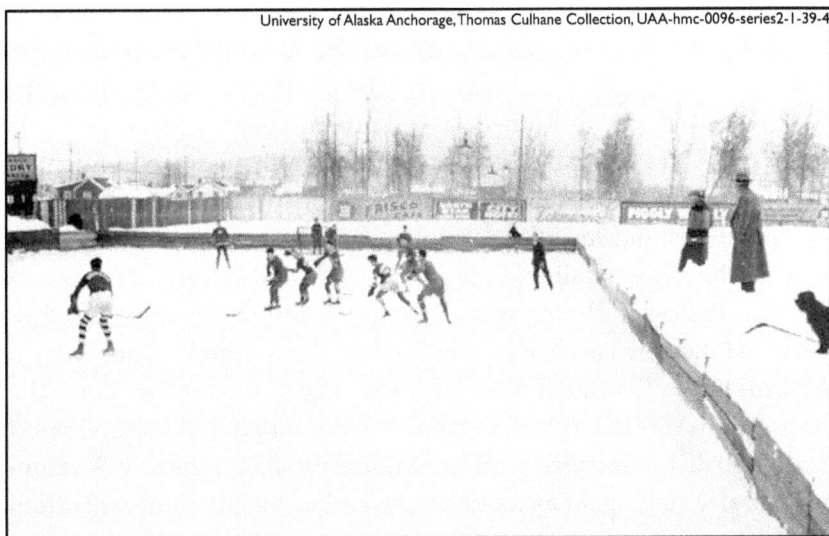

University of Alaska Anchorage, Thomas Culhane Collection, UAA-hmc-0096-series2-1-39-4

The ever-sports-minded Mulcahy also supported ice hockey as a means to keep youth occupied.

Anchorage finally outgrew the Alaska Railroad Commission's stadium and grandstand, seen here with a game under way on May 30, 1917.

treasurer and director of Recreation for the USA; he coordinated American Red Cross activities for service men at Fort Richardson and Elmendorf, and he was on The Salvation Army advisory board. For his service to the Alaska Railroad and Alaska's youth, he received a Commendable Service Award from the U.S. Department of Interior, citing "extra-curricular activities in promoting recreational organizations and facilities for young people ... created much good will for the Alaska Railroad."

The selfless Irishman was surprised when it was announced in 1951 that the new baseball field at Seventh Avenue and C Street was to bear his name. Considered one of Anchorage's "Grand Old Men," the community wanted to honor the man who, for so many years, stood for baseball in Anchorage. With seating for 750, Mulcahy Stadium held nearly half again as many as the earlier facility. A new stadium at 16th and Gambell, completed in time for the 1964 season, also was given his name.

Mulcahy retired from the railroad in 1953, and prior to departure, he and his wife – his right-hand "bat boy" – were honored at a testimonial dinner in recognition of their service to the community.

The Mulcahys returned to Connecticut, where Mr. Baseball organized the Golden Age Club and the Retired Men's Club.

On New Year's Day, 1965, Mulcahy died at 68. His wife wrote in the summer of 1972:

"His was a full and happy life – and I sometimes wonder, now that baseball season is here, if he isn't scouting for some heavenly team for All Stars to play on Cloud Nine."

In 1964, the city of Anchorage honored Mr. Baseball by naming its new stadium Mulcahy, seen here looking east with Gambell and Ingra streets running across the center.

TRAILBLAZERS ON WHEELS

13

A VERY BUMPY RIDE

On July 29, 1913, one of Alaska's trailblazers started on a historic journey – the first automobile trip over the wagon trail from Fairbanks to Valdez.

But that wasn't Robert E. "Bobby" Sheldon's first experience with a motorized vehicle. Sheldon, who'd never seen an automobile, also built the first car in Alaska. As he described his creation:

"All I knew about them was what I read in papers from the states. I was interested in mechanics, and being on the night shift at the Skagway powerhouse, I had considerable time to think it over.

"It was my job to make all kinds of emergency repairs on the equipment. My funds were limited, but I finally located four buggy wheels and built a frame over them.

"I salvaged an old marine engine from a deserted boat, put some gears on it and made a chain drive. I tested the thing late one night when no one was around. It really worked."

The car could carry two passengers at the dizzying speed of 15 mph. Back in 1905, when horse-drawn wagons and sled dogs were the popular means of land transportation, his invention caused quite a stir in Skagway, located in Southeast Alaska. It still draws a lot of attention in the University of Alaska Fairbanks museum where it's on display.

Born in Snohomish, Washington, in 1883, Sheldon landed in

University of Washington, Asahel Curtis Collection, CURl423

When Robert Sheldon arrived in Skagway, pictured above in 1897, the town was just developing as a supply center for prospectors heading to the gold fields of the Klondike.

Skagway with his father in 1897 with plans to strike it rich in the Klondike gold fields. But Sheldon's father died before the pair reached their goal, leaving the then 14-year-old boy to fend for himself.

He got a job selling newspapers and had the distinction of being the first newsboy in Alaska to sell a paper to the notorious criminal Soapy Smith. Sheldon later said:

"Soapy always gave me $1 for his paper. The regular price was two bits. As you can imagine, I was very sorry when Soapy was shot by the vigilantes!"

In his spare time, the natural mechanic read everything he could lay his hands on and quietly started taking correspondence courses. Sheldon eventually got work in the engine rooms of small steamers operating between Skagway, Dyea and Juneau.

Sheldon turned out to be a natural pile-driver operator and marine and stationary steam engineer, too. Besides working on boats, he also labored on the Bracket wagon road and the White Pass and Yukon Railroad.

In a few years, the "jack of all trades" had experience in most of the available means of transportation in Alaska. Then his imagination was caught by the new-fangled cars. As Sheldon told it:

"There was this beautiful girl there in Skagway, and I was trying to beat another fellow's time. He was the son of a banker and had the use of his father's horse and buggy, which was a luxury in those days. I didn't have a horse and buggy and had no immediate prospects of getting either. One night I had the idea of building one of those new gasoline engine-powered buggies I had been reading about. ..."

The young lady enjoyed the runabout rides with Sheldon, but she married the other fellow.

Love later smiled on the adventurer, who left Skagway in 1908 and became manager of Fairbanks' Northern Commercial Power Plant. He met and married Anne Bergman in Fairbanks in 1920. The couple had one daughter, Frances Ruth.

Sheldon continued his interest in automobiles and avidly read everything he could find on this new type of transportation. After

Anchorage Museum of History and Art, Crary-Henderson Collection, AMRC-b62-1-a-220

The first horse-drawn sleighs from Fairbanks arrived in Valdez on Dec. 20, 1905.

studying several makes through magazines and stateside catalogs, he ordered a four-passenger Model-T Ford convertible touring car.

The Detroit price was $390. But by the time it traveled by rail to Seattle, by steamship to St. Michael and by riverboat up the Yukon, Tanana and Chena rivers to Fairbanks, it cost Sheldon $1,297.

He made that sum and more in two weeks after its arrival, however, by whizzing up and down dirt wagon roads with passengers giving him gold for the privilege of riding in his car.

After friends offered him $100 to drive them 120 miles down the Richardson Trail to Donnelley Roadhouse, Sheldon realized that automobiles could be more than a novelty. The trip, which took five days by horse and wagon, took seven hours with the Model-T.

The lucrative possibilities of commercial transportation weren't lost on the entrepreneur. Sheldon quit his job with Northern

University of Washington, Alaska-Yukon Pacific Exposition Collection, AYP145

Robert Sheldon drove a Ford Model-T, similar to the one pictured here at the Alaska-Yukon-Pacific Exposition in 1909, from Fairbanks to Valdez in 1913.

Commercial, and along with three passengers, he set out on July 29, 1913, to try the impossible – travel by car over the primitive wagon trail from Fairbanks to Valdez.

They jolted over washouts, plowed through slides and mud and forded streams with no bridges. One passenger had enough and got off at Donnelley, but the other two – mining men named John Ronan and John Ferguson – stayed on until the bitter end.

The men drove into Valdez at 11 p.m. on Aug. 2. They'd covered the 370 miles in 59 hours of actual driving time.

Shortly after arriving in Valdez, Sheldon sold the Model-T for $1,300 and bought a bicycle. He then pedaled back to Fairbanks to become the first person to ride a bike from Valdez to the interior city.

When he returned to Fairbanks, Sheldon ordered more Model-Ts and organized Sheldon's Auto-Stage Line, which he operated with various partners until 1926. The company averaged three trips a month and those excursions were rugged any time of year.

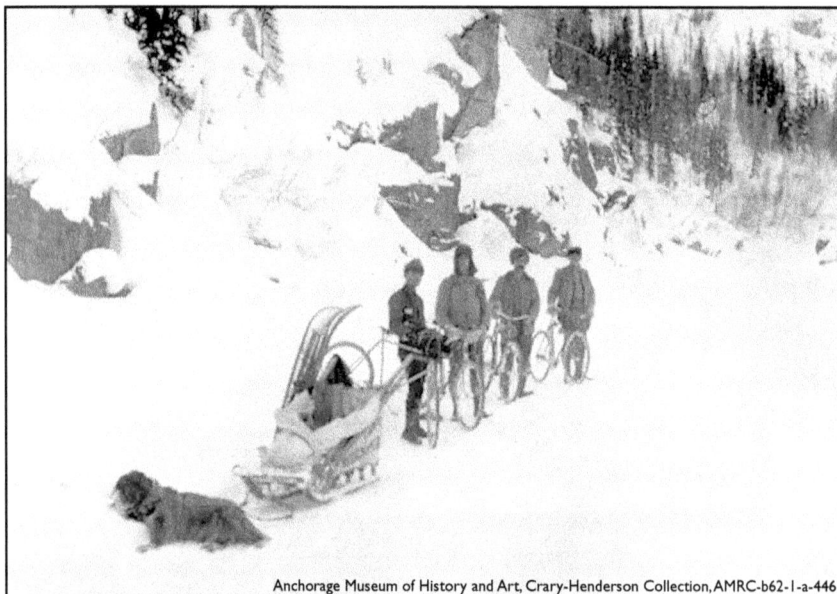

Anchorage Museum of History and Art, Crary-Henderson Collection, AMRC-b62-1-a-446

Once Robert Sheldon proved it was possible to ride from Valdez to Fairbanks via bicycle, others tried the adventure. These men are pictured in the Tiekel Canyon along the Valdez-Fairbanks Trail.

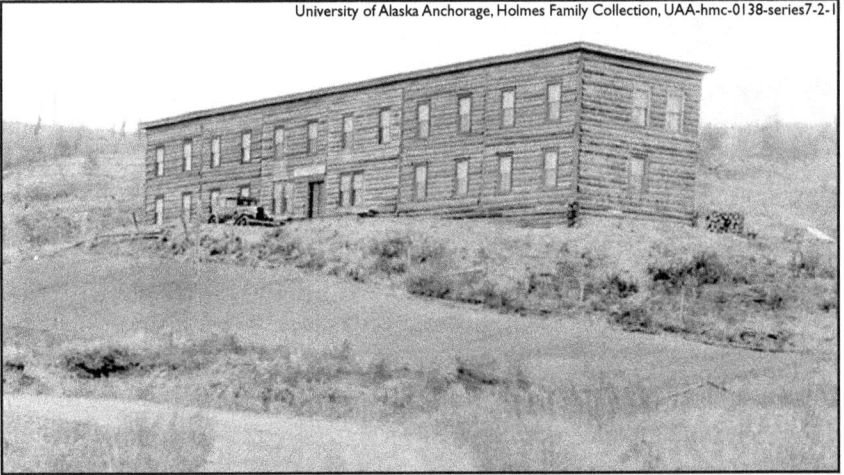

Robert Sheldon, the first person to take an automobile from Fairbanks to Valdez, proved that motorized vehicles could make the trip in a fraction of the time of horses and dogs. As a result, many overnight lodgings, like the Richardson Roadhouse – seen here on the Fairbanks-Valdez Trail – became unnecessary.

In winter, with Thompson Pass clogged with 50-foot snowdrifts, the stage line bypassed Valdez to connect with the Copper River and Northwestern Railway at Chitina. Isabelle Pass, impassable at times, often had to be portaged by horse and wagon.

But in spite of all the difficulties, the 100 miles a day made by Sheldon's fleet proved impossible competition for other outfits. Many historic roadhouses went out of business, too, for they were spaced 20 miles apart – a day's trip for horse and wagon or dogs and sled. Those means of transportation had seen their day. The age of the automobile had arrived.

Automobile races at Fairbanks fanned interest in the new mode of travel. In 1919, Sheldon raced a car specially built for him at Owen Meal's shop in Valdez. On his way to Fairbanks to enter the race, he made the trip in 32 hours racing time, but while his car ran away from all others in the beginning of the contest, it developed engine trouble and quit in the last quarter.

Sheldon left the transportation business in 1926 to chalk up another first – a tourist concession in McKinley Park (now Denali

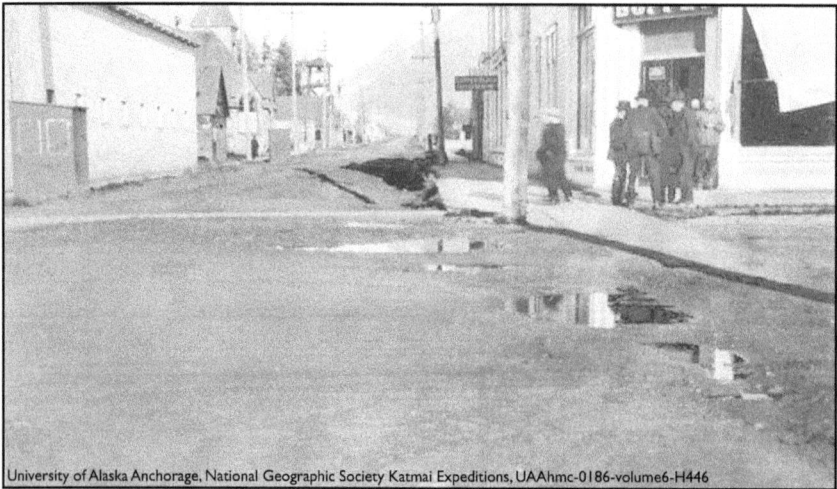

University of Alaska Anchorage, National Geographic Society Katmai Expeditions, UAAhmc-0186-volume6-H446

This view of a street in Valdez in 1919 may have met Robert Sheldon's eyes when he arrived in town to pick up his specially made racing car. The Valdez Glacier can be seen at the end of the street.

Robert Sheldon left his transportation business to run the first tourist concession in McKinley National Park in 1926. He was known as a good cook.

National Park and Preserve), which he operated until 1931. Park Superintendent Grant Pearson remembered Sheldon's tenure in his book, "My Life of High Adventure."

"Bobby is a good camp cook, and in the fall when the camp was being closed down, he always did the cooking. One day in late September, five Fairbanks businessmen arrived at the camp for a few days vacation. The first morning Bobby made hotcakes for them. One of the group decided to kid the cook by remarking that the cakes reminded him of the asbestos stove pads in his hardware store.

"Now Bobby is a keen-minded little fellow who never is at a loss for words; this time, though, he said nothing … but he made that fellow a special hotcake, cooking it long and slow, and with special ingredients. It was so tough, when served, that you not only couldn't eat it, you couldn't even cut it!"

Sheldon didn't have the last word, however. The hardware merchant got hold of a couple of medicine bottle stickers and pasted them on the hotcake. On one he wrote a Fairbanks address, and on the other he put this message:

"Bob Sheldon is our cook, the food is fine, here is a sample."

The fellow then put a stamp on the hotcake and sent it through

Robert E. Sheldon served in the Seventh Alaska Legislature House of Representatives. He's seen here fourth from the right in this April 30, 1925, photo in Juneau.

the mail unwrapped. It arrived in Fairbanks without a nick on it and was exhibited all around town.

Appointed postmaster in Fairbanks in 1933, Sheldon was popularly rated as the only "First Class Postmaster in a Second Class Post Office."

He also served two terms in the Territorial Legislature and in 1940 became executive director of the Unemployment Compensation Commission of Alaska.

Sheldon never got rich from his pioneering transportation efforts. However, he felt rich in friends, memories and engineering achievements, and as he often said:

"Who wants to be the richest man in the cemetery?"

Robert E. Sheldon, the first person to drive a vehicle from Fairbanks to Valdez and then become the first person to ride a bicycle from Valdez back to Fairbanks, also served in the Territorial Legislature. He is pictured here at his Fairbanks cabin.

14

A REO AND A RESORT

One of Anchorage's early characters drove along the new city's streets in a bright-yellow Reo truck. And he wore a yellow suit to match.

Joe Spenard moved to Anchorage from Valdez, where he'd had a small transfer business. Once he got settled in the new town, he purchased his truck – said to be the first auto truck in Anchorage.

Anchorage Museum of History and Art, General Photograph File, AMRC-b99-15-5

Joe Spenard's truck was decorated with a medical theme for the Fourth of July parade in 1916.

Joe Spenard drove his 1915 Model-T Ford City Express taxi through the streets of 1916 Anchorage. The jail can be seen in the background along Fourth Avenue.

Spenard started a taxi service with a Model-T Ford, too, and plastered lost and found notices and tide information on the sides of that vehicle. He painted "Time and Tide will not wait, but City Express is never late" on the radiator.

He became known for having a "good time," and one description of his adventurous side was printed in an early *Anchorage Daily Times* article.

"Joe Spenard caused considerable excitement Saturday afternoon when he attempted to drive his yellow car through the doors of the Robarts pool hall. He made the attempt for a box of cigars promised him by Jack Robarts if he accomplished the feat; otherwise he was to pay the damages. Joe is still smoking his pipe."

Spenard may not have won his bet with Robarts, but he stumbled across something else that kept him in cigars for a while. The feisty little man discovered a lake that soon drew clientele who wanted to take dips in its clear, clean water.

Not so long ago, the area now known as Spenard was referred to as the Miracle Mile. As part of the Chugach National Forest created by a stroke of U.S. President Theodore "Teddy" Roosevelt's pen in 1907, the land was locked in a government deep freeze.

Anchorage Museum of History and Art, Ickes Collection, AMRC-b75-175-249

While blazing a trail through wilderness near Anchorage, Joe Spenard stumbled across a beautiful lake – now called Lake Spenard – pictured above and below.

University of Alaska Fairbanks, Walter W. Hodge Collection, UAF-2003-63-138

In 1919, this piece of land was liberated after the Alaska Railroad camp of Anchorage was born, and its residents asked that the surrounding land be unshackled. The growth of Anchorage to the south would not have occurred if this "miracle" hadn't happened.

But before the land opened for private ownership, Joe Spenard had moved in. He'd been cutting wood in the area for some time and blazed a trail through the wilderness that wound around Chester and Campbell creeks.

One of the area's first homesteaders, Thomas Jeter, had built a cabin on the land in 1909. But he had been forced to give up the land by a court order five years later because the forest reserve land hadn't been open to homesteading at the time.

While wandering through the timbered land one day, Spenard found a beautiful lake a few miles from the railroad community. There he set up a camp.

Anchorage Museum of History and Art, General Photograph File, AMRC-b70-19-217

Joe Spenard cleared a trail so Anchorage residents could gather at Lake Spenard.

And regardless of laws that prohibited cutting trees in a forest reserve, he started chopping wood. Spenard eventually acquired timber rights in what he called his "homestead," although land office records don't confirm such a claim.

He also made improvements to the land, which included a full-scale resort with a roadhouse, bathhouses and a swimming beach. He opened his recreational resort in August 1916.

Unfortunately, Spenard's health was poor and he had to leave Alaska in September 1917. He sold his beloved Reo and headed for California to seek medical treatment for a heart condition.

"I'll be back in the spring," he promised.

That promise was not kept, and he died in Sacramento in 1934.

But his resort thrived, and the trail Spenard cut through the wilderness has become one of the busiest roads in Alaska. The strange, beautiful lake he claimed is now called Lake Spenard and is surrounded by business, recreation and transportation.

And although Spenard the community did not start growing until 1949, when it got a post office, it seems to have taken on some of the characteristics of its namesake – the unorthodox, hustling, spunky Joe Spenard.

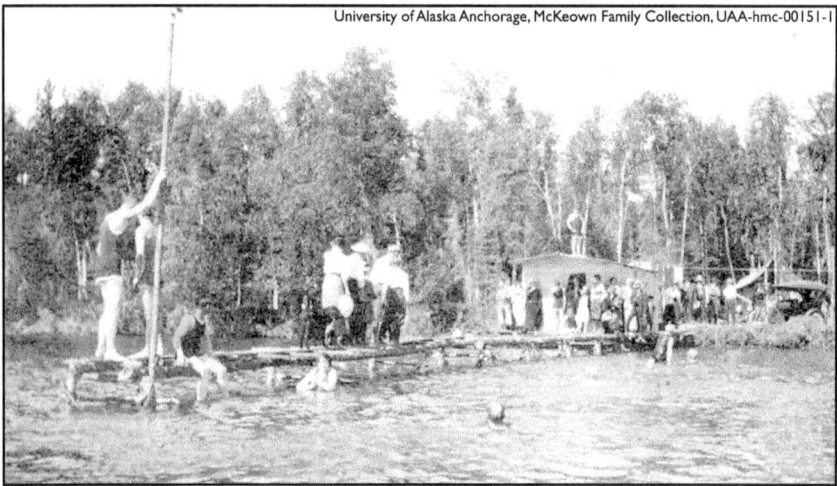

University of Alaska Anchorage, McKeown Family Collection, UAA-hmc-00151-1

Anchorage residents gathered at Lake Spenard for picnics, swimming and boating.

For years, Joe Spenard's resort gave countless hours of pleasure to Anchorage residents. U.S. President Warren G. Harding and his entourage spent a relaxing afternoon dipping into the waters at Lake Spenard when Harding came to drive the final spike into the Alaska Railroad track in Nenana in 1923.

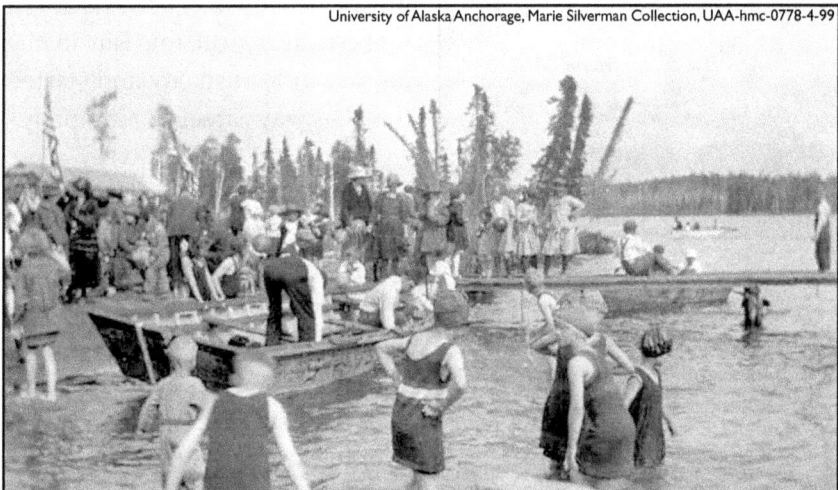

15

ALASKA'S FIRST STREETCAR

A three-hour stopover in Skagway in July 1923 by President Warren G. Harding turned into a booming business for one Alaskan sourdough. Martin Itjen, an immigrant who came north from Florida in 1898 to join the stampede in search of riches in the Klondike, took the President on an excursion in a painted coal truck.

Anchorage Museum of History and Art,
General Photograph File. AMRC-b88-3-67

Martin Itjen stands in front of the streetcar he built, owned and operated in Skagway.

After seeing how much Harding enjoyed the tour, the mustached Itjen figured he could make a living off tourism in the famous gold rush city and started the Skagway Streetcar Company.

The local coal delivery man, rooming house operator and undertaker built his first marvel of transportation on a Ford chassis. It resembled a bus and contained fanciful gadgetry.

Itjen, who also became Skagway's first Ford dealer, eventually had four streetcars

Above: Residents of Skagway relied on horses and wagons to transport items and people before motorized vehicles arrived on the scene.

Below: Martin Itjen took tourists on two-hour tours around Skagway and shared tales of the Klondike Gold Rush. His words painted pictures, such as what Broadway, seen here during the 1898 stampede, looked like at the time.

decked out with oddities to delight and amaze his clientele. One picturesque car carried a bear cub replica on the front that growled and pointed to the left or right as the car turned. He also had a life-size mannequin of Soapy Smith that performed when Itjen worked a series of foot pedals. It nodded its head, waved a flag, rang a bell and puffed exhaust smoke through a cigarette.

Itjen gave his customers quite a show as he recited poetry, told stories and related humorous anecdotes of Skagway during the gold rush.

After purchasing Soapy Smith's parlor in 1935 and converting it into a museum, Itjen decided to travel to Hollywood and extend an invitation to movie star Mae West to come north. A Seattle newspaper covered his arrival in its fair city:

"In Alaska's 'only street car,' the 65-year-old sourdough, who was Skagway's undertaker in the roaring days of the gold rush, has come to the United States to see Mae West, the movie actress.

" 'I'm just itchin' to see Mae,' said Martin Itjen on his arrival here by steamer. 'She's got something the others haven't.'

An unidentified woman and streetcar driver Martin Itjen stand on Itjen's tourist bus in Skagway. Passengers only paid 25 cents for a two-hour tour. Itjen took his streetcar to California in 1935 to see Mae West.

Although Martin Itjen visited with the legendary Mae West, seen here riding in a carriage, he could not convince her to come to Alaska and work on his streetcar.

"His vehicle, unloaded from the steamer, is a bus constructed to resemble a street car. In it he plans to drive to Hollywood to see Mae."

Itjen indeed drove his street car to California and spent two weeks with West, but he couldn't convince her to come north with him to be a hostess on his streetcar.

The sourdough tour operator died in 1942. In keeping with Itjen's sense of humor, a large rock painted gold sits next to his grave in Skagway. On it is written: "The largest nugget in the world" and "Property of Skagway Streetcar."

EPIDEMICS, RESCUES AND DISASTER

16

THE BIG SICKNESS

I had a little bird
And its name was Enza.
I opened the window
And in-flew-Enza

Schoolgirls in Massachusetts chanted this little ditty as they jumped rope in September 1918. A month later, 700 people in Philadelphia died of influenza in one day. The deadly virus then made its way to Alaska.

During the spring of 1918, a flu had spread across the world and sickened many people – some died. But by that fall, the virus had mutated and become a mass killer.

It preyed on the young and healthy.

A dull headache signaled the beginning. Then came chills so intense that no amount of blankets warmed the body. As the fever climbed, delirium followed. Lungs filled with fluid. Pneumonia took over.

Sometimes it took days. Sometimes hours. But nothing could stop the relentless march toward death for many.

Doctors and nurses soon knew the signs. Patients' faces turned brownish purple. Feet turned black. Final breaths gurgled as blood-tinged saliva bubbled out of mouths.

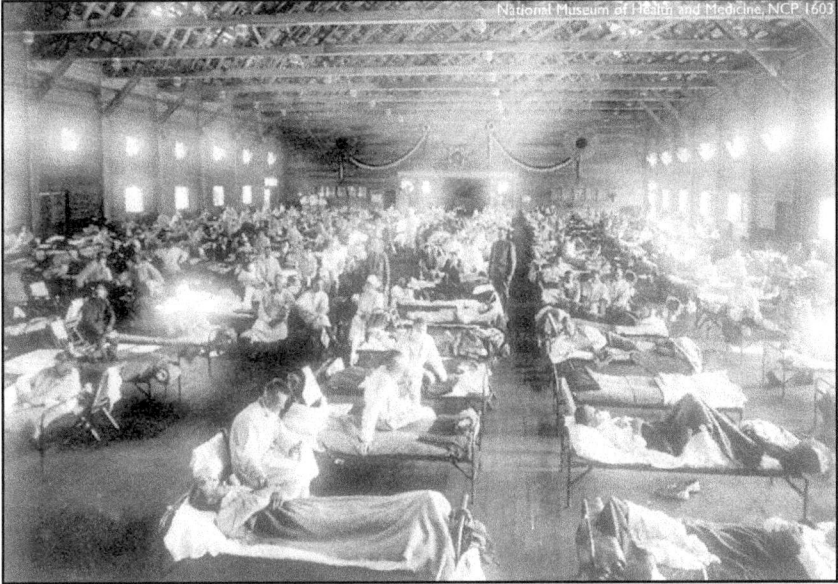

An emergency hospital set up during the 1918 influenza epidemic in Camp Funston, Kansas, is filled beyond capacity.

Because this plague developed during World War I, it spread like wildfire across battlefields, oceans and cities as troops crowded together in camps and trenches, ships and ports. Called the Spanish flu, only because the Spanish press wrote about it, the virus took more than 500,000 American lives between 1918-1919. Fatality estimates worldwide range from 20 million to 100 million.

And even though Territorial Gov. Thomas Riggs did everything in his power to keep it away from Alaska's shores, the killer still came.

When 75 citizens of Seattle died from the flu during the week of Oct. 12, Riggs asked that the steamship companies examine all passengers heading north on the final ships of the season and not allow anyone with flu symptoms to travel. He warned that anyone showing signs of influenza would be isolated at the port of debarkation and assigned physicians to meet the ships and enforce his directive.

By the end of October, Seattle's death toll had reached 350. And the panhandle of Alaska was too close to Seattle to keep the flu at bay.

University of Washington, Social Issues Collection, SOC396

Above: Seattle's public health department issued gauze masks in an effort to stop the spread of influenza.

Below: *SS Victoria*, seen here in June 1918, brought passengers and influenza to Nome in September 1918.

University of Alaska Fairbanks, John Zug Collection, UAF-1980-68-331

EPIDEMICS, RESCUES AND DISASTER

St. Ann's Catholic Hospital in Juneau filled will patients suffering from influenza during the fall and winter of 1918-1919.

Juneau's first reported case came on Oct. 14, and soon it had spread along the coast. Juneau officials advised people not to congregate in groups, which meant staying away from churches, schools, social functions and pool halls.

The panhandle came through the epidemic better than areas farther north and west, because it had services and physicians who set up quarantine areas, emergency hospitals and buried the dead immediately. It also had help from professionals in Seattle and San Francisco.

But when passengers from the *S.S. Victoria*, the last ship of the season from Seattle, docked in Nome, the killer disease enveloped the Seward Peninsula.

Before leaving Seattle, the ship's passengers and crew had been checked by three physicians, separately and independently, to assure that no one who exhibited symptoms would be traveling.

And when the *Victoria* arrived in Nome on Oct. 20, all those who came ashore were quarantined in the hospital for five days and all freight and mail were fumigated.

No one showed any signs of influenza.

But within days, Alaska Natives were sick and dying. Few escaped infection. In a single eight-day period, 162 had died.

Earlier epidemics of smallpox, measles and typhoid fever had instilled a paralyzing fear in Alaska's Native population.

"They believed in the spirit of death and feared that, if a person died in their home, that spirit would claim them next," wrote Gay and Laney Salisbury in their book, "The Cruelest Miles."

A death often caused family members to panic and flee, which helped to spread the diseases.

"Some Eskimos, hounded by superstitious horror, fled from cabin to cabin, infecting increasing numbers with disease and panic. The temperature fell below freezing, and when rescuers broke into cabins from whose chimney came no sign of smoke, they found many, sometimes whole families, who had been too sick to renew their fires and who had frozen to death," wrote Alfred Crosby in his book, "America's Forgotten Pandemic."

The influenza pandemic of 1918 devastated the Native village at Nome.

Many victims of the 1918 influenza froze to death because they were too weak to chop wood and keep fires burning.

"When a number of Eskimos were rounded up from their separate cabins and placed in a single large building so they could be cared for efficiently, several of them responded to what they apparently perceived as incarceration in a death house by hanging themselves," said Crosby.

Volunteers buried the dead.

"Bodies were removed by dogsled and piled up in abandoned houses until the spring, when a mass grave could be dug in the thawed ground. Cabins, furs, bedding and clothes were burned as a protective measure. Dogs were shot, and for the first time in Nome's recorded history, the evening malamute chorus was silent," wrote the Salisburys.

Gov. Riggs, who recognized that the deeply rooted Native culture of hospitality and gathering together might be aiding in the spread of the disease, issued a directive on Nov. 7 to try and stem the tide of Native deaths. He advised them "to stay in their own villages and repel all visitors; to avoid visiting one another's homes within their villages; indeed, to avoid all gatherings, even those most vital to their self-esteem. 'A potlatch is absolutely forbidden, and any Native

In an effort to stop the spread of influenza during the fall of 1918, Alaska Territorial Gov. Thomas Riggs banned get-togethers like this Nome dancing event.

attempting to get up a potlatch will be prosecuted,'" Riggs said, according to Crosby.

The people of Mountain Village heeded the governor's words and initiated a quarantine.

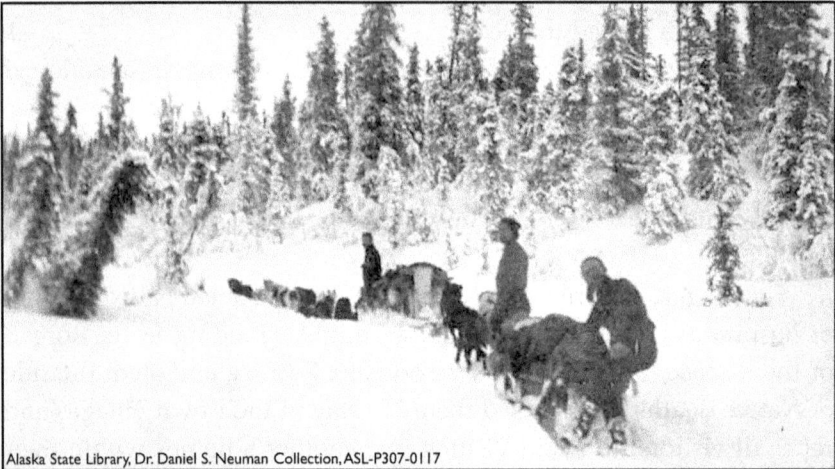

Checkpoints were set up along trails to keep travelers from entering villages in an attempt to keep influenza away.

"This was a hard thing for the Natives to do," wrote the village school teacher, "but the safety of their own families impelled them to break their habits and the customs of their ancestors."

The flu never made it to Mountain Village.

But it appears that some mail carriers who hit the trails with the governor's order delivered more than Riggs' message. The Spanish flu followed the mail carriers' routes to York and Wales.

According to Crosby, York and Wales had no warning about the flu and residents from both villages innocently attended the funeral of a boy who had died in York. Two days later the father was sick. Then the epidemic exploded. All of the villagers were sick within days. The epidemic killed everyone in York and 170 of Wales' 310 residents.

Having neither food nor medicine to deal with such an epidemic, the lone government nurse could only comfort as best she could those who flocked to the schoolhouse, many of whom remained, too sick to crawl back to their homes, recalled Henry W. Griest, a medical missionary serving in the Arctic.

"Young boys were asked to kill reindeer from nearby herds, the meat from which was turned into broth to feed the motherless babies and sick adults. As more and more died, their bodies were first removed to vacant schoolrooms and eventually to the Presbyterian

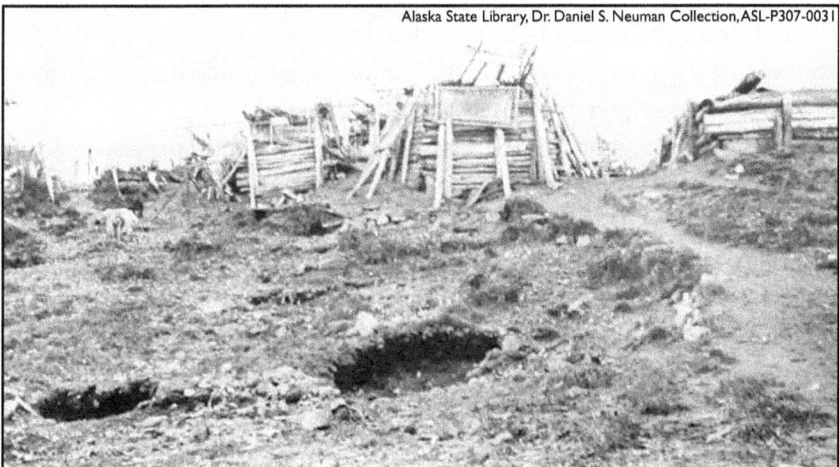

Alaska State Library, Dr. Daniel S. Neuman Collection, ASL-P307-0031

Influenza swept through the village of Wales, seen here looking from the outskirts.

Many of the children of Wales, seen here outside of the school, became orphans when influenza swept through their village in 1918.

Church where they were placed side-by-side, awaiting eventual burial. Family sled dogs, uncared for by dying adults, broke their tethers and roamed the streets seeking food where they could find it, including frozen human remains residing in abandoned Inupiat houses," Griest wrote in a manuscript titled "Seventeen Years with the Eskimo."

It took several months for a relief party to reach Wales. It brought flour, tinned milk, sugar and coffee for the survivors, along with shovels to bury the dead. All the bodies were placed in a common grave, with a large, white cross to mark the spot.

In order to give all the orphans a home, the deceased local district superintendent's replacement lined up the surviving men and women, boys and girls, and had the men pick wives. He had blank marriage licenses, signed by proper Nome authorities, with him.

"... widowers and young unmarried men were told to take a position on one side of the large room, and the widows and young unmarried girls on the other. Each man was then asked to select a wife from the facing line. If they did so, the couple would then stand aside and give their names to the secretary who would write them on the marriage certificate. If any hesitated, a spouse was selected for that person. After the licenses were duly filled out, a mass ceremony was held in which the substitute district superintendent formally pronounced each couple 'man and wife,'" wrote Griest.

"... The Eskimo are human and many are Christian men and women; and may not be mated as are horses and cattle. Unhappiness hung over Wales village for years, and it was rare that I heard singing in any home when the man was absent. Few divorces were had, for divorce now in Alaska costs a large sum, thanks to the new constitution and a few unscrupulous attorneys. Divorce also demands a trip to Nome, Fairbanks, or other legal center, which often would prove a very great hardship to the Native. And, too, wedding vows are very generally considered by the Eskimo as binding, to actually hold 'until death doth separate,'" Griest wrote.

Mail carriers or supply sleds are suspected of delivering the flu to the villages of Solomon, Golovin, Mary's Igloo and Teller, too. The population of Teller Mission, located about five miles from Teller, was decimated. The deadly virus may have reached that village, later renamed Brevig Mission, on the breath of men bringing supplies.

Teller did not escape the onslaught of influenza – 72 of 80 residents in Teller Mission, five miles away, died within five days in November 1918. The U.S. Army buried the victims with a steam-powered excavator used by gold miners.

Natives who loaded their sleds with supplies in Teller might have picked up the virus by working beside the men.

Between Nov. 15 and Nov. 20, 72 of Brevig Mission's 80 residents died. The U.S. Army buried the victims in a mass grave dug by a steam-powered excavator used by miners.

Scientists visited the common grave in the late 1990s, because they thought the permafrost may have preserved some of the lung tissue of the victims. With permission from the villagers, three of whom were survivors of the pandemic, researchers unearthed remains and obtained samples so they might study the DNA of the 1918 virus.

The last steamer of the year also brought the virus to Kodiak Island, and then severe storms cut the island off so no relief could come in for two months. Flu sickened several hundred of the island's 550 residents – 47 died.

The flu made its way to other parts of Alaska, as well, including Copper Center, Cordova, Skagway and Cook Inlet.

In the spring of 1919, it hit Fairbanks, the Aleutian Chain and Bristol Bay.

But by summer 1919, the killer disappeared. And while many white Alaskans contracted the flu, only 150 deaths were reported. Between 1,500 and 2,000 Natives had died.

"The Natives showed absolutely no resistance," said Gov. Riggs, who traveled to Washington, D.C., to try and get the government to reimburse the territory for more than $90,000 he had spent in combating the disease. His pleas fell on deaf ears.

"I doubt if similar conditions existed anywhere in the world – the intense cold of the arctic days, the long distances to be traveled by dog team, the living children huddled against their dead parents already being gnawed by wolfish dogs," he said in his annual report to the Secretary of the Interior.

Riggs suggested that those in power who should have helped Alaskans were "all too much engrossed with the woes of Europe to be able to note our wards, seemingly protected by solemn treaty with Russia, dying by swarms in the dark of the northern nights."

17

DISASTER STRIKES SOUTHEAST

"Steamer *Sophia* Is Sunk In Canal" screamed the headline in the *Dawson Daily News* on Saturday, Oct. 26, 1918. But this tragedy was quickly dropped from the news as the crisis of the influenza epidemic and the ending of World War I took center stage.

Canadian steamship *Princess Sophia* plied the waters of Southeast Alaska from 1912 until sinking in 1918.

Skagway, pictured above in 1918, was filled with miners from the Klondike gold fields and others who wanted to head south for the winter onboard the *Princess Sophia*.

Three days earlier, the Canadian Pacific Railway steamship *Princess Sophia* pulled out of the port at Skagway around 10 p.m. and headed into the Lynn Canal bound for Vancouver.

One of the last ships scheduled to leave that fall, the 245-foot ship was filled with 350 gold miners, families and others heading south for the winter. The steamship company, in an effort to hold more passengers for the voyage, had converted the *Sophia* so she could carry 100 more passengers than normal.

The Scottish-built ship, which had been traveling the inside passage route since 1912, was considered a sturdy ship.

"She was not a beautiful princess but a sturdy, somewhat chunky down to earth lady of the seas," wrote Ian MacDonald and Betty O'Keefe in their book, "The Final Voyage of the Princess Sophia."

"She was practical, comfortable and soon became popular with those who traveled the West Coast to Alaska," they wrote. "Her cabins provided an uncommon comfort compared to the primitive housing and rigors of isolated living to which they were accustomed."

And her seaworthiness had been tested several times prior to this voyage. The ship, built in 1911, had run aground three times before

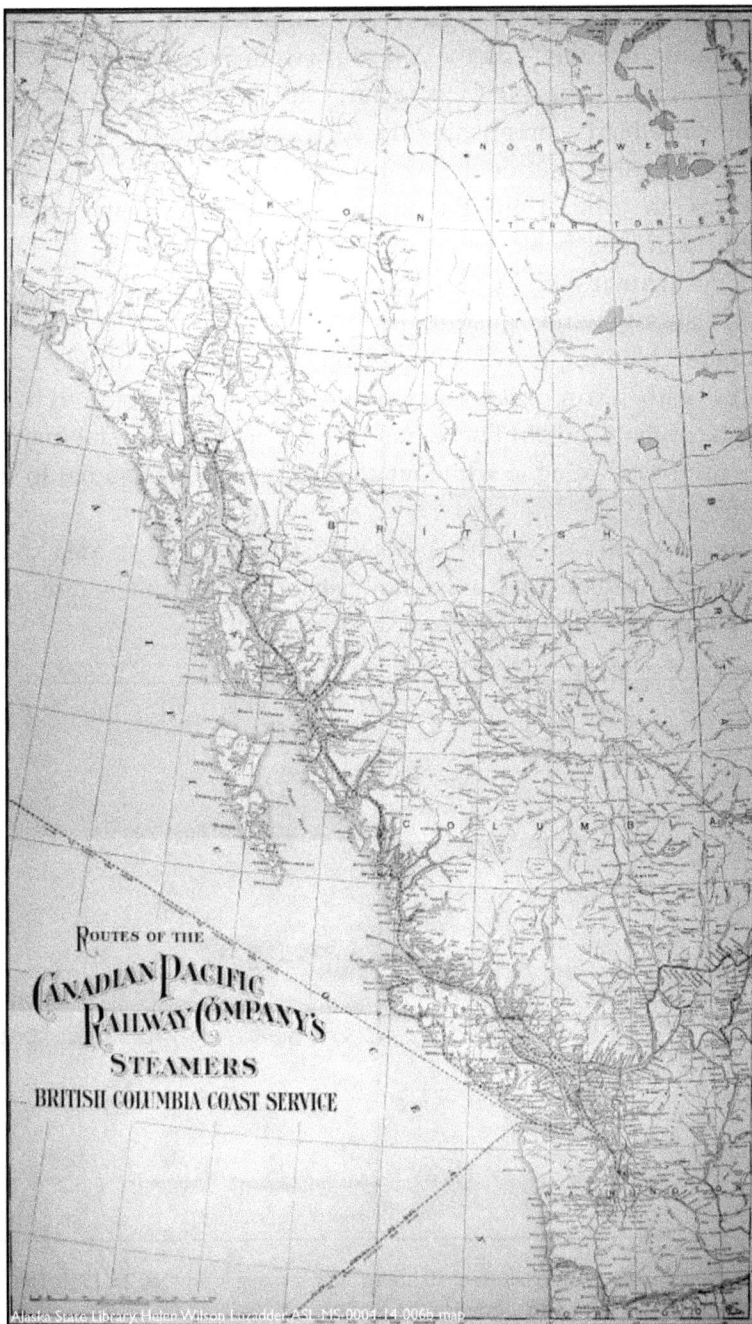

Routes of the
Canadian Pacific
Railway Company's
Steamers
British Columbia Coast Service

this ill-fated trip – most notably on Sentinel Island, just four miles from Vanderbilt Reef – on the run south from Skagway in 1913.

About four hours out of Skagway, Capt. Leonard Locke ran into a north wind that began pushing the *Sophia* southward.

"The weather suddenly worsened and a blinding snowstorm overtook the ship from the north," wrote Ken Coates and Bill Morrison in their book, "The Sinking of the Princess Sophia: Taking the North Down With Her."

"A strong wind, gusting up to 50 mph, whistled over the mountain, blowing heavy snow before it. The water turned rough, boiling with heavy rollers and whitecaps," they wrote. "It was a bad storm, but Captain Locke had faced worse and coastal mariners were used to running in whiteout conditions. He decided not to slow down."

By 2 a.m. on Oct. 24, the *Sophia* was steaming into an area known as Vanderbilt Reef. And unbeknownst to Locke, a navigation error had placed the ship two miles off course.

Alaska State Library, Winter and Pond, ASL-P87-1702

Princess Sophia sat on Vanderbilt Reef 10 hours after striking it on Oct. 24, 1918. This view is of the starboard side, with a bouy in the foreground.

EPIDEMICS, RESCUES AND DISASTER

This distant view of the steamship *Princess Sophia* was taken at 11 a.m. on Friday, Oct. 25, 1918.

Sophia struck the reef at 2:10 a.m.

"Because the reef was so low in the water the bow lifted out of the water and, with a horrible grinding and tearing, slid up and onto the rock," Coates and Morrison wrote. "Despite the terrific force of the impact, there were few if any injuries because most of the people were in bed."

The captain telegraphed company officials in Juneau and Skagway, who, in turn, dispatched ships to help the *Sophia*.

At daylight, crewmembers assessed the damage. After a careful inspection, they determined that the ship had not suffered any significant damage and that its double-hulled bottom was holding.

Several ships arrived on scene during the morning of Oct. 24, but they were unable to assist due to the heavy seas. Locke would not let his passengers off the stranded vessel until the fierce gales quieted. He was afraid that if he lowered the lifeboats, they would be smashed to bits on the rocky reef below.

Skippers of the vessels waiting to rescue the passengers estimated the wind was whipping about 100 mph and the seas were rising more than 30 feet. A sharp drop in barometric pressure as far away as Sitka signaled a major storm.

Records indicate that some thought the ship would slip off the reef at high tide, and others thought perhaps the storm was weakening and it would be safer for all concerned to wait to evacuate passengers.

But one passenger didn't think the storm was getting any milder. Jack Maskell wrote his will, and a note, to his fiancée, Dorothy Burgess.

"The boat might go to pieces, for the force of the waves are terrible, making awful noises on the side of the boat. ..."

The *Princess Sophia* seemed secure, however, sitting on an even keel and supported for much of her length by the reef itself. Her electricity failed that evening, but was eventually restored.

Observers on both Oct. 24 and 25 noted that passengers and crew came out on deck, boats were swung out, but ultimately nothing was done. Witnesses said they assumed that Locke was waiting for the weather to calm down before he began an evacuation.

But on the afternoon of Oct. 25, the storm worsened and the rescue ships standing by had to seek shelter in high seas, in a near-zero visibility blizzard.

At 4:50 p.m., David Robinson, the Sophia's 20-year-old wireless man, radioed to anyone listening.

"Ship foundering on reef. Come at once."

A second message was sent at 5:50 p.m.:

"For God's sake hurry. The water is coming in my room," said Robinson, who was in the wireless room on the top deck of the ship, next to the bridge.

That message was followed by an unintelligible transmission and then the final words received from the ship.

"You talk to me so I know you are coming."

About 40 hours after she settled on the rocks, the sea picked up Sophia's stern and turned her 180 degrees, slipping her off the reef – tearing her bottom out as she went – and eventually covered her in the frigid froth.

EPIDEMICS, RESCUES AND DISASTER

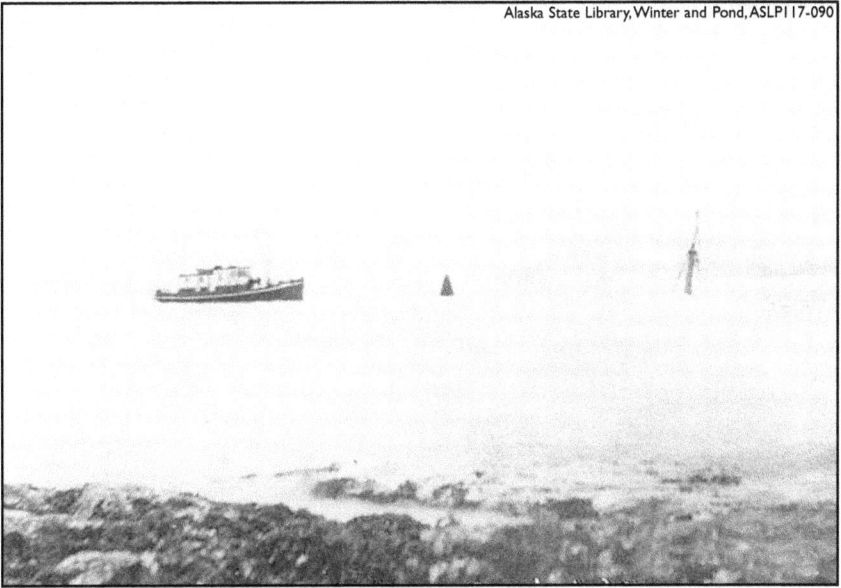

When resuers returned the next day during calm weather, the mast of the *Princess Sophia* was all they could see.

Those on support vessels returning the next day were horrified to see only her mast standing out of the water.

Divers later discovered that during the sinking her boiler had exploded, severely damaging her superstructure. Close to 100 people were trapped below decks as the ship sank.

The other 250 passengers who floated free died quickly of exposure or from the effects of ingesting fuel oil. For several weeks, bodies were recovered for miles up and down Lynn Canal. Only a few died from drowning, according to the inquest that followed.

The lone survivor of the *Princess Sophia* disaster was a small English setter who swam to Auke Bay, 12 miles from the ship, and was recovered a few days later covered in oil.

The sinking of the *Princess Sophia* devastated Dawson City, as many of its professionals and businesspeople were onboard the ill-fated steamer. It also was reported that $1 million in gold was in her hold.

Rescue workers and divers desperately searched for survivors, but except for one dog, all passengers and crew onboard died when the *Princess Sophia* sank. Her mast is sticking out of the water on the left.

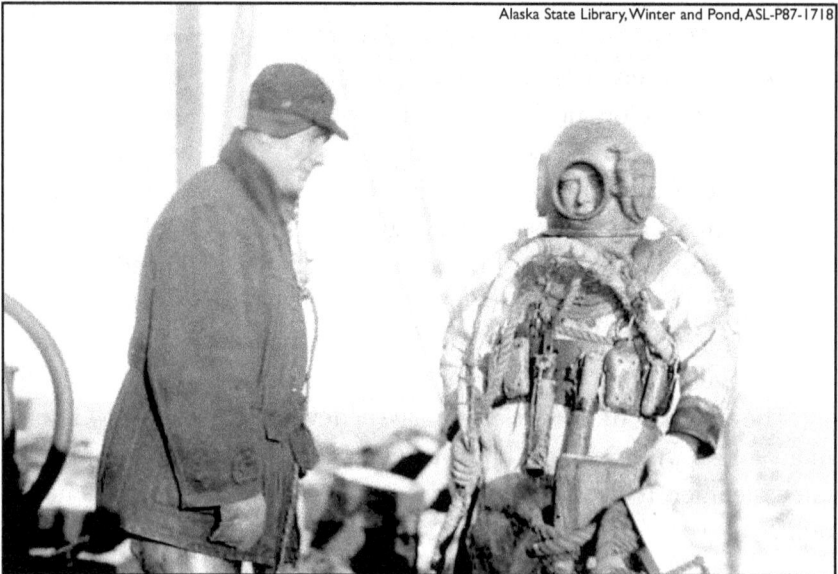

University of Washington, William E. Meed Collection, MEE 108

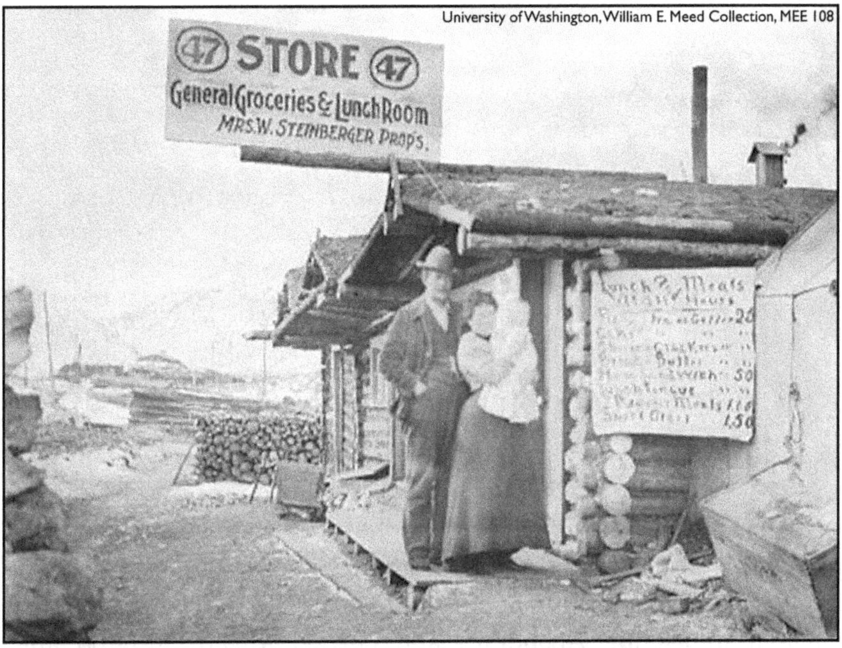

William Steinberger, pictured here with his wife at their store and lunch house on Bonanza Creek, Yukon Territory, in 1900, was one of the gold miners who died onboard the *Princess Sophia.*

Courtesy Jan Harper-Haines

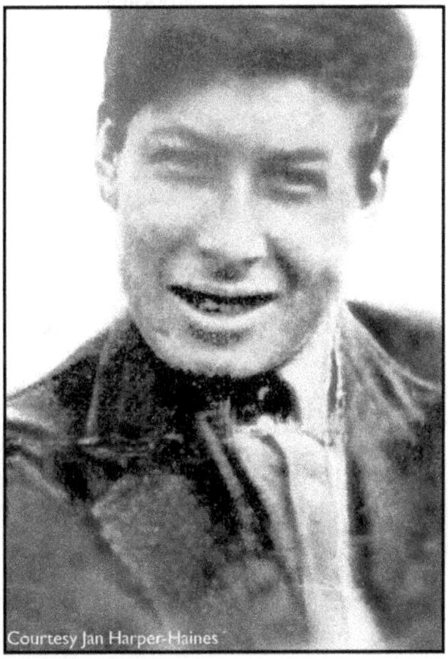

One Alaska hero also lost his life. Walter Harper, credited with being the first person to summit Denali in 1913, and his wife, Frances Wells Harper, both perished in the accident. The couple, married six weeks before, were on their honeymoon to the Lower 48.

18

FIRST RELAY RUN NORTH

One of Anchorage's most respected doctors set out on a mission of mercy to Iditarod four years before the celebrated diphtheria serum run of 1925.

Early on the morning of Jan. 24, 1921, Dr. John B. Beeson hopped on a train leaving Anchorage and headed toward Iditarod after getting word through the U.S. Army Signal Corps that Claude Baker was near death.

Anchorage Museum of History and Art, General Photograph File, AMRC-b70-19-157b

Alaska Railroad doctor John B. Beeson left the comforts of 1921 Anchorage, pictured here, to make a house call in Iditarod more than 500 miles away.

Dr. John Beeson and Bill Corey boarded a train in Anchorage and rode to the end of the track at Broad Pass, pictured here. They then hitched up Corey's dog team and raced to Healy.

Baker, a well-known Iditarod banker, was suffering from an old injury he'd received while serving as a guard on the gold trail outside of the famous mining town. He'd been thrown some distance while holding a gee-pole, which caused internal injuries. The banker also had a lung ailment.

An impromptu relay of dog teams carried the good doctor on his long-distance house call. Along with Bill Corey and his race-winning team of setters and six malamutes, Beeson's trip via dogs and sleds began with a train ride to "end of steel" near Broad Pass. The railroad crews en route laid aside all of the switching to give the mercy train clearance.

Once they hit the end of the tracks, Corey and the railroad doctor hitched up Corey's team and raced 54 miles to Healy, where a locomotive and caboose waited to take them to Nenana.

By 11 p.m. Beeson was sitting on the sled of the "Scurvy Kid," flying down the trail out of Nenana heading north. But after only a

Above: Bill Corey's winning team of dogs, seen here near Cushman Street Bridge along the Chena River in Fairbanks, raced Dr. John Beeson from Broad Pass to Healy.

Below: A locomotive and caboose carried Dr. John Beeson, Bill Corey and his dog team on their mission of mercy from Healy to Nenana, seen here.

EPIDEMICS, RESCUES AND DISASTER

few miles, the Kid misjudged a turn and crashed.

The good doctor dug the Kid out of the snow, loaded the injured musher onto the sled and jumped on the runners. His first lesson on dog mushing took him 23 miles to Bachelors Cabin, where he left the Kid and hooked up with Indian William Jimmie, who took him another 58 miles.

Exhausted after 36 hours without rest, Beeson managed to climb into a horse-drawn bobsled and continue on his mission. It was slow going, but the horse plodded along for 21 miles, bucking in the deep snow.

Courtesy John P. Bagoy

Dr. John B. Beeson

An ex-soldier and his team met Beeson on the trail and took him to Tolovana, where another relay was waiting and ready to help him on his journey.

Eleven dogs pulled with all their might, and the doctor's sled whipped down the Tanana River on its way to Fort Gibbon and the Yukon River. Guided more by instinct than by sight, the dogs sped through the darkness, until they hit an overflow of river ice four miles before Gibbon.

The musher plunged into the icy water and got soaked to above his knees.

Beeson, tied to the sled so he wouldn't be thrown off while traveling at breakneck speeds, tried desperately to untie the rope binding him to the sled. But he couldn't find the knots. As he sank into the frigid water, he thought the end had come, he later recalled.

Then the sled lurched forward. The dogs pulled him out of the stream and up the bank to safety.

With temperatures hovering at 20 below zero, and the wind blowing a gale, the musher told Beeson he thought he could keep warm by running the last few miles.

Dr. John Beeson collapsed into a bed in Fort Gibbon and slept soundly.

But once they reached Gibbon, Beeson discovered that the musher had frozen part of one foot and both big toes. He had to administer medical aid before collapsing into a bed at 8 p.m.

He arose at 4 a.m., ate breakfast and headed out again with another musher and 13 dogs. They sprinted 50 miles down the river to Birches, where Beeson was met by a soldier named Shannon. The soldier's 11-dog team made the 40-mile dash to Kokrines.

Indian Paul was waiting for Beeson at Kokrines, and sensing the sporting feature of the race, made the 30 miles into Ruby in just four hours. By the time the doctor arrived in Ruby, he'd spent 23 hours traveling 120 miles from Nenana.

An enlisted man stationed with Alaska Communications System in Ruby put Beeson into a sled and hauled him the 30 miles to Long with his 11-dog team. He then turned the doctor over to a young Scandinavian with 13 dogs, and they made the next 30-mile run to Poorman.

A wild, unmanageable team took over for the Poorman to Lone Mountain portion of the trip. Beeson later said he would never forget that mad race of 30 miles on a clear night through timber when all the dogs knew was to travel straight ahead.

EPIDEMICS, RESCUES AND DISASTER

A soldier named Burke and his team of malamutes met the doctor at Lone Mountain. Considered one of the best mushers on the Yukon, Burke delivered his cargo to Cripple where the next relay was waiting.

A new 11-dog team and musher whisked Beeson on to Ophir, 40 miles down the trail, where another team met him and mushed through a pitch-black night. They made the 60-mile trip to Shermans in record time.

The last team, driven by Charley Brink, ran the 18 miles to Iditarod and put Dr. Beeson at the bedside of Claude Baker just 130 hours after the doctor had stepped off the locomotive in Nenana.

The remarkable 512-mile adventure got Beeson to the banker and manager of the Otter Creek Dredge Company in time to save his life. The banker was in the advanced stages of pulmonary tuberculosis, according to Gay and Laney Salisbury, authors of "The Cruelest Miles."

Thanks to the headquarters' managers of the Northern Commercial Company, Messrs. Goss at Tanana, Parsons at Ruby and Sam Applebaum at Iditarod, teams had been ready and equipped at points along the way to aid Beeson on his journey to Iditarod.

University of Alaska Fairbanks, John Zug Album, UAF-1980-68-343

Dr. John Beeson pulled into Iditarod, pictured here during summer, 5-1/2 days after stepping off the train in Nenana.

"Not a man failed and we were not delayed a minute by having to wait for the next team to arrive," Beeson later reported.

But the return trip was a different matter.

It took Beeson 14 days to reach the railroad on his trip out with his patient.

He traveled over the trail from Iditarod through Rainy Pass with Charley Brink, and later was joined on the trail by mushing legend Leonhard Seppala, who was taking out Col. John C. Gotwals and Anton Eide of the Alaska Road Commission.

"Dr. Beeson proved himself a real sourdough and musher," Col. Gotwals said of the doctor. "Breaking trail all day, especially when at the Salmon River, the temperature was 51 below during the day and 40 below at night."

With four teams and 43 dogs, the party traveled along the Kuskokwim River to near the south fork, where an overflow forced them to turn back 13 miles and take the route through the hills. Near the mouth of the Post River, the trail led over a glacier at least 150 feet high. The men had to unhitch the dogs, except Seppala's 1916 Nome Sweepstakes leader, and coast down the glare ice on about a 40 percent grade.

Seppala later recounted his experience with Beeson.

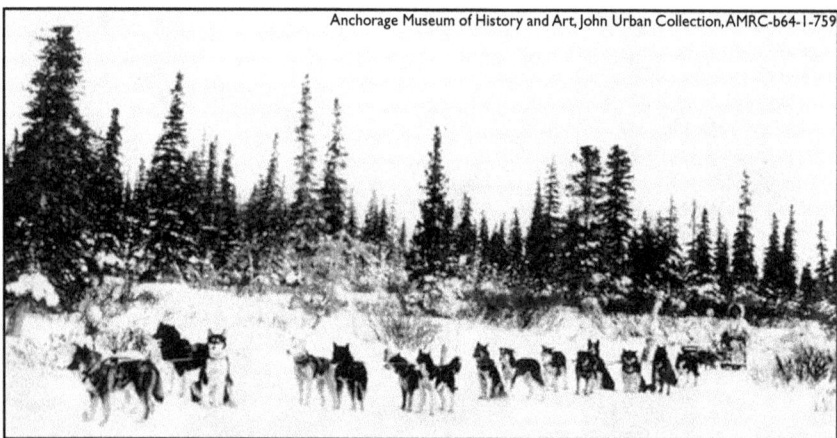

Anchorage Museum of History and Art, John Urban Collection, AMRC-b64-1-759

Dr. John Beeson met legendary Alaska musher Leonhard Seppala and his team, seen here, along the route back to Anchorage.

EPIDEMICS, RESCUES AND DISASTER

After his life-saving mission north, Dr. John Beeson returned to his position as chief surgeon at the Alaska Railroad Hospital near Ship Creek in Anchorage, seen here on the left looking north toward Government Hill.

"...When we started out from McGrath, Doctor Beeson was on his way back to his patients at the hospital at Anchorage, and though they had a two days' start on us, we caught up with them. ...

"... We all traveled close together, taking turns in leading the way, and one man from each outfit going ahead on snowshoes or skis breaking trail. At Susitna Station the doctor found it necessary for him to continue on through the night, as he was in a hurry to get back to Anchorage. His dogs were pretty well used up by this time, so the Major offered to change teams with him, and I was to take the doctor through. The next day we arrived at Anchorage, making the last lap of what was known as the first relay drive ever undertaken in Alaska."

Once he completed his 1,146-mile mushing adventure, Dr. Beeson returned to his job as chief surgeon at the Alaska Railroad Hospital. He later returned to his hometown of Wooster, Ohio, and founded a medical clinic there in 1933.

Beeson, who'd received his Alaska medical license in 1916, died in La Jolla, Calif., in 1969 at 97.

19

DIPHTHERIA THREATENS NOME

Nome's only physician was puzzled when a two-year- old Inuit girl from Holy Cross died in November 1924 after displaying symptoms of tonsillitis. Then many more children were diagnosed with tonsillitis during December – one died.

Two more Native children with sore throats from the Sandspit district of Nome died in January.

When Dr. Curtis Welch saw the grayish patches of diphtheria membranes in 7-year-old Bessie Stanley on Jan. 21, he sounded the alarm that triggered a race against time to stop a massive outbreak.

Diphtheria is highly contagious, easily passing from one person to another. Through coughs, sneezes, or even laughs, Dr. Welch knew the disease would spread quickly through the town unless he could get a large batch of diphtheria antitoxin as soon as possible.

He only had enough antitoxin, which is made from the serum of immunized horses, for a few people. So along with instituting quarantines, Welch sent radio telegrams via the U.S. Army Signal Corps to all the major towns and officials in Alaska. He desperately needed serum.

He also sent the following message to the U.S. Public Health Service in Washington, D.C.:

It didn't take long for diphtheria to spread among Alaska Natives in Nome, seen here.

> An epidemic of diphtheria is almost inevitable here STOP I am
> in urgent need of one million units of diphtheria antitoxin
> STOP Mail is the only form of transportation STOP I have
> made application to Commissioner of Heath of the Territories
> for antitoxin already STOP

Bessie Stanley died. By Jan. 24 there were two more fatalities. Welch and nurse Emily Morgan diagnosed 20 more confirmed cases and 50 more at risk.

The doctor knew that Alaska's first people lacked resistance to white man's diseases. A previous influenza epidemic in 1918-1919 wiped out about 50 percent of the Native residents in Nome, and 8 percent of the Native population throughout Alaska. Without antitoxin, expected deaths from this diphtheria outbreak was high.

Within a week, headlines in newspapers across the country highlighted Nome's plight. Radio sets announced the crisis, too.

Public Health officials found 1.1 million units of the much-needed serum, but it would take weeks to get it from the West Coast by steamship to Seward, Alaska's deepwater port, and then on to the isolated community of Nome.

Luckily, on Jan. 26 Anchorage physician John B. Beeson found 300,000 units of serum in the Alaska Railroad Hospital. While not sufficient to defeat the epidemic, the units could hold it at bay until the larger shipment arrived.

Beeson sent a telegram to Territorial Gov. Scott C. Bone stating that he could send the antitoxin by train to Nenana, the closest point on the railroad to Nome, and mail drivers and their dogs might carry it the rest of the way.

The governor instructed Beeson to prepare the package. He then had to decide if it would continue on to Nome by dog team or by plane – the Bering Sea was icebound so a sea voyage was out of the question.

There were only a couple airplanes in Alaska at the time – World War I-vintage Standard J-1 biplanes that belonged to James Rodebaugh's Fairbanks Airplane Corp. The planes, which had been dismantled and stored for the winter, used water-cooled engines that

University of Alaska Fairbanks, Kay J. Kennedy Aviation Collection, UAF-1991-98-464

The only planes operating in Alaska in 1925 were World War I-vintage Standard J-1 biplanes that had open cockpits – not suitable for cold-weather flight.

were unreliable in cold weather. And the planes had open cockpits. With temperatures hovering around minus 50 degrees Fahrenheit, Bone doubted any pilot could survive the flight to Nome.

He had to consider the limited number of daylight hours, too. Early aviators relied on line of sight to fly their planes.

The governor also learned that experienced pilots for the Fairbanks-based planes were in the Lower 48, so an inexperienced pilot named Roy Darling would have to be used for the mission.

After much thought, Bone decided to forego the new technology and stick with traditional Alaska transportation. Sled dogs would carry the precious cargo to the remote community near the Bering Sea. He ordered U.S. Post Office inspector Edward Wetzler to arrange a relay of the best mail drivers and dogs across the Interior.

Wetzler contacted Tom Parson, an agent of the Northern Commercial Company, which contracted mail delivery between Fairbanks and Unalakleet. Messages through telephone and telegrams turned the drivers back to their assigned roadhouses to prepare for the relay.

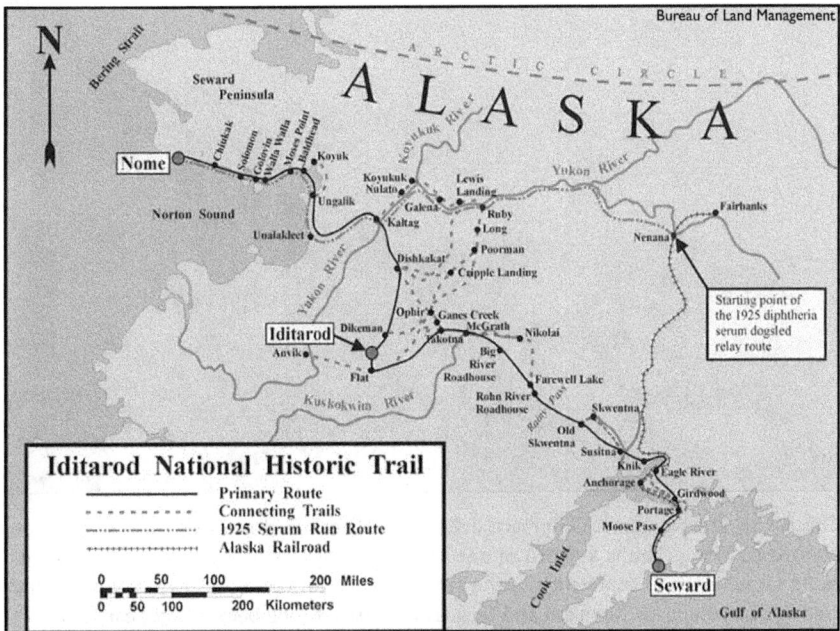

Bureau of Land Management

Iditarod National Historic Trail

———— Primary Route
- - - - - - - Connecting Trails
···—··—··—·· 1925 Serum Run Route
················· Alaska Railroad

0 50 100   200 Miles
0 50 100   200 Kilometers

The dog teams would follow the mail route from Nenana to Nome, which crossed the barren Alaska Interior, following the Tanana River for 137 miles to the village of Tanana at the junction with the Yukon River. It then followed the Yukon for 230 miles to Kaltag.

The route continued west 90 miles over the Kaltag Portage and the forests and plateaus of the Kuskokwim Mountains to Unalakleet on the shores of Norton Sound. It then wound 208 miles northwest around the southern shore of the Seward Peninsula with no protection from gale-force winds and snow blizzards, including a 42-mile stretch across the shifting ice of the Bering Sea.

Twenty courageous men and their dedicated dogs answered the call to relay the life-saving serum from Nenana across those 674 miles of vast, frozen tundra. Jack London once described the land that these mushers would cross as a "pitiless" expanse of "the bright White Silence."

In Anchorage, Dr. Beeson handed the precious 20-pound package of antitoxin, wrapped in fur and canvas, to Alaska Railroad conductor

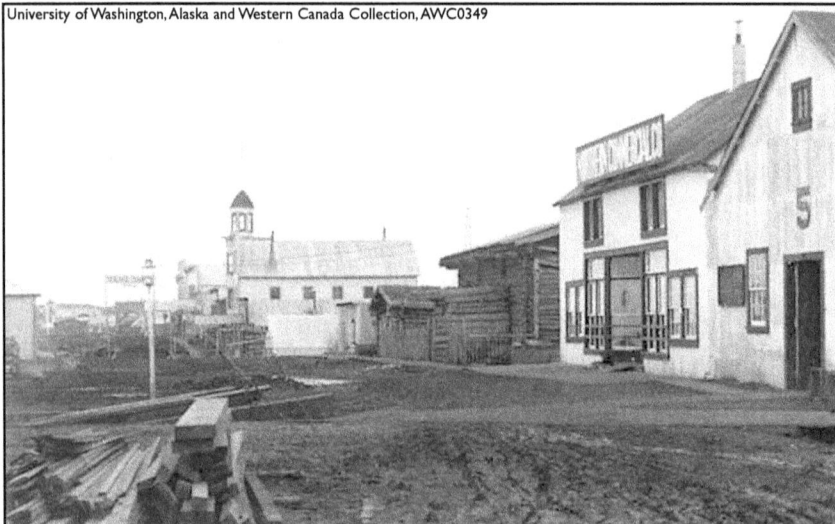

University of Washington, Alaska and Western Canada Collection, AWC0349

Officials of the Northern Commercial Company lined up drivers to relay serum from Nenana to Nome. This is a photo of one of the company's stores located at Tanana. Due to its location at the confluence of the Tanana and Yukon rivers, Tanana was a traditional trading settlement for Koyukon and Tanana Athabascans long before European contact.

An Alaska Railroad train carried precious serum from Anchorage to Nenana in 1925. This photo shows a train bound for Nenana crossing a trestle bridge in 1923.

Frank Night, along with instructions for the care of the serum. Knight took the bundle onboard the train and headed north to Nenana, 300 miles away.

Knight gave the serum to "Wild Bill" Shannon at the train station in Nenana at 9 p.m. Tuesday, Jan. 27, almost 24 hours after leaving Anchorage.

Shannon lashed the khaki-colored package to his sled and left immediately with his team of nine inexperienced dogs, all 2-year-olds, except leader Blackie, a 5-year-old husky. The temperature dropped to minus 62 during his leg of the trip, and despite jogging alongside the sled to keep warm, Shannon developed hypothermia. He reached Minto at 3 a.m., with parts of his face black from frostbite.

After warming the serum and himself by the fire of Johnny Campbell's roadhouse for four hours, Shannon dropped three dogs that were too tired to make the remaining 22 miles and left with the remaining six. The three dogs died shortly after Shannon returned for them.

"What those dogs did on the run to Nome is above valuation. I claim no credit for myself," Shannon later told a reporter. "The real heroes of that run ... were the dogs of the teams that did the pulling, dogs like Cub, and Jack and Jet that gave their lives on an errand of mercy."

Shannon, who traveled a total of 52 miles, pulled into Tolovana at 11 a.m. Jan. 28 and gave the serum to Athabaskan Edgar Kallands.

After warming the serum in the roadhouse, Kallands headed into the wilderness onboard his 16-foot mail sled. He traveled 31 miles to Manley Hot Springs, arriving at 4 p.m. The owner of the roadhouse later said he had to pour hot water over the musher's hands to get them off the sled's birch-wood handlebar.

From Manley Hot Springs, the serum traveled with Dan Green 28 miles to Fish Lake, Johnny Folger 26 miles to Tanana – the geographical center of Alaska where the Yukon and Tanana rivers meet – Sam Joseph 34 miles to Kallands, Titus Nikolai 24 miles to Nine Mile Cabin and Dave Corning 30 miles to Kokrines.

Corning handed the serum off to Harry Pitka, who mushed 30 miles to Ruby, then Bill McCarty carried it 28 miles to Whiskey Creek.

University of Alaska Fairbanks, Walter W. Hodge Papers, UAF-2003-63-261

Relay teams traveled at breakneck speeds through Alaska's rugged wilderness to get diphtheria serum to Nome.

Johnny Folger raced the serum 26 miles to Tanana, seen here in the 1920s.

The Nollner brothers raced the serum farther along the trail. Edgar took it from Whiskey Creek to Galena, a distance of 24 miles, and George mushed the serum 18 miles from Galena to Bishop Mountain, arriving at 3 a.m. Jan. 30.

He handed the serum off to Charlie Evans, a half-Athabaskan descendant of a long line of powerful Koyukon chiefs. After warming the serum, Evans left the fish camp around 4:30 a.m.

Evans knew this section of the trail well, but with the temperature at minus 62, he had to rely on his lead dogs when he passed through ice fog where the Koyukuk River had broken through and flooded over the ice.

But the 22-year-old musher forgot to bring rabbit skins to protect the groins of his two shorthaired mixed-breed lead dogs. Both dogs collapsed with severe frostbite along the trail, so Evans put them in the sled's basket and helped the remaining dogs pull the sled over the last bit of the trail to Nulato.

Evans covered 30 miles in seven hours and arrived at 10 a.m. But his two lead dogs died.

The relay runners still had 318 miles to go, so Tommy Patsy departed within half an hour and carried the serum 36 miles to Kaltag. There he handed it off to "Jackscrew," who mushed on to the Old Woman shelter cabin, a distance of 40 miles.

Inuit Eskimo Victor Anagick next carried the precious cargo on to Unalakleet, 34 miles, and handed it to his fellow Inuit, Myles Gonangnan, at 5 a.m. Saturday, Jan. 31.

Gonangnan saw the signs of a storm brewing, so he didn't take the shortcut across the dangerous ice of the Sound. He left at 5:30 a.m., and as he crossed the hills, "the eddies of drifting, swirling snow passing between the dog's legs and under the bellies made them appear to be fording a fast running river," according to Gay and Laney Salisbury, authors of "The Cruelest Miles."

The whiteout conditions cleared as Gonangnan reached the shore, but 40 mph gale-force winds drove the wind chill to minus 70. He arrived at Shaktoolik, a distance of 40 miles, at 3 p.m. and handed the serum to Henry Ivanoff, a Russian Eskimo who captained a schooner on Norton Sound in the summers.

Ivanoff met Leonhard Seppala along the trail, just after his team ran into a reindeer and got tangled up outside of Shaktoolik.

Seppala didn't see Ivanoff at first. He still believed he had more than 100 miles to go and was racing to get off the Sound before the storm hit. He was passing the team when Ivanoff shouted, "The serum! The serum! I have it here!" according to the Salisburys.

Seppala was an experienced musher – 48 in 1925 but still in his prime. He originally had been chosen to carry the serum all the way from Nulato to Nome. But as the plan developed, more teams were added to the relay route so they could push on day and night.

The scrappy Norwegian had previously made the run from Nome to Nulato in a record-breaking four days, won the All-Alaska Sweepstakes three times and had become a legend for his athletic ability and rapport with his Siberian huskies.

And although he'd earned his nickname, King of the Trail, his lead dog, a Siberian husky named Togo, was equally famous for his leadership, intelligence and ability to sense danger.

By the time Seppala whipped around and met up with Ivanoff, he had already driven 170 miles from Nome. He'd mushed into the oncoming storm, with a wind chill estimated at minus 85, to meet the life-saving package along the trail.

EPIDEMICS, RESCUES AND DISASTER

Mushing legend Leonhard Seppala, above, first was slated to carry the serum from Nulato to Nome. But when more drivers were added to the relay, he and his dog team only carried it 91 miles from Shaktoolik to Golovin – a distance two to three times longer than any other team in the relay.

After transferring the serum to his sled, Seppala decided to brave the storm and once again set out across the exposed open ice of Norton Sound. He reached Ungalik, a fishing camp 23 miles to the north, after dark.

His faithful 12-year-old Togo then led the team in a straight line through the dark, and they arrived at the roadhouse in Isaac's Point on the other side of the Sound at 8 p.m. In one day, they had traveled 84 miles, averaging 8 mph.

The team ate salmon and seal blubber, rested and departed at 2 a.m. into the full power of the storm. The dogs ran across the breaking ice a few hundred feet from land, then they returned to shore to cross Little McKinley Mountain, crossing a series of ridges to the 1,200- foot summit.

After descending to the next roadhouse in Golovin, Seppala, who had traveled 50 miles on this leg, passed the serum to Charlie Olsen on Feb. 1 at 3 p.m.

With the powerful blizzard raging and 65-80 mph winds, Welch ordered a stop to the relay until the storm passed. He thought that a delay was better than the risk of losing the serum. Messages from Nome were left at Solomon and Port Safety before the lines went dead.

University of Alaska Fairbanks, Otto Nordling , UAF-1974-135-4

Leonhard Seppala's dog team, seen here in 1915, was known as the fastest in Alaska.

EPIDEMICS, RESCUES AND DISASTER

Relay mushers sometimes found themselves on bare, windswept ice on their race to Nome with the precious serum.

But the next drivers on the relay never received the message.

Olsen was blown off the trail, and suffered severe frostbite in his hands while putting blankets on his dogs. The wind chill was minus 70. He arrived at Bluff, a distance of 25 miles, in poor shape at 7 p.m.

Gunnar Kaasen took over at the tiny mining village. He waited a couple of hours for the storm to break, but it only got worse. When it looked like the drifts soon would block the trail, he departed into a headwind.

Wearing seal mukluks that went to his hips, sealskin pants, a hooded reindeer parka and another parka over that, the 6-foot, 2-inch Kaasen plowed through the storm. He traveled all night, through drifts and overflow, and up and over the 600-foot Topkok Mountain. His lead dog, Balto, led the team when visibility was so poor that Kaasen couldn't see the dogs harnessed closest to the sled.

"A dog's sense of smell is at least 600 to 700 times more powerful than that of a human and Balto was capable of smelling the tracks

Dog team relays sped through a snow blizzard with gale-force winds to get to Nome with live-saving diphtheria serum in 1925.

left behind by other dogs several feet beneath the snow," wrote the Salisburys. "A canine's paws, too, are sensitive and would help Balto feel the hard-packed surface of a trail that had been covered over by new snow."

The blowing snow was so thick that Kaasen was two miles past Solomon before he knew it. He and his team kept going.

The winds after Solomon were so severe that his sled flipped over, and he almost lost the cylinder containing the serum when it fell off and became buried in the snow. Kaasen suffered frostbite when he had to use his bare hands to find the cylinder.

He reached Point Safety at 3 a.m.

Ed Rohn, the next scheduled driver, believed that Kaasen and the relay had stopped at Solomon, so he was sleeping soundly when Kaasen pulled near.

Kaasen decided not to disturb Rohn, as it would take time to prepare Rohn's team, and Balto and the other dogs were moving well.

He pressed on the remaining 25 miles to Nome, reaching Front Street at 5:30 a.m. on Monday, Feb. 2.

Not a single vial of serum had broken, and the antitoxin was thawed and ready by noon. In a few hours, more than 10 percent of the serum had been used. By Feb. 3, it looked as though even those who were seriously ill would recover. The quarantine was lifted on Feb. 21, two weeks after Kaasen pulled into town with the serum.

Together, the teams covered the route in 127-1/2 hours, which was considered a world record, all driven in subzero temperatures in near-blizzard conditions and hurricane-force winds.

The 1.1 million units of serum from the West Coast left Seattle on Jan. 31 and arrived in Seward onboard the *Admiral Watson* on Feb. 7.

Dr. Welch asked for half the serum to be delivered by airplane from Fairbanks, even though the original 300,000 units had kept the epidemic under control.

Gov. Bone agreed to Welch's request, and sent the other half of the second shipment by sled dog on Feb. 8. Many of the same drivers faced harsh conditions again as they relayed the second batch of serum, which arrived in Nome on Feb. 15.

Anchorage Museum of History and Art, O.D. Goetze Collection, AMRC-b01-41-76

Gunnar Kaasen, the final driver of the diphtheria serum run, pulled into a snow-bound Nome at 5:30 a.m. on Feb. 2, 1925.

The half destined to be airlifted never got off the ground. After assembling the plane and getting it ready to fly, the plane failed to start when a broken radiator shutter caused the engine to overheat. The mission was scrapped when the plane failed to start the next day, too.

The death toll of the diphtheria epidemic is officially listed between five and seven, but Welch later estimated there were probably at least 100 additional cases among "the Eskimo camps outside the city. The Natives have a habit of burying their children without reporting the death."

Forty-three new cases were diagnosed in 1926, but they were easily managed with the fresh supply of serum.

In late February 1925, Kaasen and his wife took Balto and the rest of the team to the Lower 48 for a whirlwind media-fest.

After the unveiling of a statue of Balto in New York City's Central Park, Kaasen left his dogs with a promoter and returned to Alaska and his job hauling supplies for Hammon Consolidated Gold Fields.

After a stint of vaudeville acts, the dogs ended up as part of a sideshow in Los Angeles. They lived in horrible conditions for several months, until being rescued by George Kimble, a businessman from Cleveland who recognized them.

Anchorage Museum of History and Art, John Urban Collection, AMRC-b64-1-188

The second batch of diphtheria serum, 1.1 million units, traveled from Seattle and arrived in Seward on Feb. 7 onboard the steamship *Admiral Watson*, seen here.

Balto, who originally had been one of Seppala's dogs, received a hero's welcome as he and six of his serum-run teammates paraded through downtown Cleveland pulling a sled rigged with wheels driven by Mary Berne, a former gold rush stampeder. The dogs padded to their new home at the Brookside Zoo, where 15,000 people came to see them that first day.

The famous sled dog died on March 14, 1933. His body was preserved and is part of a collection at Cleveland's Natural History Museum.

Togo, who many consider to be the real hero of the serum run, also enjoyed a bit of celebrity.

He and Seppala made a round trip of 261 miles from Nome to Shaktoolik and back to Golovin, and delivered the serum a total of 91 miles, almost double the distance of any other team.

"… it was almost more than I could bear when the 'newspaper dog' Balto received a statue for his 'glorious achievements,'" Seppala said after some of Togo's achievements were attributed to Balto.

Courtesy New York City Parks Department

A statue of Balto was erected in New York City's Central Park in 1925.

Seppala took Togo and his team on a tour from Seattle to California in October 1926, and then across the Midwest to New England. They consistently drew huge crowds and were featured at Madison Square Garden in New York City for 10 days. Former Nome resident and then-current Garden manager Tex Rickard arranged the exhibition.

During a break at a hockey game, explorer Roald Amundsen walked out on the ice and presented Togo with a gold medal, while thousands of spectators cheered.

Seppala raced his Siberians in New England in January 1927, easily beating the competition. He sold the majority of his team to a kennel in Maine and now most huskies in the states can trace their descent from one of those dogs.

Togo died on Dec. 5, 1929, at 16.

Upon his death, *The New York Times Magazine* wrote:

"Every once in a while a dog breaks through the daily routine of feeding and barking and tugging at a leash, and for some deed of super-canine heroism wins the adoring regard of every one who hears of him ... His was the kind of life that catches men by the throat and sets them to hero worshipping."

Seppala had Togo's body preserved and mounted, and today the dog is on display in a glass case at the Iditarod museum in Wasilla, Alaska.

Anchorage, Museum of History and Art, John Urban, AMRC-b64-1-744

EPIDEMICS, RESCUES AND DISASTER

Seppala lived in Seattle until his death in 1967 at 90. His wife, Constance, died a few years later at 85. Both are buried in Nome.

University of Washington, Museum of History and Industry Collection, MOHAI-1986/G.2757

In 1926, Leonhard Seppala traveled onboard the steamship *Alameda* to the Lower 48 with several of his Siberian huskies that made the famous serum run to Nome.

Leonhard Seppala trained Siberian huskies for racing, and most of the Siberians now in America can trace their heritage to his dogs.

EARLY ALASKA AVIATION

20

MAGNIFICENT FLYING MACHINES

an first ventured into Alaska's skies on July 4, 1899.
Juneau residents were treated to a spectacle when
"Professor" Leonard ascended to 1,000 feet in a hot-
air balloon he designed, according to Robert W. Stevens, author of
"Alaskan Aviation History."

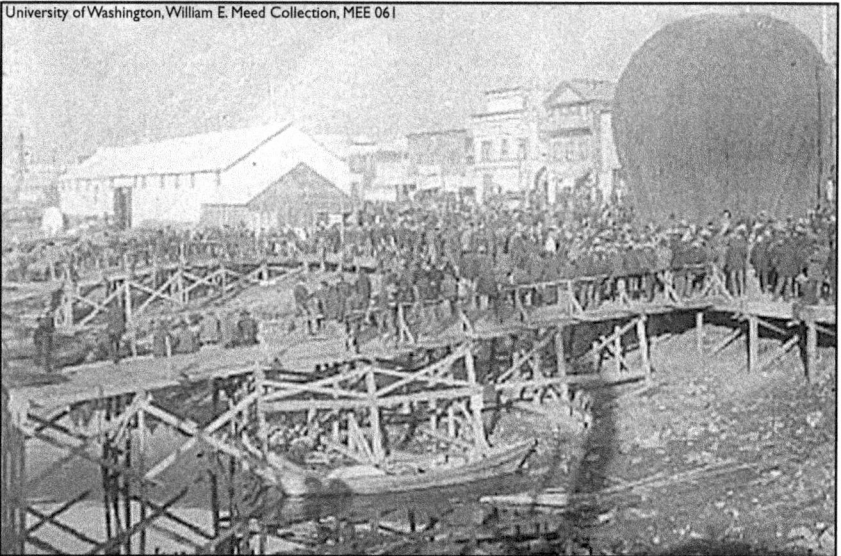

University of Washington, William E. Meed Collection, MEE 061

"Professor" Leonard climbed high above Juneau in 1899 in a hot-air balloon, similar to the
one pictured here in Dawson at the turn-of-the-last century.

But after Orville and Wilbur Wright made the first controlled, powered and sustained heavier-than-air human flight on Dec. 17, 1903, many other people's imaginations took flight, too.

By 1911, flying events and air shows across the country were making news. And that's when one Nome resident decided to build Alaska's first airplane.

Henry Peterson, who gave piano lessons to Nome's children and organized operettas for local entertainment, ordered a set of plans and a motor from Outside. He then built his machine inside the old Ames Mercantile Company warehouse.

On May 9, 1911, Peterson and his helpers towed the Bleriot monoplane, which had been equipped with sled runners for mobility, to an open area.

The would-be pilot, who had no flying experience but had read much about constructing and operating the plane, attempted lift off.

But the machine did not budge. It moved a bit after Peterson's assistants gave it a push, but it didn't accelerate enough to get into the air.

The biplane was pushed back into its shed.

Unlike this early Bleriot monoplane that did make it off the ground, Henry Peterson's home-built model did not.

James V. Martin was the first to fly in Alaska's skies. He brought his Gage-biplane, similar to the one shown here in Seattle over The Meadows, and performed air shows in Fairbanks in 1913.

The first actual flight in Alaska soared in Fairbanks two years later, when Arthur Williams, owner of the Arcade Café, and R.S. McDonald brought aviator James V. Martin north. The promoters thought they'd make a hefty profit with a Fourth of July air show.

Martin and his wife, Lily Irvine Martin – also an experienced aviatrix – crated their Gage-Martin tractor biplane and boarded a ship in Seattle. After landing in Skagway, they and their cargo traveled via the narrow-gauge White Pass and Yukon Railroad to Whitehorse, then wound their way down the Yukon River to Tanana by boat. From there, the pilots followed the Tanana River to Chena and up the Chena Slough to Fairbanks, arriving on Saturday, June 21, 1913.

While the Martins assembled the plane and gave lectures on aviation, Williams and McDonald sold tickets for the flying event – $2.50 for adults, $1 for children over 6.

The air shows were a resounding success, with Martin making five flights between July 3 and July 5.

University of Alaska Fairbanks, Frederick B. Drane Collection, UAF-1991-46-769

Above: Fairbanks' Exposition Park, seen here in 1920, was transformed from a horse- and auto-racing track into a makeshift airfield for the first flight in Alaska in 1913.

Below: Curious Fairbanks residents crowd around an early airplane.

University of Alaska Fairbanks, George Lounsbury Collection, UAF-2006-102-56

The promoters didn't make much money, however, because most of the spectators viewed the aerial maneuvers from their own rooftops and woodpiles and didn't buy tickets to watch the shows from the makeshift airfield at the racetrack in Exposition Park.

At the end of the exhibition, Martin offered to sell the airplane. But with no takers, he and his wife disassembled the craft and shipped it back to the Lower 48.

Brig. Gen. William Mitchell had a hand in the next event that brought airplanes to the Great Land.

Soon after the end of World War I, Mitchell organized a flight of four De Havilland DH-4B aircraft from Mineola, New York, to Nome. The general wanted to show that airplanes could play an integral part in the nation's defense.

The Alaska flying expedition was named the Black Wolf Squadron. The group set out from New York on July 15, 1920, to "demonstrate that we could establish an airway to Alaska and Asia," according to "Alaska Aviation History" author Stevens.

Due to a multitude of stops, inclement weather and a few mechanical problems, it took a month for the planes to fly across America and Canada. The squadron landed in Wrangell on Aug. 14.

Anchorage Museum of History and Art, Crary-Henderson Collection, AMRC-b62-1-1911

Nome, pictured above, was the destination for U.S. Army Black Wolf Squadron in 1920.

Alaska State Library, Winter and Pond Collection, ASL-P87-1089

This biplane over the Juneau waterfront was one of four U.S. Army Black Wolf Squadron planes that flew from Mineola, New York, to Nome in 1920. This plane, en route from Wrangell to Whitehorse, dropped a message for Alaska Territorial Gov. Thomas Riggs.

The pilots then had a couple more stops on their way to Nome, including layovers in Fairbanks and Ruby. One pilot made a side trip after the planes left Wrangell and became the first ever to fly over Juneau. He dipped down over the city and dropped a package to Territorial Gov. Thomas Riggs.

The Black Wolf Squadron finally touched down on the old parade ground at abandoned Fort Davis, three miles east of Nome at the mouth of the Nome River, at 5:30 p.m. on Aug. 23. The citizens of Nome had readied a strip 400 yards long and 100 yards wide for the event.

University of Alaska Fairbanks, Charles S. Hamlin Collection, UAF-1964-74-109

The U.S. Army Black Wolf Squadron landed near Nome at Fort Davis, seen here, 39 days after leaving New York.

EARLY ALASKA AVIATION

Fairbanks residents inspected one of the planes of the U.S. Army Black Wolf Squadron in September 1920 during the squadron's return flight.

The squadron had traveled 4,500 miles in 55 hours flying time, proving that air travel to the northwest corner of America was possible – and that air transportation in Alaska could become more than a dream.

The four airplanes arrived back in New York on Oct. 20, 1920, three months and five days after their departure.

Next came Clarence Oliver Prest, who in the summer of 1922 decided to fly from New York to Nome in his biplane named *Polar Bear II*. All went well until Prest departed from Dawson City, Yukon Territory.

After having engine trouble, he crash-landed on an isolated beach near Fort Yukon.

Prest, who had failed a year earlier to fly *Polar Bear I* from Mexico to Siberia – an idea conceived in a darkened saloon with friend "Mort" Bach – was transported by riverboat operator Gilbert Cook to Tanana and then made his way to Fairbanks.

Prest became the first in a long and famous list of aviators to crash in the unforgiving terrain of Alaska's wilderness.

Above: Early aviators could not call ahead and ask if a community had a suitable landing area. They just looked for good spots to land their planes. And although many early pilots crash-landed, most walked away relatively unscathed due to the slow speeds of the aircraft.

Below: Unless bad weather arose, seaplanes had numerous places to land. This is the first seaplane built by William Boeing and Conrad Westervelt in 1915 in Seattle. In 1922, two Boeing seaplanes would make their way to Alaska – one by ship and one by flight.

21

AVIATORS HEAD NORTH

In 1922, two Boeing seaplanes flew over Alaska's waters within days of each other. The first arrived in Anchorage by ship from Seattle, and the second was flown from Seattle to Ketchikan.

World War I aviator and machine-shop operator Charles Otis Hammontree was the first to bring an amphibian aircraft into the territory.

Hammontree, who moved to Anchorage in late 1921, sent for his airplane, which he'd stored in a floating hangar in Bremerton, Washington.

Boeing's Model C seaplane, built in 1916, was the first "all-Boeing" design and the company's first financial success.

A crane from the Alaska Engineering Commission hoisted Charles Hammontree's biplane from the old dock, seen here, into the waters of Cook Inlet. Note the mudflats in the foreground.

The Boeing C-11S biplane with a 100-horsepower motor arrived onboard the Alaska Steamship Company freighter *Juneau* at 4 p.m. on April 24, 1922.

While curious onlookers watched his every move, Hammontree assembled the plane on the Old Dock. He also built a platform and shed from which to operate the plane on the waters of Cook Inlet.

He christened the plane *Mudhen*, in honor of the mudflats surrounding Anchorage. And although it was missing the airspeed indicator and altimeter, he deemed the plane ready for its initial flight in Alaska airspace.

On Monday, May 22, an Alaska Engineering Commission crane lowered the 2,400-pound seaplane into the water. Hammontree ran the new motor for several hours to break it in.

On Friday, June 24, with Hammontree at the controls, the Boeing rose from the water at the west end of Fourth Avenue and flew for a bit with Arthur Marsh, of Brown and Hawkins, as a passenger.

Anchorage's first flight proved successful.

The plane flew several more times during the next year, but was dismantled and stored after Hammontree sold his garage and business and left Alaska in August 1923.

Twenty-three days after Hammontree soared over Cook Inlet, pilot Roy Franklin Jones was touching down in the waters of Ketchikan in his Boeing Curtiss MF flying boat.

Jones had come to Alaska during the springs of 1915 and 1916 as a rod man and deckhand for the hydrographic section of the U.S. Coast and Geodetic Survey.

He learned to fly after World War I started, graduating as a second lieutenant from the U.S. Army Air Service at March Field in California in 1918. Like many young men of his time, he was placed on inactive service after the Armistice to end the war was signed.

The young aviator moved to Ketchikan, and after seeing a need for aerial surveys for the fishery, timber and other resources, he decided the area could use a flying service.

Alaska State Library, William R. Norton Collection, ASL-P226-390

Seaplanes seemed a natural fit for Ketchikan, seen here, when the first amphibian touched down in July 1922 with Roy Franklin Jones, aviator, and Gerald J. Smith in the cockpit of a Curtiss MF flying boat.

Roy Franklin Jones took his Boeing Curtiss MF flying boat, similar to the one shown above, out for a few test flights in Seattle before heading to Ketchikan in July 1922.

Jones purchased a surplus U.S. Navy Curtiss MF flying boat from Philadelphia for $500, and then located a 180-horsepower Hispano-Suiza motor. He had both shipped to Seattle.

The flying ship's hull was built from solid mahogany, and the freight bill for the 1,980-pound open-cockpit plane from the Northern Pacific Railway Company was $1,036.

On the day Hammontree was taking off in Cook Inlet, Jones was arriving in Seattle to assemble and test his new machine at Boeing pilot Eddie Hubbard's hangar on Lake Union. Once the craft was deemed in tip-top shape, Jones christened it *Northbird*.

The airman and Gerald Smith, a student mechanic, took off for Ketchikan on July 8. Jones wanted to be back home in time for his first payload – a flight slated for July 15 with the Bureau of Fisheries and for the Forest Service to locate lakes and power sites.

After running into a lot of smoke from forest fires, losing their way and taking a side trip in Canada, the pair finally landed in Ketchikan on July 17 to thunderous cheers of the town's residents.

"Teams were running from the field, the bleachers emptying. The wharves, normally deserted, were thick with people, and white columns of steam were rising from the mill, laundry, the canneries and boats as their whistles sounded," wrote Robert W. Stevens in his book, "Alaskan Aviation History."

The pilot and the mechanic had no idea that all the hullabaloo was for them.

"Puzzled by this activity, the airmen swung twice over town but could see no fire in evidence."

After enjoying the town's celebration, Jones threw himself into operating his Northbird Aviation Company. He lasted for a year and a half before throwing in the pontoons.

In a letter written to the Ketchikan Alaska Chronicle on Dec. 1, 1923, Jones said he was getting out of the flying business, according to Stevens. It appears that the problems of operating those early planes,

University of Washington, Museum of History & Industry. MOHAI 1983.10.LJ611.1

Even though Roy Franklin Jones found it too difficult to continue operating his flying service in Ketchikan in the early 1920s, it wouldn't be long before amphibious aircraft became one of the main modes of transportation in Southeast Alaska.

along with the liquid-cooled motors, were too difficult in Southeast Alaska.

But as Jones slipped out of the aviation business in Alaska, other aviators were just beginning to test Alaska's skies.

In the summer of 1923, Anchorage resident Arthur A. Shonbeck believed that his community needed to enter the air age. And he knew that bush pilots, flying open-cockpit planes, needed a place to land.

Shonbeck organized and led the entire town in clearing a field of trees, stumps and moss just beyond civilization. The cleared strip along Ninth and 10th avenues not only became an airstrip for bush pilots, it also turned into a nine-hole golf course.

It would be another year before the new airstrip saw any action, though.

But then a few young men, who would soon make aviation history and are covered in the next few chapters, headed north.

Anchorage Museum of History and Art, General Photograph File, AMRC-b65-2-6

Businessman Arthur A. Shonbeck organized residents to clear a strip of land at Ninth and 10th avenues in 1923 so new-fangled flying machines could land in Anchorage.

One of these two Hisso Standards, seen here at Weeks Field in Fairbanks, was the first airplane to fly in 1924 from the Anchorage airfield cleared near town in 1923. From left, James Rodebough, owner of the two planes, Eddie Hudson, a Fairbanks-born man taking flying lessons, and pilot Noel Wien.

Noel Wien, the first to use the landing field, came to town with a disassembled World War I Standard J1 biplane on June 27, 1924. Wien had traveled north with his crated plane, reassembled the craft and soon was taking paying passengers into the air for 15-minute rides. The young aviator moved the plane, named *Anchorage*, to its home base in Fairbanks on July 15.

The town's first local airline made the new airfield home a couple of years later.

Anchorage Air Transport Inc., formed by Shonbeck, Oscar Anderson, Gus Gelles and Ray Southworth in 1926, used the strip for several years. Its chief pilot, Russell Hyde Merrill, made countless successful take-offs and landings.

But some pilots, like well-known bush pilot Merle Sasseen, also had a few mishaps.

Aviators like Carl Ben Eielson, seen here during his heyday of flying, dressed in layers of warm clothing. A typical outfit included two pairs of heavy wool socks, one pair of caribou-skin socks, moccasins that reached over the knees, heavy underwear, a pair of breeches, a pair of heavy trousers, a shirt and sweater, a skin cap and goggles. The whole outfit then was covered with a knee-length fur or skin parka. Wool gloves covered with heavy fur mitts protected their hands.

Sasseen, who had survived three crashes in as many months, two of which while landing on the "runway" at the out-of-town field, had to fill out a detailed federal report to describe his last accident.

The final, crucial question on the form made him think.

"General ability as a pilot?" it asked.

While most pilots lost no time responding to the ego-challenging question and filled in the blank with "Excellent," Sasseen was weighed down with chagrin at his third aviation smashup.

He studied the question.

"General ability as a pilot?" he asked.

Then, after scratching his head, he wrote: "I used to think I was pretty good, but lately I've begun to wonder."

Bush pilots used what's now called the Park Strip, or Delaney Park, as an aviation field for about seven years. And even after the completion of Merrill Field in 1930-31, spring breakup occasionally forced pilots to use the more solid town strip.

Anchorage Museum of History and Art, General Photograph File, AMRC-b65-2-12

Anchorage quickly outgrew its landing strip off Ninth and 10th avenues, so another field was cleared in 1929 and named after Russell Hyde Merrill in 1930.

22

STRANGE SIGHT SOARS OVER TELLER

The people of Nome were planning a grand celebration in mid-May 1926. They'd decorated their fine city, set up committees, arranged receptions and lined up wagon teams to take schoolchildren to the airfield to see the landing of the dirigible *Norge* N-1.

Slated to be the event to top all events, Nome residents were none too pleased when they learned that the huge craft – which had left Norway to fly over the North Pole a few days earlier – had missed their beautiful town and landed in Teller instead.

Famous explorer Roald Amundsen, who twice before had attempted to reach the North Pole in conventional aircraft, realized his dream in the 348-foot airship after he joined forces with a couple other men who were familiar with dirigibles.

Lt. Riiser-Larsen of the Royal Norwegian Navy steered him toward the N-1, of Italian construction, because it was small enough

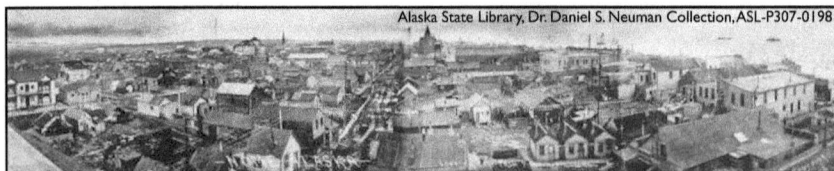

Alaska State Library, Dr. Daniel S. Neuman Collection, ASL-P307-0198

The residents of Nome pulled out all the stops to ready their city for the arrival of the dirigible *Norge*. This photo depicts Nome in the early 1920s.

The dirigible *Norge* left Norway to travel across the North Pole on May 11, 1926.

to be economical. After contacting Col. Umberto Nobile, who had built and flown the airship, Amundsen agreed to pay $75,000 for its use – with $46,000 to be refunded if the craft was returned intact after the voyage.

Financial support of $90,000 came from Lincoln Ellsworth, son of an American industrialist, as well as the Aero Club of Norway. Nobile agreed to supply the crew for the trip for $11,000.

The airship, which left Rome on April 10, 1925, was filled with highly flammable hydrogen held in envelopes of rubberized silk. Balloons filled with air through an opening in the nose helped the ship retain its shape.

After landing in Spitsbergen, Norway, on May 7, the expedition prepared for its flight over the North Pole with 16 men aboard. And one dog. Nobile's terrier, Titina, was the token female.

The dirigible was pulled from the hangar on the morning of Sunday, May 11, and Nobile ordered the crew to cast off the moorings.

"The *Norge* was fueled with 13,700 pounds of petrol and carried 7,500 pounds of lubricating oil and 834 pounds of emergency rations,"

Umberto Nobile, who piloted the *Norge*, brought his dog, Titina, along for the ride.

wrote Robert W. Stevens in his book, "Alaskan Aviation History."

"Forty thermoses of coffee and tea were stacked in the crowded control cabin," Stevens wrote. "Of water, there was little; it had been forgotten."

The airship reached the Geographical North Pole at 1:25 a.m. on May 12, and the men – who had readied flags on weighted staffs in advance – tossed out the flag of Norway first, then the American flag and lastly the flag of Italy.

The *Norge* then made its way to the coast of Alaska, traveling at altitudes of between 1,800 and 2,400 feet. After several hours, it ran into fog and suffered icing problems. Then harsh winds blew it off course.

By May 13, the crew had been awake for more than 60 hours, and in danger for half that time.

The next morning, they spotted a few houses along the shore,

The dirigible *Norge* traveled from Norway over the North Pole to Alaska and is seen here settling on the ground in Teller on May 13, 1926.

which they did not know was Teller. They continued on for a couple more hours, and then ended up back at that spot again.

"The men prepared a long canvas sleeve as a drag and filled it with heavy cans of oil, pemmican, and other weighty material; two ice anchors were attached to the end," according to Stevens. "The strong winds they had been experiencing suddenly ceased as they neared the ice, but the anchors did not hold, dragging rapidly along the ice toward shore as a gust caught the airship. Tom Peterson of the Teller Lighterage Company, upon recognizing the *Norge*, had quickly organized the villagers into a landing force.

"He and another ran forth and leaped onto the anchors, forcing them into the ice; other men seized the mooring ropes flung from the craft and the airship came to a halt some 300 feet from the nearest building as Nobile valved gas from the envelopes," Stevens wrote.

And so ended the historic flight of Amundsen, who had conquered the South Pole on Dec. 14, 1911, and now added the North Pole to his list of accomplishments.

The renowned explorer Roald Amundsen arrived in Teller aboard the dirigible *Norge* on May 13, 1926. He and his fellow team members became the first to cross the North Pole traveling from Norway to Alaska – although Admiral Richard Byrd had claimed he'd flown an airplane over the pole on May 9, two days prior to Amundsen's departure.

Amundsen also was the first person to navigate the Northwest Passage. After that historic feat in the winter of 1906, he reportedly traveled more than 1,000 miles by skiis, sleds and dogs through Alaska, stopping at places like Eagle City, Point Barrow and Nome.

News crews immediately chartered flights to Teller to capture this event on film.

The Pathé News and the *New York Times* hired Fairbanks Airplane Corporation's new pilot Joe Crosson, who later became famous for his daring rescues throughout Alaska. He also made the first commercial flight from Fairbanks to Point Barrow and the first flight over Denali's 20,320-foot summit. Crosson arrived in Nome on May 16 in the company's Standard *Fairbanks 1* with Andy Hufford onboard.

A new Waco aircraft owned by a new company landed a short time later.

Just weeks before, both James Rodebaugh and A.A. Bennett had left the Fairbanks Airplane Corporation, bought a new Waco Model 9 biplane, and formed the Bennett-Rodebaugh Company. This Waco, piloted by A.A. Bennett with Ed Young, touched down in Nome under contract with International Newsreel.

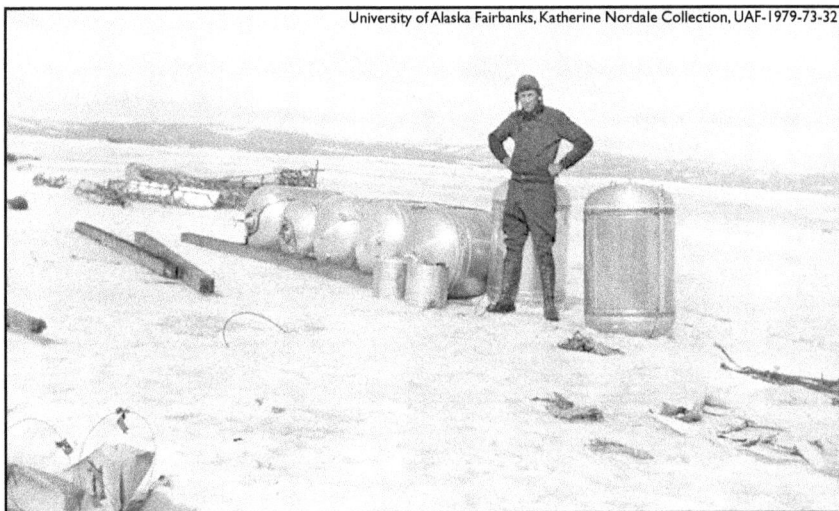

Above: Pilot Joe Crosson was among those who witnessed the salvaging of parts from the *Norge*.

Below: A.A. Bennett flew a Waco Model 9 aircraft from Fairbanks to Nome and then ferried a cameraman to capture the historic landing of the *Norge* in Teller. He and James Rodenbaugh started the Bennett-Rodebaugh Company in 1926 after severing ties with the Fairbanks Airplane Corporation.

The crew of the *Norge* salvaged the main components of the dirigible after landing in Teller. Those parts then were shipped back to Europe. The silver fabric that covered the craft was cut into pieces, and many Alaskans ended up with a piece of material as a souvenir of the event.

The pilots carried cameramen to Teller to record the dismantling of the now-famous airship, as Nobile and other crewmembers packed up its components for shipment.

While many Alaskans ended up with a piece of the silver fabric that covered the ship, its frame traveled in crates aboard the Alaska Steamship Company's *Tanana* to Seattle. The crates then were shipped to Italy.

Amundsen and his team's expedition over the North Pole confirmed that no land lay between the pole and Alaska in the Arctic Ocean. And his prophecy that commercial air service would someday cross the North Pole on a regular basis came true about 30 years later when the first Scandinavian Airlines System plane landed at the Anchorage International Airport on Feb. 24, 1957.

23

CORDOVA FINALLY ENTERS AIR AGE

The first flight in Alaska soared in the skies of Fairbanks in July 1913. The Black Wolf Squadron touched down in Wrangell, flew over Juneau and made its way to Nome in 1920. Then a seaplane made its debut in the waters of Cook Inlet near Anchorage in June 1922, and another flying boat landed in Ketchikan a few weeks later.

Even Teller had seen a huge dirigible land on its shores in 1926.

But by 1929, Cordova had yet to see its first aircraft landing.

The town had been left "waiting at the church" in 1924. The first Round the World fliers, who were scheduled to stop in Cordova,

Alaska State Library, Place File, ASL-P01-2622

The Round the World fliers stopped in Sitka on April 13, 1924.

passed up the town because of hazardous weather and flying conditions over the Gulf of Alaska.

The four amphibian planes, which had taken off from Seattle on April 6, had planned to touch down in Cordova after departing Sitka, but strong winds whipped up and created unstable wave action so that plan was scrapped.

After the U.S. Army Black Wolf Squadron flyers blazed the way in 1920, aviation started to become important in the territory. Seward, Anchorage, Nenana and Fairbanks built landing fields – Southeast Alaska had amphibians – and in Nome and the Far North people were taking advantage of the time and effort saved by flying instead of dog mushing.

But by the late 1920s, Cordova residents still were waiting. The Gulf of Alaska frightened the boldest aerial navigators, and although aviators sometimes circled the town, none had ever landed.

Then on May 1, 1929, news came through that planes from Seattle-based Gorst Air Transport Company were to land in Cordova that week.

The aircraft were scheduled to leave Seattle on May 1, the article

Gorst Air Transport Company out of Seattle made plans to cross the Gulf of Alaska and be the first to land an aircraft in Cordova.

By 1929, Cordova residents were ready to see an airplane land in their community. They made plans for a big celebration to welcome Gorst Air Transport Company's aircraft.

said, and proceed to Juneau to pick up six legislators and bring them to Cordova. If all went well, it would be the first commercial air trip ever made over the Gulf of Alaska to Cordova.

The officials of the Gorst Transport Company said that an aviation craze had seized Alaska. They also said that although the Gulf had for several years been considered a hazardous barrier to flying, they had made a careful study and thought the difficulties had been overrated. The flight should not be too hazardous, they concluded, and expected they could make it over the Gulf – a distance of 450 miles – in about four or five hours.

Cordova residents laid plans to do everything possible to entertain the aviators. Harry O'Neil, president of the Chamber of Commerce, appointed a special committee that included then-mayor Dr. Chase.

The committee planned a banquet, and the Cordova Tennis Club proposed entertaining the fliers, passengers and crew at the theater where they would take over the loge seats to see the show "Ace High," which the club considered most appropriate.

By May 2, it was thought that the fliers would arrive late Saturday afternoon. They had landed in Juneau on Thursday, but had to wait until Saturday to take off, as the legislators were attending a banquet in Juneau on Friday evening.

The names of the legislators making the Cordova trip were not known, but Cordovans kept preparations going at a great pace. The committee in charge of the arrangements announced that the arrival of the planes would be one of the most outstanding events in the history of the town.

The committee arranged for a huge welcome to sound when the planes were within sight. Whistles bellowing from the two fire engines, as well as every cannery and boat, would alert the residents that the planes had been spotted. The New England Cannery tender, Caleb Haley, the largest available, was to meet them.

A banquet with places set for 150 people was planned at the Elks Hall. Walter Hodge, in charge of music, had an orchestra lined up to play during the banquet, as well as many solo numbers by local talent. The mayor would be toastmaster and Harry O'Neil would preside over the gathering.

The entire town was asked to attend and businesses planned to close. The American Legion Auxiliary scheduled an Aviation Ball.

"Please, everyone, display the American Flag," the committee asked.

On May 3, big black headlines spread across the newspaper.

"Gulf of Alaska remains unconquered by air as Gorst trip abandoned."

Cordova, it seems, was destined again to be left with a royal welcome ready and nobody to receive it. The article in *The Cordova*

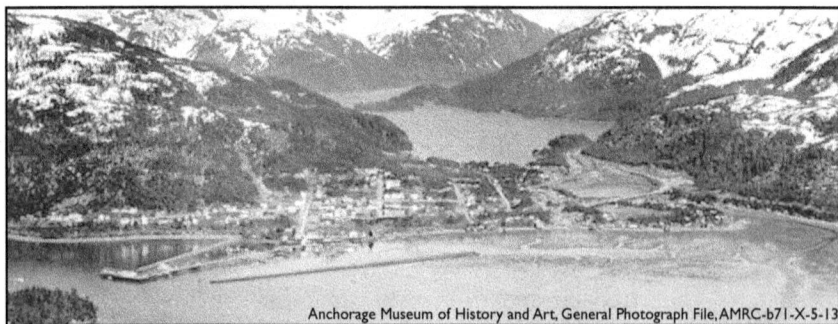

Anchorage Museum of History and Art, General Photograph File, AMRC-b71-X-5-13

Gorst Air Transport Company canceled its plans to land in Cordova, shown above, after bad weather kicked up winds in May 1929.

Times announcing the blow was written with great feeling.

"Nature's immobile barriers victorious again today in the thunderous answer of the winds and waves to man's peremptory challenge to dispel distance, and the mighty Gulf of Alaska remains unconquered by man-made wings which have soared bird-like over practically every other section of the world. This section of Alaska remains, for the time being at least, the un-welded link in the chain of airways which extend now from the States to the Arctic – a chain broken by the sullen Gulf."

All reception plans were abandoned, and Cordova's citizens felt a little sour over the whole aviation business.

The weather was blamed, again, for this latest fiasco – it was too unfavorable for a pioneer flight, it was said, although the rumor flew that the price asked, $150 for the trip, discouraged the would-be passengers. At any rate, Cordovans went to bed that night in the same frame of mind as when the Round the World Fliers failed to stop in their town.

But the residents were cheered the next day when they received a report that one Gorst pilot, Clayton Scott, offered to come to Cordova if four passengers could be secured.

Cordovans got busy – while keeping their fingers crossed – and wired Scott that they would put up a bonus of $250 if he would make the trip.

A wire from the aviator to Mayor Chase gave them cause for a little optimism – he asked if aviation fuel was available in the town, and if appropriate weather reports from Cordova could be given him.

The Chamber of Commerce and Mayor Chase wired Scott, stating "Weather conditions ideal – no plane ever visited Cordova, and you can easily pick up more than $1,000 taking people up, we promise you a royal welcome."

On Monday, May 6, it was announced that the Gorst plane would head for Cordova the next day.

"Gulf of Alaska Conquered by air – the last link of airways between South America and Arctic complete!" stated an article in the May 7 Cordova Times.

"Gorst flier ends special flight from Juneau to Cordova. The entire city joins in welcome as the plane swoops gracefully over the bay, and settles down on the water like a big, red bird."

The trip had taken four hours and 36 minutes. Cordova was finally on the map in the air age.

The town went wild – almost before the plane had been sighted the entire city joined in wild celebration. Steam whistles, electric sirens, horns of every description blew frantically. The reception committee went out to greet the plane in the launch, *Ittewake,* and almost half of the town's population was there at the dock when the plane landed on the calm water of the bay.

As each man came out of the plane, he was greeted by a wild ovation from the spectators, who at last were witnessing the first commercial fliers to cross the dreaded Gulf and could show their unstinted praise of these men pioneering a route that would put Cordova on the flying map of Alaska.

Scott's passengers were Joe Murray, H.W. McDurmont and Paul Abbott, Alaska representative of the DuPont Company, and the first

Alaska State Library, Winter and Pond Collection, ASL-P87-1087

Pilot Clayton Scott and mechanic Gordon Graham take off from the harbor in Juneau on May 7, 1929, in a Loening amphibious plane, owned by Gorst Air Transport Company. The pair made the first commercial flight across the Gulf of Alaska and landed in Cordova.

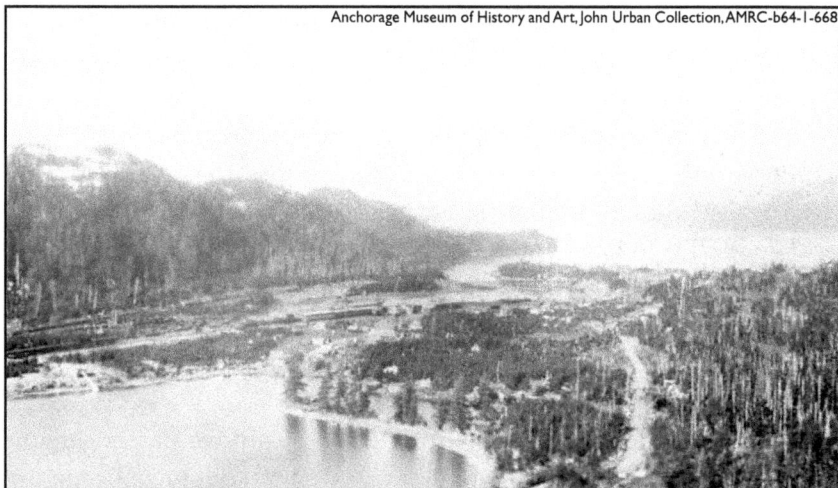

The first plane to land in Cordova on May 7, 1929, was anchored in Lake Eyak, shown above, to keep it safe from an impending storm.

traveling representative of a firm to make a business trip by air over the Gulf.

With the tide running strongly, it was decided to anchor the plane at Lake Eyak. With some adventuresome Cordova residents aboard – Mayor Chase, Dorothy Dooley, E.W. Sandell, L.C. Pratt and Alan Craig Faith – the amphibian rose from the bay, circled the town, and anchored in the protected lake.

The weather, which had dealt Cordova some pretty hard blows, had finally relented and allowed the plane to land safely. But then a deluge hit that threatened to keep the plane grounded.

But in spite of the rain, Scott managed to fly excursion trips for $5 and $10. Phil Lydick, Lew Cochran, and Mr. and Mrs. Joe Whitehead were among the first to take advantage of the opportunity to see Cordova from the air.

A banquet was held to honor the occasion on May 9. It was one of the most successful affairs ever held in Cordova, according to The Times.

In a speech, Scott said that the country between Cordova and Juneau was not a barrier, but ideal for flying. He said that during the trip there was no place where they could not have dropped down to the beach and trundled to shore.

He prophesied that Cordova would have regular air service within two years and he promised numerous excursions between Cordova and Juneau that summer. The proper thing, he said, for Cordova would be a seaport rather than a landing field, but it would be a good idea to have both, if possible.

On May 10 the first aerial wedding was celebrated. Cordova schoolteacher Henrietta Brown and H.W. Steward, a local photographer, were married by the Rev. Bert Bingle in Scott's plane while flying almost two miles a minute.

Scott then took the plane with a load of Cordova passengers on to Anchorage on May 11, where that city went all out to welcome the conqueror of the Gulf. A few miles from town, two Anchorage planes flew out to meet the inbound party and led them into the city, where a big celebration was held in their honor.

It took one hour and 40 minutes to fly over, and two hours to fly back.

An all-out drive commenced two weeks later to paint "Cordova" on the roofs of the most prominent buildings – Scott, when his advice was asked, said it would be very helpful to aviators who had never been through this section before.

The townspeople certainly did not want any aviators to miss Cordova, now that it had a successful landing under its wings.

The first southbound aerial trip ever to be made by a commercial airplane came on June 3.

Scott left his mooring at Eyak Lake at 10:45 a.m. with Harry Seidenverg, an Anchorage clothing merchant who needed to travel to Portland, Oregon, to be at the bedside of his seriously ill 8-year-old daughter.

Also onboard were Joe Ibeck, fox rancher on Middleton Island, who flew as far as Juneau, and a New York businessman, who had been hunting but was called back home on business.

Scott arrived in Ketchikan at 8:30 p.m. and stayed overnight. The plane touched down in Seattle at 3:30 p.m. the next day.

Cordova's first plane landed in Ketchikan, seen above in the late 1920s, on its way back to Seattle on June 3, 1929.

The plane also carried 500 airmail letters – the first airmail ever to be taken over the Gulf from Cordova to Seattle. The mail carrying was unofficial, as no government contract for the route had been awarded, but Scott posted the mail in Seattle on Tuesday morning.

The pilot reiterated his appreciation for the cooperation given him by the citizens of Cordova. He declared that the town had shown not only that its location was ideal for an airport connecting interior and coastal cities, but that it had shown, in its spirit of friendliness, that the townspeople would aid in every way to have Cordova established as a leading air city of the North.

His own company, he said, would endeavor to have a plane based there, and he, himself, would return in the amphibian *Alaska* to be stationed in Cordova for the summer, at least.

Carl Benjamin Eielson became Alaska's first full-fledged pilot in 1923 when he joined Farthest-North Airplane Company in Fairbanks. He's seen here on one of his expeditions with Australian explorer Sir G. Hubert Wilkins to cross the North Pole and land in Norway.

DARING FLYBOYS

24

EIELSON: ALASKA'S PIONEER AVIATOR

O ne of Alaska's earliest aviators turned wilderness landings into an art form – until he lost his life in a crash in 1929.

Carl Benjamin Eielson, born in 1897 in Hatton, North Dakota, earned his wings after joining the U.S. Air Service in 1918. After completing flight training in 1919, he was commissioned second lieutenant, Aviation Section, Signal Officers Corps, just as the Armistice ending World War I was signed.

Eielson longed to get back into the air after his release from government service, so he organized the Hatton Aero Club. The club purchased a Curtiss J-1, and soon the aviator was aloft – teaching club members to fly and performing air shows.

In 1921, after enrolling to study law at Georgetown University in Washington, D.C., he hired on as a congressional guard at the Capitol Building. There he met a man who would steer his life north.

Dan Sutherland, a former miner and Alaska's delegate to Congress, persuaded Eielson to head to Alaska for a career as a schoolteacher.

The 25-year-old traveled onboard the *Northwestern* out of Seattle. After arriving in Seward, he rode an Alaska Railroad train to Anchorage. From there he took another train ride on the still-under-construction tracks to Nenana, where he hopped on a riverboat and arrived in Fairbanks in the summer of 1922.

Eielson soon met another man who planted more flying dreams in the young aviator's head.

Clarence Oliver Prest showed up in Fairbanks on Aug. 11, after wrecking his airplane, *Polar Bear II*, near Fort Yukon. Prest, who had been scheduled to put on air shows for the Fourth of July celebrations in Fairbanks, told Eielson all about his flying experiences in the wilderness.

After Prest departed for the Lower 48, Eielson drummed up interest in getting an airplane to Fairbanks and putting on a flying show himself.

The idea intrigued local businesspeople and government officials. On March 14, 1923, the Fairbanks City Council announced that an airfield would be constructed and named Weeks Field – after U.S. Secretary of War John Wingate Weeks.

Nenana City Council soon followed with the decision to survey open tracts and lay out an airfield. Anchorage also began plans to create a landing strip for the new-fangled flying machines.

By the end of March, Eielson and a group of businessmen formed the Farthest-North Airplane Company. First National Bank of Fairbanks President Richard C. Wood and *Daily News Miner* Editor William F. Thompson were named directors and Eielson became the sole pilot.

Early aviators got a bird's-eye view of Fairbanks, seen here around 1923.

Alaska's first commercial aircraft arrived aboard the *Alameda*, pictured here docked at Anchorage, on June 23, 1923.

The directors fronted $1,000 for the new company, of which $750 was wired to Minneapolis to purchase a Curtiss OX-5 plane, a spare motor and other spare parts.

The plane and spares arrived in Anchorage onboard the *Alameda* on June 23, 1923, accompanied by Eielson and mechanic William S. Ambler. The men and machine boarded the north-bound Alaska Railroad and arrived in Fairbanks on June 30.

"Ben Eielson and Ira Farnsworth, proprietor of the New Era Garage in Fairbanks, began uncrating the shipment on Garden Island, assembling the plane the same day," wrote Robert W. Stevens in his book, "Alaskan Aviation History."

"With wings still in crates, the plane, now on wheels, was towed to the ball park airfield. The two men installed and rigged the wings, tested the motor and made other adjustments during the next three days," Stevens wrote. "As a finishing touch, *Fairbanks*, in large white letters, was painted on the olive-drab side of the fuselage."

Eielson test-flew the craft on July 3, almost 10 years to the day of James Martin's first flight over the city.

It took directionally challenged Carl Ben Eielson three times as long to find the Nenana ball field, seen here, on his first flight there on July 4, 1923, as it did to return to Fairbanks the next day.

All set for the Fourth of July exhibition, Eielson left Fairbanks for Nenana at 9 p.m. July 4 with stockholder Dick Wood seated in the rear of the open cockpit. The pilot, plagued with a poor sense of direction, wandered around the skies for an hour and a half until he found the Nenana ball field and landed.

On July 5, Eielson treated the spectators to a one-man aerial show, performing acrobatics and dives. After the spectacle, it only took him 30 minutes to find his way back to Fairbanks.

Eielson then made news on July 16 when he flew the first commercial flight in Alaska. Carrying attorney R.F. Roth and supplies, he landed at the Denhart mines on Caribou Creek. Not only did it cost the Salchaket Mining Company $450 less for the plane ride compared to travel along the trail from Fairbanks, but it also saved time. The trail route took about six days, and the airplane trip took just a little more than an hour.

The young pilot flew paying passengers to various destinations for the remainder of the summer and fall, and in October put the Curtiss "Jenny" into the Stewart warehouse on Third Avenue for the winter.

While on vacation in the Lower 48, Eielson traveled to Washington, D.C., to visit Sutherland. By late 1923, rumors were circulating that a possible mail contract might be awarded to the Farthest-North Airplane Company.

On Dec. 20, the superintendent of the Railway Mail Service of the Pacific Northwest announced that a contract would be issued for airplane mail service between Nenana and McGrath. Ten mail flights along the 230-mile route, on a trial basis only, would begin in February 1924, and Eielson's company would receive $2 per pound for the deliveries.

The government sent a De Havilland DH-4BM airplane – the type of aircraft used for mail routes in the Lower 48 – to Fairbanks from Washington, D.C.

The plane "had all the latest improvements to plane and motor, including special equipment for cold weather operation," Stevens wrote. "The body was of yellow maple veneer which, with silver-painted wings, made a very attractive appearance as compared to the customary olive drab of military planes. A pair of skis and a spare motor were included in the shipment, which consisted of three large crates containing the fuselage, engine and wings, and a fourth crate containing spare parts."

Anchorage Museum of History and Art, General Photograph File, AMRC-b65-2-20

The U.S. government sent a De Havilland DH-4BM aircraft, shown above, to Alaska for Carl Ben Eielson to use for experimental airmail runs between Nenana and McGrath.

Above: Pilots learned to dress for the frigid winter weather. Note Carl Ben Eielson's long leather boots. Early aviators always wore suitable footwear because they often had to hike out of remote spots after making emergency landings.

Below: Carl Ben Eielson, left, completed the first experimental mail flight between Fairbanks and Nenana on Feb. 21, 1924, using a De Havilland plane with a 400-horsepower 12-cylinder water-cooled Liberty engine.

After the plane arrived in the Interior and was reassembled, Eielson prepared for his historic flight.

At 8:45 a.m. on Feb. 21, 1924, the aviator took off from Weeks Field carrying 164 pounds of mail, emergency gear, 10 days of provisions and five gallons of oil. He landed at McGrath two hours and 50 minutes later.

He lifted off at 2:35 p.m., but with the airspeed indicator broken and the compass reading 40 degrees off course because of magnetism in the plane, Eielson became lost. He finally found his way through the pitch-black night to his home field, where a bonfire burned brightly in front of the hangar.

"Guessing at the edge of the field, the pilot went on in," Stevens wrote of Eielson, who landed at 6:45 p.m. "He struck a tree during the glide and broke off one ski. On landing, the De Havilland nosed over – breaking the prop in front of the entire town whose citizens had been awaiting his arrival for the past hour."

University of Alaska Fairbanks, Edward Lewis Bartlett Collection, UAF-1969-95-74

Fairbanks residents cleared land and created Weeks Field, shown above, for the territory's new flyboys.

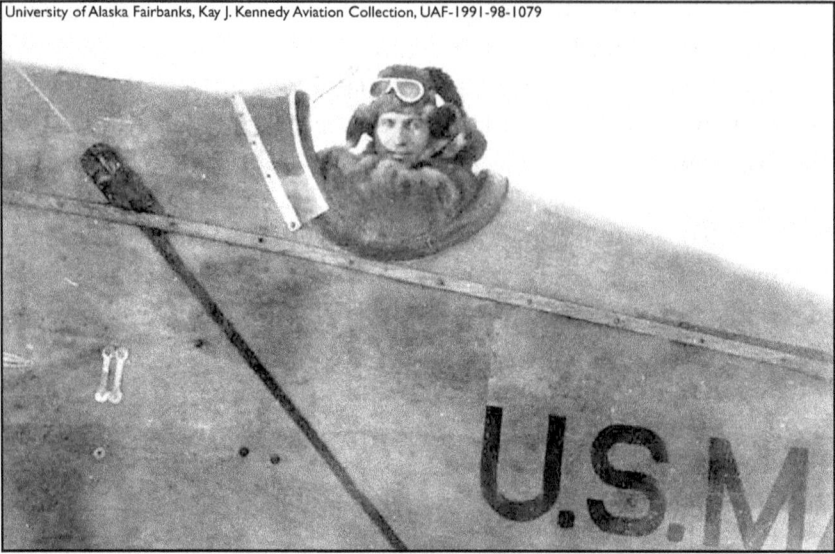

Carl Ben Eielson completed eight of 10 planned airmail runs - then a mishap caused substantial damage to the plane and ended any more flights with the De Havilland.

During the next three months, Eielson completed six more trips without any major mishaps. But while returning to Fairbanks from the eighth trip on May 28, the plane's wheels sunk into a boggy spot close to the center of the runway, and the plane nosed up and flipped over onto its back. The accident broke the propeller, rudder and two wing struts.

Eielson already had used spare parts sent with the plane, so the government recalled the airplane and ended the first airmail contract in Alaska. But the diphtheria epidemic in early 1925 pushed the need for air service in the Last Frontier to the forefront once again. Congress passed the Kelly Act in February 1925, which authorized the Postmaster General to contract for airmail service.

In that same year, Australian explorer Sir G. Hubert Wilkins enlisted Eielson to join him in an exploratory expedition to the North Pole and a possible trans-polar flight from the northern coast of Alaska to Greenland.

Although the expedition was unsuccessful, the Fairbanks pilot

Sir G. Hubert Wilkins and Carl Ben Eielson land in Barrow to begin their circumpolar flight on April 15, 1928. The pair flew 2,500 miles to Spitsbergen, Norway.

did become the first aviator to cross the Arctic Circle and land a plane on the North Slope.

He joined Wilkins again in 1927, and again the expedition failed.

But the April 1927 expedition may have been one of the greatest arctic survival tales of all time, according to Dorothy Page, author of "Polar Pilot – The Carl Ben Eielson Story."

Engine trouble forced them down twice on the ice floes. After making what were believed to have been the first-ever landings and takeoffs on floating ice, the men's Stinson plane ran out of gas, and Eielson made a third emergency landing on moving ice the same day.

The men abandoned the plane and walked 125 miles on the ice in 13 days. They made crude sleds from airplane parts and pulled them across the ice. They soon abandoned the sleds, continuing with backpacks – which they eventually downsized to one.

Despite Wilkins falling in the icy water and frozen fingers for Eielson, the pair finally reached land near Beechy Point, about 25 miles northwest of today's Prudhoe Bay.

One of Eielson's fingers was so frostbitten that it had to be amputated.

The men's third attempt in 1928 proved to be the charm. On April 15, they took off from Barrow in a small orange Vega loaded with 3,000 pounds – mostly gasoline.

Although famous Norwegian explorer Roald Amundsen had said their attempt was "beyond the possibility of human endeavor," Eielson and Wilkins successfully flew the 2,200-mile route from the North Slope over the polar ice cap to Spitzbergen Island, Norway.

The now-famous pilot flew again with Wilkins to the Antarctic in 1929, in the same Lockheed Vega, becoming the first pilot to fly over both polar regions.

Eielson then formed his own air service, Alaskan Airways Inc. He built three hangars, bought 12 planes and staffed his company with a crew of experienced Alaska pilots and mechanics.

But his success was short-lived. That winter, while attempting to rescue stranded passengers aboard the freight ship *Nanuk*, which was caught in the ice off the Siberian coast, Eielson and his mechanic, Earl Borland, ran into trouble.

They had made one successful trip from the ship back to Nome, but after leaving on the second flight on Nov. 9, they encountered a

University of Alaska Fairbanks, George Lounsbury Collection, UAF-2006-102-30

Following his successful trans-polar flight with Sir G. Hubert Wilkins in 1928, Carl Ben Eielson started his own company. This Hamilton sports the new company's name, Alaskan Airways Inc.

The wreckage of Carl Ben Eielsen's aircraft was located more than two months after it had been reported missing. Men can be seen in the upper middle of the photo searching for the bodies.

storm about 400 miles northwest of Nome. Both men and their plane disappeared.

Aviators from the United States, Canada and Russia soon began searching.

The *Nanuk* sent word that a plane had been spotted flying in the fog about 60 miles from the ship on the day Eielson's Hamilton went missing. Another report came from a Russian trapper who said he'd heard an airplane in the fog about 50 miles from the *Nanuk.*

Searchers finally discovered the wreckage on Jan. 26, 1930. It took another three weeks to find the bodies.

Eielson was only 32 years old.

A mountain peak near Denali National Park and Preserve and a U.S. Air Force base near Fairbanks were named in his honor.

A massive search was launched involving fliers from America, Canada and Russia. On Jan. 26, 1930 - 77 days after the search began - they found the plane at a point about 30 miles west of Cape Vankarem and about 90 miles from the icebound ship *Nanuk*.

The bodies, discovered on Feb. 18, 1930, are seen here loaded onto sleds and covered with American flags.

25

WIEN: A LEGEND IN THE NORTH

Traveling by steamship and rail, a young pilot from Minnesota arrived in Anchorage in June 1924, bringing with him a disassembled World War I Standard J-1 airplane. Noel Wien, recently hired by James S. Rodebaugh of Fairbanks as a pilot for a new flying venture – Alaska Aerial Transportation Company – was eager to earn his $300 monthly paycheck flying over the Alaska wilderness.

Alaska State Library, Mary Nan Gamble Collection, ASL-P270-ARRC-Album Cover

Anchorage residents helped clear land for an airstrip in 1923.

Noel Wien took Anchorage residents up for rides in this Hisso Standard J-1 and then flew it from Anchorage to Fairbanks on July 15, 1924.

The airplane, with its Hispano-Suiza 150-horsepower motor, was lifted from an Alaska Railroad flatcar by a huge crane and transported along with its propeller and wheels to the garage of MacDonald and Gill. The wings were taken to the new Anchorage Aviation Field.

Townspeople had turned out in force in the spring of 1923 to clear 16 acres of land between Ninth and 10th avenues and C and L streets. That strip of land had served as a firebreak between downtown Anchorage and the south.

The May 27 issue of the *Anchorage Daily Times* reported the event:

"Men whose hands had not been soiled by anything heavier than a pen for many years, grappled the mattock or the axe and shook the kinks out of their flabby muscles. Ladies with rakes and other implements cleared away the small debris while others piled it upon the small mountain of stumps ready for the torch."

Now the airstrip was to be put to use for the first time, when on June 27, Wien took off to test fly the reassembled craft. He climbed to 2,000 feet, circled over the city and performed a few stunts to check for any weaknesses in the plane.

The airplane, which had been christened *Anchorage*, was ready to take on passengers. For the next few days, Wien took Anchorage residents on 15-minute flights for $10 apiece. And on July 4, the young airman wowed the crowd with aerial loops, stalls and spins.

Rodebaugh sent word that he wanted the airplane flown to Fairbanks, so local mechanic Oscar Gill fabricated an auxiliary gas tank for the craft. It allowed the plane to travel several hundred miles without needing to refuel.

"An air pump, mounted on the Hisso motor, supplied fuel from this tank to the carburetor by pressurizing the fuel tank to a low pressure," wrote Robert W. Stevens in his book, "Alaskan Aviation History." "An additional thirty gallons from the center section tank could be drained by gravity into the fuselage tank, when it became depleted, by opening a valve, giving the Standard an effective range of 400 miles."

The plane was ready for its historic flight by mid-July with Wien at the controls.

On July 15, the 24-year-old barnstormer took off at 2:30 a.m. in the open-cockpit biplane and followed the railroad north.

Although the gutsy aviator encountered thick smoke from wildfires near Healy that hampered his visibility, he landed safely at Weeks Field in Fairbanks at 7:20 a.m. The flight, which traveled at 65-75 mph, took almost five hours.

Wien's first-ever flight between Anchorage and Fairbanks changed the way Alaskans thought about transportation forever. That same journey by train took two days.

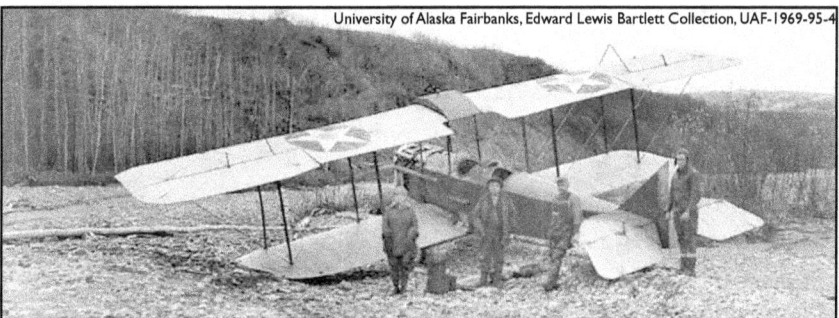

University of Alaska Fairbanks, Edward Lewis Bartlett Collection, UAF-1969-95-4

Noel Wien, far right, became adept at putting his Standard J-1 "Jenny" down on sandbars, like this 300-foot strip near Kantishna.

Noel Wien squeezed into the captain's seat of a Fokker F-3 six-place cabin monoplane in June 1925, just minutes before taking off on the first commercial flight to Nome.

The young aviator flew 34 trips during the summer of 1924 to places like Livengood, Eagle, Circle Hot Springs and McGrath. But by September, The Alaska Aerial Transportation Company had lost its chief mechanic and second pilot – both of whom returned to the Lower 48. That left Wien as the sole flier in the Interior, as Eielson also was Outside.

By spring 1925, James Rodebaugh of Alaska Aerial Transportation Company and banker Richard Wood of the Farthest-North Airplane Company had merged their assets to become the Fairbanks Airplane Corporation.

With the passage of the Kelly Act, which authorized mail to be flown to destinations in Alaska, along with demand from businesses for air transport increasing, the company needed a new airplane.

It chose a Fokker F-3, built in Holland in 1921, located in New Jersey.

Wien traveled to the East Coast and learned to fly the craft, which could carry a payload of 1,200 pounds, including five passengers and a pilot, at 90 mph.

After Wien became familiar with it, the Fokker employees crated the plane and sent it to Alaska via ship through the Panama Canal and on to the West Coast.

Rodebaugh also needed a new mechanic, and Wien – now director of flying for the new company – hired his older brother, Ralph.

Alaska State Library, Portrait File, ASL-P01-468?

Noel Wien pioneered flying routes in Alaska's vast wilderness.

The summer of 1925 brought a milestone in Alaska aviation when two mining operators wanted to travel from Fairbanks to Wiseman. Noel Wien flew them to the village, located about 80 miles north of the Arctic Circle, thus making the first flight across the Arctic.

That year also proved quite busy for the Wien brothers and the Fairbanks Airplane Corporation. Management decided the growing business needed another pilot.

Almer Acie "A.A." Bennett, a pilot from California, arrived in Fairbanks in September. By December, the Wien brothers had quit due to disputes over maintenance as well as pressure to fly when Noel Wien didn't feel comfortable with conditions.

Noel and Ralph Wien, along with Gene Miller, started Wien Brothers, and in 1927, began the first scheduled air service between Fairbanks and Nome.

"Miners, traders, salesmen and missionaries were eager to fly. They didn't question the plane's airworthiness or the pilot's ability to

The Wien Brothers' plane, shown above in June 1927, was the first airplane to serve the Nome and Seward Peninsula area. Notice the spare propeller tied on the side of the fuselage on the wing.

land safely on Arctic beaches, river bars or mountain domes," wrote Kay Kennedy in her book, "The Wien Brothers' Story."

"When the weather permitted, the plane was in the air all hours of the day or night. During the summer, three round trips between Nome and Fairbanks were made carrying passengers, one or two at a time, and letter mail."

Like many pilots during Alaska's fledgling days of flying, the Wien brothers had a few crash-landings and lived to tell their stories. But Ralph Wien's luck ran out on Oct. 12, 1930, when he crashed at Kotzebue. He and two priests died.

Noel Wien continued to take to the skies and flew many history-making flights during those early years. He was the first pilot to land above the Arctic Circle, made the first transcontinental flight between Alaska and Asia when he flew from Nome to Siberia, and completed the first commercial flight from Fairbanks to Seattle when he rushed pictures of the airplane crash that killed Will Rogers and pilot Wiley

Post to the world in the 1930s.

Wien Air Alaska was formed in the mid-1930s, and by 1972 the airline had grown to 800 employees and served almost 190 communities in Alaska and Canada. It closed in 1984.

"The business just sort of grew around the fact that there was a need for his (Noel's) services," said Wien's son Richard in a profile written by Catherine Evanelista for *Alaska Business* in January 1989.

"In his case, he was really a pilot first and a businessman second."

Anchorage Museum of History and Art, Wien Collection, AMRC-b85-27-1849

Ralph Wien, seen here near a biplane, died on Oct. 12, 1930, after crash-landing near Kotzebue.

In 1975, Noel Wien was named Alaskan of the Year.

"I sometimes think that the stern necessities of Alaska have been the best of all teachers," Wien told Evanelista before his death in 1977.

26

MERRILL: BLAZING TRAILS IN THE SKY

On Sunday, Sept. 25, 1932, the Russell Hyde Merrill Memorial Beacon was dedicated at Merrill Field in Anchorage. Bought with money raised by the Anchorage Women's Club, it was a memorial to a pioneer airman. Three years before, he had disappeared almost without a trace.

The name of this early commercial pilot has been given not only to the beacon and Anchorage's Merrill Field, but also to the pass he discovered in the towering peaks of the Alaska Range. He'd blazed many trails across Alaska skies before the day he disappeared, and many firsts had been chalked up by the young flier – only 35 years old when his life was tragically cut short.

University of Alaska Fairbanks, Kay J. Kennedy Aviation Collection, UAF-1991-98-33

Russell Hyde Merrill arrived in Alaska in 1925. He died in the wilderness he loved four years later.

DARING FLYBOYS

The Gastineau Channel between Juneau and Douglas made a fine landing area for Russell Merrill when he arrived in Southeast Alaska in 1925.

Even before coming North, Merrill's life had been adventuresome and eventful. Born in Des Moines, Iowa, on April 8, 1894, his heritage included a Samuel Merrill who was a governor of Iowa. The young Merrill attended Cornell University and joined the U.S. Navy when America entered World War I. He earned his wings in March 1918 and for a while was with a sub-chaser squadron. When the Armistice came, Merrill was chief pilot at the Naval Air Station in Cape May, New Jersey.

He returned to Cornell at the end of his service and received a degree in chemistry in 1919. The flyboy headed west after graduation and worked for a while in the Crown Paper Company plant at Camas, Washington. He also worked in Oregon and California, but he kept up with his flying.

Merrill made his first appearance in Alaska when he flew from Portland, Oregon, to Juneau in July 1925. In August, along with Roy

Seward residents were fascinated with floatplanes landing in Resurrection Bay in 1925.

Davis, he flew a Curtiss F Flying Boat to Seward in the first attempt by a single-engine plane to cross the Gulf of Alaska. It was the first commercial air flight westward from Juneau, as well.

After arriving in Seward, he started flying commercially from that little town, but the venture lasted only a month. On Sept. 4, he had to make an emergency landing at the entrance of Cook Inlet. A sudden windstorm tore the plane loose from its moorings and damaged it beyond repair.

The adventurer returned to Portland that fall in good spirits, however, impressed with the new land. In spring 1926, he bought another plane at Vancouver, British Columbia, and again with Davis, flew up the Canadian coast, across the Gulf of Alaska and landed near Anchorage.

Flying passengers and freight across the sparsely settled country kept Merrill busy all that summer. He returned again to Portland in the fall, but early in 1927 he came North for the last time with his wife and two sons, Richard Kendrick and Robert Ludlow. Merrill landed a job with the newly organized Anchorage Air Transportation Corporation.

His first flight was typical of many others in this new land — an errand of mercy, a plane accident and then a long, difficult attempt to get home.

University of Alaska Fairbanks, Kay J. Kennedy Aviation Collection, UAF-1991-98-30

Russell Merrill, working for the Anchorage Air Transport Company, flew a biplane named *Anchorage 1* off the cleared field between Ninth and 10th avenues in Anchorage.

Anchorage 2 was fitted with skis on the snow-covered ground during Alaska winters.

On May 4, he and Alonzo Cope, his mechanic, left Anchorage for Savoonga on St. Lawrence Island to try to save the life of an Eskimo. After flying for seven and a half hours, they landed on the Bering Sea ice in front of Nome, only to find that their passenger was beyond help.

Instead of proceeding to Savoonga, Merrill, with two passengers, took off for Candle. A blizzard came up, so he landed on Selawick Lake, but the plane nosed over and was damaged. They were missing four days that time. On May 10, he and Cope finally made it back to Anchorage.

That winter, on Nov. 8, Merrill discovered the pass that later was named for him. It opened up a new and shorter route to the Kuskokwim area.

Then a few weeks later, he made the first night landing at the Anchorage field.

On Nov. 24, Merrill was returning from an emergency flight from Ninilchik with a schoolteacher who was in critical condition from a revolver wound. Darkness had descended, so Merrill circled the town.

Quickly bonfires and flares were lighted and automobiles turned their headlights on to help illuminate the landing field, which is now the Park Strip. Merrill landed safely, and the school teacher recovered.

In May 1928, Merrill had one of his most narrow brushes with death. It was on the first commercial flight to Barrow for the Fox Film Expedition to Alaska to photograph Arctic scenes to be used later in a screen story. Noel Wien had the contract and needed another pilot. Merrill, eager for an Arctic adventure, jumped at the chance to fly for Wien.

When he took off on that warm, sunny May 13 in his Travel Aire, the Fairbanks field was free of snow. Wiseman, their only communication on a direct route to Barrow, reported clear skies, little wind and the ground covered with snow and ice.

There was no way to judge weather conditions beyond Wiseman. The Arctic Slope wasn't surveyed and only sketchily mapped, but Wien and Merrill hoped to reach Barrow, 560 miles away, by evening. Merrill's plane carried two passengers, famous bow and arrow expert Capt. Jack Robertson and cameraman Charles Clarke.

The planes arrived in Wiseman on schedule, refueled and took off again. They planned on being back the next day, but three and a half weeks passed with no word from Merrill.

Anchorage Museum of History and Art, Wien Collection, AMRC-b85-27-699

Russell Merrill joined Noel Wien, seen here with his Hisso Standard J-1 airplane at Wiseman, on the first-ever commercial flight to Barrow and first flight to cross the Arctic Circle in 1928.

After leaving Wiseman, they climbed to an altitude of 9,000 feet to get over the Endicotts before hitting the Anaktuvuk River, which runs into the Colville River. Maps of the area were nearly useless, so they were navigating partly by compass and partly by the "seat of their pants."

They flew into a wall of fog when they reached the Colville. They couldn't fly under it, so they tried getting over it. The farther they went, the thicker, higher and heavier the fog became. They were past the point of no return, however, and couldn't fly back to Wiseman. Nor could they continue on to Barrow, so they landed on a small ice-covered pond.

Wien's plane had balloon tires, so he was able to get off later by lightening his load. There was so much fog that he could not pick up any landmarks to guide him back, however, and Merrill's plane was grounded until the other plane could get back with shovels and equipment to clear a strip for takeoff.

Pilot Matt Nieminen arrived from Anchorage to help Wien search for Merrill's plane, but when they finally spotted the craft, it was empty. Merrill's two passengers left the plane on May 22 and were picked up by Nieminen on June 1. They said Merrill had stayed with the plane. However, it later came out that Merrill had left two days after his passengers, carrying a four-day supply of cooked rice and a .22 revolver.

A dog musher found the pilot snow blind, exhausted and unable to travel any farther on June 4. Merrill said after he'd eaten all the food he'd brought with him, he'd killed lemmings and eaten them raw.

U.S. Fish and Wildlife Service

Merrill recovered from his blindness while in the Barrow hospital, but he almost died from Rocky Mountain spotted fever, caused by his diet of lemmings. With a nurse from

Russell Merrill survied his ordeal in the wilderness by eating raw lemmings.

After rescuers found him, Russell Merrill was brought to the Presbyterian Hospital in Barrow, pictured here in 1920.

Barrow accompanying him, Merrill was finally placed on a mattress on the floor of Wien's plane and flown to Nome. There the plane was grounded by two weeks of bad flying weather.

After arriving in Fairbanks, he had a few day's rest in the hospital before he was flown home. He'd been gone three months. His wife and sons awaited him, and the grateful residents of Anchorage gave him a watch to commemorate his safe return.

It was some time before he recovered enough to resume flying, but in 1929 commercial flying was becoming increasingly important in Alaska, and Merrill became increasingly busy, too. On Sept. 16, his flying day started at 5:30 a.m. when he flew down the Kenai Peninsula, returning around 9:30 a.m. He refueled and took some hunters to Rainy Pass.

Back to the field by 2 p.m., he again loaded up. This time it was a heavy piece of machinery. He took off alone in his float-equipped Travel Aire for Sleetemute and Bethel. No one ever saw him again.

Although Carl Ben Eielson, Joe Crossen and Frank Dorbrandt flew more than 10,000 miles in two weeks searching for him, no trace of the missing aviator was found.

The only clue came on Oct. 3, when a piece of fabric was found on a Cook Inlet beach. The material, apparently cut away by a knife, was identified as coming from the tail section of Merrill's plane. Had he fallen asleep and flown into the Inlet? There were some who thought so, but that wouldn't explain the cut fabric.

Others thought he'd been forced down in the Inlet and had cut the fabric to use as a sail before the plane was swamped and sunk by the gale that raged the night of Sept. 17. His fate, however, is still unknown. But his name lives on.

Air travel around Anchorage had grown so much that city leaders decided it was time to create a new, improved airfield for Alaska's aviators.

Mayor J.J. Delaney wrote a letter to the Commissioner of the General Land Office in Washington, D.C., requesting full title to the property that is now Merrill Field. He asked that the federal government give its immediate and active attention to an aviation field.

Anchorage Museum of History and Art, General Photograph File, AMRC-b65-2-17

Anchorage city leaders approved a larger runway on the northern side of town, which later was named in honor of Russell Hyde Merrill.

Extended mail service within Alaska – as well as between Alaska and the Lower 48 – and the possibilities of aviation services between the United States and Asia, would make Anchorage a hub for international commerce.

Delaney and the Chamber of Commerce's efforts paid off. By August 1929, Aviation Field was cleared and plowed.

In May 1930, the Anchorage City Council approved the expenditure of $500 in matching funds to cover the city's share of leveling and seeding the field.

Merrill had joined in petitioning for the establishment of an airfield for Anchorage before his death, so in June, the airfield was renamed Merrill Field.

The Anchorage Women's club volunteered a beacon for the field in September 1931, and the following year a 52-foot steel girder tower and beacon were presented. The club placed a plaque in memory of Merrill at the base of the tower. It was later moved to the front of the Federal Aviation Administration Building when the new control tower was completed.

By 1935, six airlines were operating at Merrill Field, which was then handling more than 25 percent of Alaska's air traffic.

Merrill Field is now one of the busiest small plane airports in the nation.

And not only were a field, beacon and pass named after this pioneer airman, but Noel Wien named his eldest son Merrill. The young man's mother is quoted as saying: "If he can emulate the courage and character of Russell Merrill, we will always be proud of him."

Pioneer aviators like Russell Hyde Merrill, Carl Benjamin Eielson and Noel and Ralph Wien helped to blaze the trails in Alaska's skies. And their legacy continues through pilots who still fly across Alaska's vast wilderness.

This aerial view of Merrill Field in 1970 shows a bustling airport and is a testament to the early flyboys.

FROM THE NEWSROOM: 1930s

27

NATIVES GAIN RECOGNITION

After decades of not being recognized by the federal government, Alaska Natives marked a milestone in the mid-1930s.

Amended in 1936 to include Alaska, the Indian Reorganization Act of 1935 allowed American Indians to locally govern their affairs by a tribal government that was established by constitution and bylaws for each tribe.

University of Alaska Fairbanks, Frederick B. Drane, UAF-1991-46-563

Natives who continued to live traditional lifestyles were not considered "civilized" and therefore not recognized as U.S. citizens after America purchased Alaska in 1867.

Through its enactment, tribes were allowed to manage their own affairs, such as ownership and transfer of title to land and to keep records of vital events, establish their own police and court systems and set the terms of enrollment in their tribes.

Alaska Natives had been working toward recognition decades before the law was passed.

They were not considered citizens when America purchased Alaska from Russia in 1867 because they were not "civilized."

And only citizens of the new American possession could own land, operate a business or vote.

In 1912, tribes in Southeast organized the Alaska Native Brotherhood; three years later the Alaska Native Sisterhood held its first meeting in Sitka.

Although the groups originated in Southeast Alaska – primarily among Tlingit and Haida Indians – the organizations included Natives from all regions, as well as some white members.

Alaska State Library, Alaska Native Organizations, ASL-P33-01

A group of Alaska Natives from Southeast Alaska formed the Alaska Native Brotherhood in 1912. Founding fathers, pictured here from the left, include Paul Liberty, James Watson, Ralph Young, Eli Kalanvok (Katinook), Peter Simpson, Frank Mercer, James C. Jackson, Chester Worthington, George Fields, William Hobson and Frank Price. Seward Kunz is not pictured.

University of Alaska Fairbanks, Mary Cox Collection, UAF-2001-129-111

Only Natives who wore Western clothing and met other conditions could vote in 1922.

It took years of hard work, but Alaska Natives were given the right to vote in 1922.

However, certain conditions had to be met.

"Wear Western clothing; not eat Indian foods or speak Indian languages; and live apart from Indian village communities" were among the list of criteria that would make an Alaska Native eligible to vote.

This was nothing new. Alaska Natives were familiar with restrictions put upon them by the U.S. and territorial governments.

In 1915, the Alaska Territorial Legislature had passed a law that allowed a Native to become a citizen only if five white people testified that the Native person had met legal criteria – meaning he or she had given up Native culture in favor of Western ways.

But early Native leaders knew that the only way to improve their situation in the white man's world was to work within the system.

An article titled "Alaska Native civil rights history shaped the state," which appeared in the Dec. 4, 2007, issue of *The Northern Light* newspaper, described what life was like behind the scenes.

"What was done in public and what was done in the home, was not necessarily the same," Helen McNeil, a Tlingit in the Alaska Native Sisterhood, told reporter Mary Lochner. "Many (Tlingits) would speak only English in public, but still speak Tlingit in the home."

Alaska Native leaders used the power of the vote to influence policies that affected Natives' lives.

They sent advocates for anti-discrimination legislation to testify before the Territorial Legislature and pushed for equal education and recognition of land ownership for their people.

A milestone was passed in 1924 when Congress extended citizenship to all Indians in the United States and Tlingit William L. Paul Sr. was elected as the first Native to the Territorial Legislature.

Alaska State Library, Portrait File, ASL-P01-2568

But all was not rosy for the Alaska Native population following these two historic events.

The Alaska Territorial Legislature put its own restrictions on Alaska Native citizens.

William Lewis Paul Sr., a Tlingit Indian and leader in the Alaska Native Brotherhood, became the first Alaska Native to serve in the Territorial Legislature in 1924.

It passed a law requiring a literacy test be passed before a Native would be allowed to vote. That requirement was in effect until Alaska adopted its constitution in the late 1950s.

But another milestone was achieved when the Alaska Native Townsite Act was passed in 1926. It allowed Natives to obtain restricted deeds to village lots.

And in 1928, a court case resolved the right of Native children to attend public school.

The "civilized persons" mentality in the territory persevered, however. Native children were instructed to speak only English.

And those who attended Bureau of Indian Affairs schools in their own villages often were forcibly sent to BIA boarding schools elsewhere if they were caught speaking their indigenous language.

"Growing up speaking Yup'ik Eskimo was very special," said Mary Lou Beaver of Kongiganak in "Our Language Our Soul," edited by Delena Norris of the University of Alaska Fairbanks.

"I remember what my grandmother told me. She said, 'Your spoken language is God-given; use it with pride.' She also said,

Alaska State Library, Dr. Daniel S. Neuman Collection, ASL-P307-0104

Many Alaska Native children were told only to speak in English while in school.

Above: Native children, dressed in Western wear, boarded planes that took them to boarding schools far from their villages.

Below: Many students from remote villages attended boarding schools, like the Wrangell Institute in Southeast Alaska.

Above: Some Alaska students attended the Eklutna Vocational School in Southcentral Alaska near Anchorage.

Below: Student Joe Husaik, seen here carving ivory, was one of many students attending the popular Eklutna Vocational School.

'When you raise your children, speak to them in Yup'ik. '"

Beaver said that Yup'ik was the dominant language in her Western Alaska home, with English "immersion" at the village school, which went up to fifth grade. Students then were sent to a BIA boarding school in Wrangell.

"Our transition from Yup'ik to English began the moment we stepped off the plane," Beaver said. "Everything was in English only."

As Alaska's Native children struggled to retain their identities in the BIA school system, Alaska's Native leaders pushed to regain lands lost to the federal government.

In 1929, at the Alaska Native Brotherhood convention in Haines, Native leaders resolved to pursue land claims settlement in Southeast Alaska.

Their efforts paid off when the Jurisdictional Act of June 1935 allowed the Tlingit and Haida Indians to pursue land claims in the U.S. Court of Claims. That set the stage for the future Alaska Native Claims Settlement Act several decades later.

28

COLONISTS SETTLE VALLEY

L ong before the Matanuska Valley in Southcentral Alaska became one of the fastest-growing regions in the nation, Russians experimented in its fertile soil. They taught the Tanaina to grow crops like potatoes, carrots, radishes and turnips.

In 1844, Russians founded settlements at Matanuska and Knik, as well as Kachemak, Kasilof and Kenai.

University of Alaska Fairbanks, Gordon Picotte Collection, UAF-1986-189-13

Potato plants have blossomed in the Matanuska Valley for almost 200 years.

Few homesteads dotted the Matanuska Valley landscape in 1918.

"A handful of Cossacks and a few hundred homeless mujiks [peasants] crossed oceans of ice at their own risk, and wherever timeworn groups of them settled in the cold steppes forsaken by nature, the places would begin to teem with life, the fields would sprout forth with grain and herds ...," wrote Russian Alexander Herzen in 1859.

Then prospectors and entrepreneurs dabbled in basic agriculture after America purchased Alaska from the Russians in 1867. Sometimes they even planted crops in the sod that insulated the roofs of their log cabins. Early photographs show hotels in Knik growing their own potatoes, residents cultivating oats and miners cutting hay for their horses.

The U.S. Department of Agriculture established an experimental station one mile northwest of the town of Matanuska in 1917 and appointed Frederick Rader as its first agent. He oversaw the clearing of four acres of land, planting two with oats. Rader ran the station until Milton D. Snodgrass took over in 1923. Snodgrass, who stayed with the project until 1929, continued the effort to attract more farmers and ranchers to the area.

Col. Otto F. Ohlson, general manager of the Alaska Railroad since 1928, also had been trying to entice farmers to the Matanuska Valley in an effort to spur railbelt settlement toward Palmer, which had been founded in 1916 as a stop on the branch of railroad that went to the Chickaloon coalfields. More passengers along the route meant more money in the railroad's pockets.

But despite the area's fertile valleys and abundant sources of fresh water, settlers didn't stream into the area. By 1929, only about 4,000 acres were under cultivation and about 117 families had settled, according to records from the U.S. Department of Interior.

Ironically, it took the Great Depression of the 1930s to jump-start the population growth of the valley. In an effort to take people away from rural districts, where poverty had prevailed long before the Depression, and move them into areas where they might lead more productive lives, President Franklin D. Roosevelt's administration designed many resettlement projects.

Ohlson convinced the U.S. Interior Department to distribute pamphlets explaining the agricultural possibilities in Alaska and

The government experimental station near Palmer had success growing grain.

Col. Otto F. Ohlson, general manager of the Alaska Railroad, encouraged people to settle along the railroad route that traveled to the Chickaloon coal mine in the Matanuska Valley.

pointing out its similarities to Scandinavian countries. In 1930, the agricultural experimental station staff published an enlarged and illustrated version of Ohlson's pamphlet called "Alaska, the Newest Homeland," which was distributed to agricultural states. Ohlson also negotiated with steamship lines to offer special rates to potential settlers.

His efforts resulted in a few colonists moving to Alaska by 1931. Not all stayed, but when U.S. government officials visited Alaska in the summer of 1934 to inspect emergency public works and relief projects in the territory, they were impressed with the possibilities for more agricultural settlement in the Matanuska Valley.

Ohlson helped the Department of Interior and the Federal Emergency Rehabilitation Administration plan a farming community, and Roosevelt approved the project known as the Matanuska Valley Colony in his New Deal in 1935.

The idea of moving families from Midwestern states to a

community in the wilderness north of Anchorage stirred imaginations across the country. The federal government, which wanted to increase Alaska's population for defense purposes as well as help farmers in depressed areas, had high expectations for the project.

Although the Great Depression of the 1930s didn't affect Alaskans as traumatically as those who lived in the Lower 48, they did reap a significant benefit through Roosevelt's Matanuska Valley Colony. Two hundred and two colonists were plucked from drought-stricken areas in Minnesota, Wisconsin and Michigan and sent north to the planned community.

By May 1935, the first group of colonists had been selected and was heading north. A group of laborers sailed before them aboard the *North Star*. These transients were to clear some land and set up temporary lodging for the new settlers.

The steamship *St. Mihiel* was refurbished for the trip out of San Francisco. Originally used as a transport for cattle and horses from Argentina to the United States during World War I, it needed some work to make it comfortable for families.

Alaska State Library, Mary Nan Gamble, ASL-P270-186

The U.S. government refurbished the *St. Mihiel*, seen here pulling into Seward, to carry the Matanuska Valley colonists and their families.

Laborers bound from Seattle to the Matanuska Valley listened to a guitarist while onboard the *North Star*. The ship docked in Seward around midnight on May 5, 1935.

The ship arrived in Seward at the end of April 1935, but due to a measles epidemic onboard, the passengers were quarantined for a week.

They finally boarded an Alaska Railroad train and headed toward the Matanuska Valley, with a welcome stop in Anchorage. They reached Palmer at 6 p.m. on May 10.

When the colonists found that all the tents were not quite ready, they built fires by the railroad tracks and made themselves as comfortable as possible.

The American Legion Community Band at Seward welcomed the colonists.

University of Alaska Anchorage, Thomas Culhane, UAA-hmc-0096-series2-1-63-5

Above: Anchorage residents turned out in force to greet the Matanuska Valley colonists arriving on the train from Seward.

Below: The colonists received their first Alaska meal, prepared by the Construction Division, on May 10, 1935, onboard an Alaska Railroad dining car.

Alaska State Library, Mary Nan Gamble Collection, ASL-P270-137

Alaska State Library, Mary Nan Gamble Collection, ASL-P270-124

Above: Mrs. Elvi Kerttula and daughter Ester, along with the rest of the first batch of colonists, disembarked from the train in Palmer at 5:20 p.m. on May 10, 1935.

Below: A tent city awaited the colonists.

Alaska State Library, Mary Nan Gamble Collection, ASL-P270-130

A little colonist tried to handle a box camera in Palmer's tent city, while a young boy peeked through the door flap of the tent behind.

"We took the kids and put them on cot mattresses in 24 x 36 tents right where Koslosky's is," Lauren Smith recounted in "Matanuska Colony, Fifty Years," by Brigitte Lively.

"At midnight, a truckload of heavy comforters arrived, of which we put seven on the kids," Smith said. "They were as warm as could be."

The farmers drew lots for 40 acres and a homestead, a deal that included a house, barn, outbuildings, a well and livestock. They also received loans for $3,000 at 3 percent interest to pay for it all. In addition, each family was given temporary housing, a food allowance of $75, medical care and help clearing the land and building a home.

Several months later, in an effort to keep track of colonists' expenditures at the commissary, the government minted tokens in various denominations. Called Bingles, they could be used as money between themselves and at the commissary.

The government issued Bingles (tokens) to the colonists in Palmer as a way to simplify bookkeeping.

Each family was issued a certain amount of Bingles, based on family size. The accrued value of these tokens would eventually have to be paid back to the government.

While Anchorage enjoyed the nationwide publicity sparked by the Matanuska Colony, the citizens derived little monetary benefit from its initial establishment because the federal government didn't hire any local carpenters to construct facilities for the newcomers. It instead recruited more than 400 Civilian Conservation Corps men from outside of Alaska to set up camps before the colonists arrived.

These transients, officially called the California Transients Alaska Expedition, also were victims of the Great Depression who found work with the government building the experimental colony.

Some Alaskans were nervous about so many men flooding into the territory.

"The presence of 300 unmarried transients on board the transport going up to be on the construction crew already at work in the Valley did not meet with the approval of the pioneer fathers," according

Transient workers from California cleared brush before setting up a tent city for the Matanuska Colony.

to a report titled "History of the Matanuska Valley," by the Palmer Territorial School in 1940-1941.

"Some asked, with indignant voices and expressions, where were the necessary guns and knives to protect themselves, their families and herds against the wild and woolly North?"

But most of the colonists thought the workers, who received $2 a week in spending money and room and board – and an additional $100 a month after they left in the fall – were fine men.

"Lots of good men in there," said Phil O'Neill in "Matanuska Colony, Fifty Years."

"The bunch we had up here were very, very good," he said. "Excellent mechanics and carpenters."

But since the workers didn't get paid until they left the territory, Anchorage residents claimed they did nothing to benefit the local economy.

Alaska Railroad General Manager Col. Otto F. Ohlsen spoke to the colonists.

Anchorage residents did embrace the colonists, however.

Shortly after their arrival in the Valley, Ohlson gathered the group together and held a drawing for 40-acre homesteads.

And with a short growing season upon them, the colonists immediately went to work tilling and planting while temporarily living in tents in "Valley City" near Palmer – named for G.W. Palmer, who started the Knik trading post in 1880.

The second batch of settlers arrived on May 23. And within weeks of arriving in their new home, farmers already were selling radishes to Anchorage grocers.

Walter G. Pippel, a Minnesota gardener, wrote:

"My first year in the Matanuska Valley has thoroughly convinced me that climate, soil and other conditions tend to make this one of the safest and surest spots under the United States flag for a farmer to make his home and ply his vocation. ..."

Colonists immediately started hauling logs to build houses and planting crops after clearing farmland in the wilderness.

Alaska State Library, Mary Nan Gamble, ASL-P270-876

Colonist Gordon Astrole walked down the railroad track dressed in his official uniform, issued to all men in the project.

Women of the Matanuska Valley Colony visited while they hung the family laundry.

And a traveler named Dan Noonan wrote an account of his observations in the developing settlement during the fall of 1935, which appeared in the February 1936 issue of The *Alaska Sportsman*.

"Everywhere, everyone was busy. The entire place was one great, outdoor workshop. Tractors, trucks, steam shovels – all seemed to litter up the landscape. They made a picture of industry, transforming the wilderness into a garden of hope and human habitation.

"Most of the families were living in tents. The men were out clearing the fields. Evidence that women were there was principally in the number of family wash lines in use. ..."

There were 176 families in the colony, Noonan wrote in the article. He said many of the permanent homes were being occupied, and it was expected that all colonists would be in their homes by the end of November.

"The tents were arranged in rows, on streets, and the whole settlement had the appearance of one of Alaska's early stampede towns such as Ruby or Iditarod," Noonan wrote. "In one field, near the tent city, lumber was piled in piles almost as far as the eye could see. There were stacks and stacks of it."

The colonists had a regular monthly allowance for provisions, and clothing and household articles were issued from a warehouse. Allowances for food ranged from $45 for a family of two to $125 for the largest family of 13. Included was a cash allowance of $5 "pocket money."

"Every purchase is acknowledged and recorded, for the colonists are expected to repay the government within 30 years with interest," Noonan wrote. "The total allotment is $3,000 per family."

"The personnel of the staff in charge seemed to be capable and the actual management of the project was in control of the Territory of Alaska. There is a Board of Directors appointed by the Governor of Alaska," Noonan's article stated. "The set up, since a recent

Alaska State Library, Mary Nan Gamble, ASL-P270-610

Colonists shopped for groceries and supplies at the commissary, pictured here.

reorganization, is such that the colony can practically organize and manage itself. It is expected that in the spring and summer there should be well over 1,000 people in or near Palmer."

But along with the glowing reports, the colonists faced some snags, as well. While 150 horses were shipped to the area to help with the farming effort, no wagons were sent. Instead, the colonists received five tons of paper towels and 18 miles of mosquito netting, according to Lively.

Other shipping snafus occurred, too.

"There was hundreds of sacks of cement – long before the colony was ready for it – and only one cement mixer that wouldn't take more than half a sack a load," Lively wrote. "There were retorts for a cannery, but there was no time to build one. There were radiators for the schoolhouse, but no intention of putting up a school the first year."

Alaska State Library, Mary Nan Gamble, ASL-P270-619

While some colonists complained that the progress of building the community was going too slowly, others worked diligently to learn how to adapt - like these women canning a crop of carrots.

Thanks to the U.S. government, the colonists had plenty of horses – but no wagons.

Some colonists also bitterly complained that officials were taking too long to build their homes and barns and that conditions at the colony were less than ideal.

A telegram sent to Congress by Patrick Hemmer and a woman with a last name of Sandvik shows their level of dissatisfaction.

"Six weeks passed; nothing done. No houses, wells, roads, inadequate machinery, tools. Government food undelivered; commissary prices exorbitant; educational facilities for season doubtful. Apparently men sent to pick political plums. Irwin and Washington officials O.K. Hands tied. Colonists cooperating. Request immediate investigation."

Eugene J. Carr, representative of the Rural Rehabilitation Division of the FERA, was immediately sent to Alaska. He assured the colonists that "construction would be speeded and that there would be adequate shelter for families, livestock, and supplies before winter," according to "The Frontier in Alaska and the Matanuska Colony," by Orlando W. Miller.

Nine families called it quits and left the colony at the end of June. A few more left by the end of October.

But not all colonists were dissatisfied with the progress of the colony and were determined to stay.

By the end of September, 28 houses had been finished and were occupied by families. By the end of October, another 140 houses were available. And by the end of December, all the colonists were in completed homes. In fact, since the number of colonists had declined to 164, there were 10 vacant houses.

Other projects had been hurried along, as well, including the warehouse trading post and diesel-powered electric generating plant. Buildings under construction and close to completion included the school, gymnasium, dormitory, staff house and hospital.

And 249 wells had been drilled and 106 barns raised.

The original crew of 400 transient workers had increased to more than 600 people after the government hired laborers from Alaska and Outside.

Workers at the Matanuska Colony were kept busy drilling wells for the colonists.

Then rumors started spreading that it cost around $125,000 to bring each colonist to the valley. With taxpayers still reeling from the devastation of the Great Depression, it is little wonder that many of them questioned the wisdom of establishing an agricultural community in remote Alaska.

But Anthony J. Dimond, Alaska's Delegate to Congress at the time, stood firmly behind the colonization of the Valley.

"The Matanuska Valley farm settlement plan is both humane and economically sound," he said. "The fact is, if it be a fact, that mistakes made in the setting up of the colony give no reason to condemn it. The settlers are being helped to get into a position to help themselves and this is the best sort of aid."

The mayor of Seward during that time agreed.

"I was in Washington, D.C., during the time of organization of the Matanuska Colonization Project and did all I could to help it,"

Some colonists worked in fields of oats and peas with a Caterpillar tractor and a reaper.

Above: Several colonists moved their tents to their homesteads so they could build their houses while they worked the land.

Below: A boy holds the bridles of horses hitched to a wagon containing possessions of a colonist family getting ready to move from the tent city to a new home in the Matanuska Valley. The wagon is loaded with household items, including a stove, benches, mattresses and a bed frame.

Some colonists built log cabins, like the one picture above, while others chose to build frame cottages, like the one shown below.

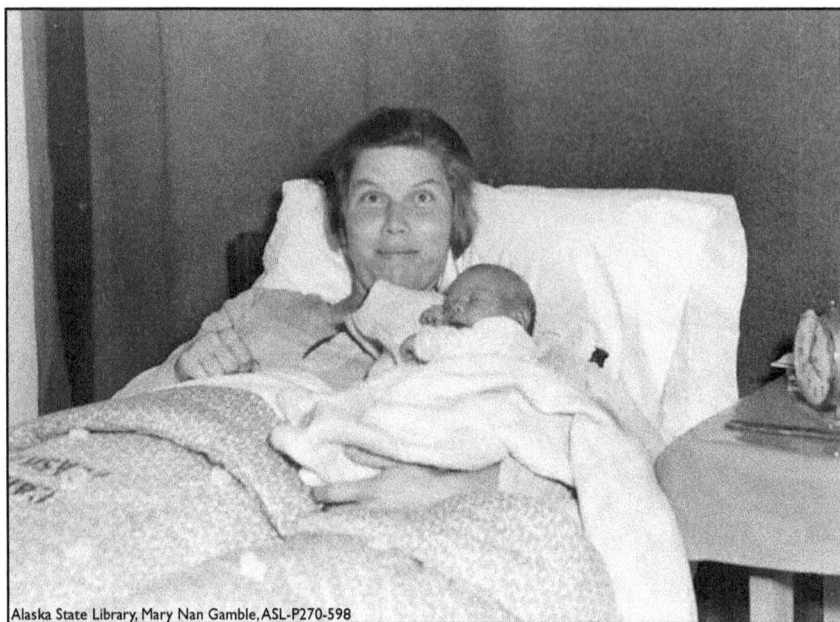

Mrs. Howard van Wormer delivered her daughter, Laura Morena, on July 11, 1935. Laura, weighing 6-1/2 pounds, was the first child born in the new Matanuska Valley project.

Don Carlos Brownell said. "I consider the colony now working so perfectly at Matanuska to be the greatest single enterprise ever put into operation by the government for the future development and growth of Alaska."

Noonan thought the experiment was a good use of taxpayers' money, too.

"Every new venture has its pitfalls, every undertaking where things are done which really amount to something has its mistakes, but after the din and controversies have died down and this colony is functioning as it is intended it shall function, all Alaskans will be glad that the Territory at last has a 'bread basket.' "

However, since local produce wasn't competitive with food shipped from Seattle, the Matanuska cooperative ran into problems marketing. Many colonists eventually abandoned the project to pursue other ventures like mining; some left the territory, and a few remained and eked out a living through the land.

By winter 1936-37, colonists were shopping at the Palmer Trading Post.

29

SOURDOUGH GOVERNOR APPOINTED

Old-timers considered John Weir Troy a real sourdough, a pioneer who toted his bit of sour dough from camp to camp to "start" his bread and flapjacks. And they believed in his vision that a large, permanent population would help Alaska become a state instead of just a territory of Uncle Sam's.

Alaska State Library, Portrait File, ASL-P01-1981

John Weir Troy served as Alaska's 12th territorial governor from 1933-1939.

When Troy was appointed the territory's 12th governor in 1933, Alaskans heaved a collective sigh of relief. Troy knew Alaska and knew what to do to make it stronger. He'd mined, mushed, trapped and fished with the masses. He'd been rich and poor, and he'd lived through hardships and knew about luxury. Gov. "Johnny" was a true Alaskan through and through.

Born in Dungeness, Washington, Troy worked as an apprentice at his uncle's newspaper in Port Townsend

John Weir Troy, wearing a derby in the center of this group, published the Daily Alaska Empire in Juneau for 27 years. His linotype operator, Arthur Bringdale, is wearing an apron at the far right, and Elmer Friend, managing editor, is second from the left.

following graduation from high school. He learned about type, galleys, picas and presses. But when he heard the tales of gold nuggets lining the ground in Alaska, the then 24-year-old set sail for Skagway in 1897 on a boat carrying "other mules and some horses."

He didn't find nuggets, but instead found work hauling gold seekers from Skagway over the mountains and waterways into Whitehorse, where they then floated down the Yukon River to Dawson.

After the gold fever subsided, he became editor of the Skagway Daily Alaskan. When it folded, he moved to Juneau and became editor of the Daily Alaska Empire, which he soon purchased and ran for 27 years.

Alaska's governor from 1933 to 1939 was a firm believer that the territory should become a state. And Troy thought a larger population and a better road system would help achieve that goal.

"More people for Alaska is her greatest need," said the former pack-train worker. "But they won't come and we could not take care

Gov. John Weir Troy supported building roads to help increase Alaska's population. Alaska Road Commission workers blazed a road through the wilderness, above, to connect the Matanuska colonists to Anchorage. By September 1938, the Palmer-Anchorage highway offered Alaskans a scenic and direct route between the Valley and the railroad town on Ship Creek.

FROM THE NEWSROOM: 1930s

Don L. Irwin, right, shows Gov. John W. Troy a Matanuska Valley turnip.

of them if they did until we have roads to take them to the valleys, hills and mountains where gold is locked in.

"... People coming to Alaska to farm or to prospect for gold and find employment in public works would furnish population that would make markets for agricultural products, timber, and other of the vast resources of the Territory."

Troy thought President Franklin D. Roosevelt's New Deal project in the Matanuska Valley was a great idea.

"The success being worked out through the Matanuska Colonization Project has added a promising outlook for the Territory. Not only has it added to the population in the vicinity of the Matanuska Valley and along the Alaska Railroad, but it has caused the people in other districts to become agricultural minded ... I believe that agricultural colonization should be carried further with the establishment of more colonies in other parts of Alaska."

University of Alaska Fairbanks,
General File, UAF-1958-1026-794

With a stroke of his pen, Territorial Gov. John W. Troy signed the law that created the University of Alaska on March 12, 1935. From left are James Wickersham, Charles Bunnell, Senate President Luther Hess, Reps. Andrew Nerland and A. A. Shonbeck (both members of the Board of Regents) and Speaker of the House J. S. Hoffman. Seated are Regent Grace Wickersham, Troy and Rep. George Lingo, who was both an alumnus and a regent. The other woman seated is unidentified.

Had Troy not been forced to leave his position as the territory's governor because of illness, more colonization projects might have dotted Alaska's landscape during the 1940s.

Troy also believed in boosting centers of learning in the territory. In 1935, he signed the law that changed the name of the college in Fairbanks and started the illustrious University of Alaska.

The institution officially began in 1917 as a college, but its origins lie in the creation in 1906 of a federal agricultural experiment station in Fairbanks, the sixth in Alaska. The station set the stage for the university that developed later, which is strongly research-oriented.

Congress approved funds in 1915 to establish a school of higher education and transferred land from the station for that purpose. The federal land grant was accepted by Territorial Gov. John Strong in 1917.

The new institution was established as the Alaska Agricultural

University of Alaska Fairbanks, Vertical File, UAF-1958-1026-1998

This aerial view of the campus shows a growing facility.

College and School of Mines in 1922. It offered 16 classes to a student body of six – with a ratio of one faculty member per student. In 1923 the first commencement graduated one student, John Sexton Shanly.

The rest of the Alaska Agricultural Experiment Station was transferred to the college in 1931.

Ill health forced Troy to leave office in 1939. He died in Juneau on May 2, 1942.

Flora Jane Harper of Rampart became the first Alaska Native to graduate from the University of Alaska in Fairbanks in 1935.

Courtesy Jan Harper-Haines

30

BLACK FOG OVER BARROW

When rescuers arrived on the scene of an airplane crash near Point Barrow on Aug. 15, 1935, they found Will Rogers dead. A typewriter recovered in the wreckage had Rogers' unfinished last "piece for the papers," and the final word he'd typed was "death."

But Rogers didn't seem to have had a premonition that his trip to Alaska would end in disaster. In an interview in Portland, Oregon, a short time before the tragedy, he was asked, "When are you going to write a book on your life?"

University of Washington, J. Willis Sayre Collection, SAY06023

"I don't know," Rogers replied. "I ain't near dead enough yet. One publisher has been after me a long time to write my memoirs. But, shucks, you got to be old and pretty near dead to have anything to look back on. I'm a long ways from being dead. Feel just as frisky as a colt!"

Will Rogers, seen here in 1912, entertained audiences with a rope and his wit on the Vaudeville circuit.

Wiley Post had this plane beefed up to his specifications for a long trip to Alaska and Siberia. It was a hybrid with a Lockheed Orion fuselage and Lockheed Explorer wings equipped with a 550-horsepower Wasp engine and oversize 260-gallon gas tanks. The large pontoons were installed by Northwest Air Service in Renton, Washington.

Not only was he frisky, but the spring of 1935 found him beginning to get fiddle-footed. The famous humorist was restless, and thought of going to Rio De Janeiro, catching the German Zeppelin and flying up the coast of Africa – he had never been in a Zeppelin and thought it would be fun. Then, in Los Angeles, he ran into friend Wiley Post, who Rogers greatly admired and considered the greatest flier in the world.

Post had a new plane to show off and was as proud of it as a boy with a new cowboy suit. It had been built for him after his own ideas, and one of the fancy features was the compensatory tanks, one on each wing. The operator was supposed to watch, and when the gasoline got low in one tank, take hold of the handle and move it over so the gas would flow in from the other tank. Later, this would prove to be important.

Rogers was eager to see how the fine, new, sleek plane worked, and made a flight with Post to a friend's ranch in New Mexico. It was discovered that the plane was nose-heavy and some scrap iron was wired into the tail. Everything then seemed to be all right, and Rogers dismissed a twinge of concern.

"If it's good enough for Wiley, it's good enough for me," he said.

Post was full of his plans to fly to Alaska. He had been there before and wanted to go back and see if it would be feasible to lay out a mail and passenger route between Alaska and Russia to avoid the long Pacific flight. Rogers, who had never been there, had once written:

"I have never been to that Alaska … I am crazy to go up there sometime. I would like to go in the winter when those old boys are all snowed 'in and I could sit around and hear 'em tell some of those old tales … they do a lot of flying up there; there is some crack aviators. Wiley Post went back up there this last summer to visit one of them that had helped him and they went hunting in a plane. Fred Stone and Rex (Beach) each have been up there a lot, but I never did get further North up that way than about a block north of Main Street in Seattle."

Listening to Post fired his imagination and revived his desire to see Alaska. Maybe he should head North instead of South.

Post had to go to Seattle to have pontoons put on the plane, and some other changes made, so Rogers told him to keep in touch.

"Call me from Seattle," Rogers said. "Maybe by then I'll know what I want to do."

When Post called, Rogers

University of Alaska Fairbanks, Wiley Post-Flat Alaska Collection, 1933, UAF-1998-129-3

Aviator Wiley Post, pictured here in 1933, invited humorist Will Rogers to travel to Alaska and beyond with him in 1935.

Miners from Flat, Alaska, set a tripod in place to get Wiley Post's plane upright after he crash-landed in 1933. Named the *Winnie Mae*, the plane hit a patch of mining tailings during Post's solo around the world flight and nosed over.

made up his mind. That was his nature – make a sudden decision and then plunge into carrying it out. His wife tried to dissuade him, but he was excited about the trip by now. And, besides, he didn't want to throw Post out. He packed two bags – packing them like always by stuffing things in. He wore one suit, and the only other one he took was stuffed into one of the bags.

On his last night in Los Angeles, he and Betty went to a rodeo. She later described that last time she was ever to have with her husband:

"Will was having a good time ... someone gave him a little wooden and paper puzzle while we sat there. Quite unconsciously he toyed with it throughout the evening. I saw him stuff the puzzle in the pocket of his suit ... his pockets were like that of a boy, always holding trinkets or souvenirs of some kind." (The puzzle was still in his pocket when he died and his blood-stained clothing cut from his broken body.)

Betty Rogers remembered how they drove from Gilmore Stadium to the airport to say goodbye. As the ship nosed up, she caught her last fleeting glimpse of her husband through the window. He smiled and waved.

Will Rogers and aviation pioneer Wiley Post rested at Renton Field in Washington shortly before leaving on their ill-fated journey on Aug. 7, 1935. The two men planned to explore a new route to Europe over Alaska and Siberia.

He telegraphed the next day from San Francisco: "Everything just fine; don't nobody worry about me."

The next day he wired from Seattle.

"Yep, everything all right. Going to play a game of polo this afternoon." (The field where he played was later named in his honor).

The plane was loaded for its trip north in Seattle. There had been no official inspection of the plane after its changes had been made.

Post and Rogers' plans were vague when they took off from Seattle early in August for the "Roof of the World," Point Barrow. They had no particular destination and planned to make it a vacation trip by easy stages. Rogers was paying the expenses, and they had half-formed plans of flying around the world by way of Siberia, China, Ethiopia, Europe and Greenland.

"Marvelous trip," Rogers wrote of the Inside Passage. "No danger with this guy. Thousand mile hop from Seattle to Juneau. Was going to stop in Ketchikan for fun, but mist and rain and he breezed through not over 100 feet off the water ... millions of channels and they all look alike to me, but this old boy turns up the right alley all the time."

A trip to Skagway to see the famous Chilkoot Pass had to be postponed because of weather, and they went on to Juneau. Here Rogers got a chance to visit with his old friend Rex Beach. Beach had heard that Rogers and Post had made it through the overhead mists, and tracked them down. They were eating dinner at a café with Post's friend, Joe Crosson.

In his autobiography, "Personal Exposures," Beach wrote that it proved a memorable evening. He listened spellbound to the tales of Crosson and Post.

Rogers himself was in magnificent spirits, more entertaining even than usual. He told Beach that he and Wiley were out for no definite purpose, and after seeing Alaska they might fly across Siberia, possibly coming home by way of Greenland.

Alaska State Library, Portrait Files, ASL-P87-2531

From left, Walter Hall, Wiley Post, Rex Beach, Joe Crosson and Will Rogers visited at an airplane hangar in Juneau in August 1935.

Beach said it sounded decidedly risky. He tried to discourage Rogers from flying to Point Barrow.

"… the Alaska summer weather is unpredictable, and furthermore, there's nothing to see either going or coming."

Rogers laughed, however.

"No danger with old Wiley," Rogers said. "He's the most careful pilot I know. Amelia Earhart told me she considered him the greatest flier in the world!"

Beach wrote that Rogers said something about having to sit well back toward the tail of Post's plane during take off because its balance had been altered in changing from wheels to pontoons, but, "I thought nothing of it at the time," Beach said.

The men had breakfast together the next morning, and Beach was one of the small group at the float who said goodbye to the pair.

The weather had cleared so they made a quick dash for the Yukon country.

"Made the Chilkoot Pass in 10 minutes," Rogers wrote. "It took the pioneers two or three months."

Then on to Anchorage, where Rogers wrote:

"Had a day, and we went flying with friends, Joe Crosson and Joe Barrows, another fine pilot. In a Lockheed Electra we scaled Mt. McKinley, the highest mountain on the North American continent. Bright, sunny day and the most beautiful sight I ever saw … Crosson landed on a glacier over half way up it … flew over hundreds of mountain sheep … flew low over moose and bear right down in the valley."

In his last published weekly column, Rogers described a visit with some trappers.

"Well, that's one thing I don't believe I could ever be, that trapping animals. On the other hand, I expect I do things every day a trapper couldn't do … here we pass up folks every day … that old trapper would mush through the winter 50 below for days to help a friend … we think they punish animals … we punish humans only we don't think so."

Rogers and Post took time out to visit the new Matanuska colony.

Wiley Post and Will Rogers stopped off in the Matanuska Valley to check out the new agricultural colony. True to his nature, Rogers left the colonists laughing when the plane took off and headed to Fairbanks.

Rogers was in high spirits and even before he was out of the plane there was a crowd around him, standing in weeds almost knee high. They wanted to laugh, and Rogers never disappointed an audience.

"Anybody here from Claremore?" he shouted.

"The Valley looks great," he told the pioneers. "You've a mighty nice place here."

A cook from a transient worker's camp came up and presented him with six brown, thick cookies.

"Looks great," he said, brushing the crumbs away from his lips with his coat sleeve. "But I'll toss 'em out if we can't get the plane off the ground."

That crowd of hardy pioneers was Will Rogers' last audience. Showman that he was, as usual he left his audience laughing.

After the flight to the Matanuska project, which was made in a

Alaska State Library, Harry T. Becker, ASL-P67-135

Wiley Post scurried across a board as he tried to keep his feet dry after landing in Fairbanks from a side trip to the Matanuska Valley in 1935.

Lockheed plane placed at their disposal by Crosson, they flew on to Fairbanks and found Crosson waiting for them. They went to a hotel and soon were having a fine time again, telling stories and swapping experiences. Rogers was in high humor, as he was reported to be throughout the trip. He joked about the salmon fishing of which the residents boasted.

"All these boys do is brag about who caught the biggest salmon ... I can't see the use of catching them when they crawl out of the water to meet you! The first handshake I got when I stepped ashore was from a big coho. A coho, they tell me, is a king salmon on relief."

While in Fairbanks, Rogers began another weekly column but never finished it. The last page was still in his typewriter when the plane crashed. The column was about dogs and the part they play in Alaskan life. The last sentence Rogers wrote was:

"... so there is two kinds of bear dogs – the ones that drive 'em away and the ones that bring 'em to you ... little Mickey thought he had done it, as the miner said he chewed all the hair off the bear after death."

Here the narrative ends.

The two soon decided it was time to head north. They were getting impatient to be on their way, although the weather reports from Barrow continued to be unpromising. Stanley Morgan, in charge of the weather station there, warned that the fog was impossible, but Post finally made the decision.

"I think I can make it," he said.

"If it's good enough for you, it's good enough for me," Rogers replied.

Crosson counseled against it. However, he said, there was a notch in the mountain and when they got through it they should turn right and head for the northeast coast. All pilots hugged the coastline.

Post and Rogers optimistically took off and headed toward Barrow. But something went horribly wrong on this leg of their trip.

After clearing through the mountains, they eventually got lost in the fog.

When they spotted a lone figure standing by a camp near a lagoon,

Post brought the plane down and landed on the water. The pair then waded ashore and asked the man, an Eskimo named Claire Okpeha, how far they were from Barrow.

On learning it was only 12 miles away, the adventurers returned to the plane and took off. According to Okpeha, everything seemed to go all right until they were up about 400 or 500 feet. Then suddenly their engine sputtered and died.

As Okpeha watched, the plane went into a nose dive, hitting the shallow lagoon with the speed of a rocket and turning completely over so that engine and fuselage were buried under three feet of water. It had happened so quickly, Okpeha said, he just stood there a minute hardly able to believe his eyes. He began yelling to the men to see if they were alive.

There was no answer, and convinced that he had just witnessed

Eskimo Claire Okpeha ran 12 miles to the village of Barrow, seen here, and told the residents that he had witnessed a horrible airplane crash. He took rescuers to the site.

a terrible tragedy, the Eskimo started running for Barrow to get help, never stopping until he reached the settlement.

That was how the first news of the tragedy reached Barrow.

But it didn't dawn on the people at Barrow that it might be Wiley Post and Will Rogers. Planes bringing strangers to the north coast were frequent and the residents of Barrow thought that it was probably some hunters who had neglected to get weather reports from their side of the mountain. But Okpeha's story called for quick action, and two launches were dispatched with blankets, sleeping bags, tackle – anything that might be needed.

Around 3 a.m. the launches returned with an umiak in tow. The fact that their motors were throttled down to normal speed was ominous. A glance at two heavily blanketed forms lying in the bottom of the umiak revealed that the worst had happened. And yet no one was prepared for the shock that came when the townspeople learned it was Rogers and Post.

"The tragedy threw a pall over all of us," said Charles "Charlie" Brower, a well-respected village leader. "It seemed so needless. Whether our weather warning reached the men is something I have never been able to discover. One finds it hard to believe that so experienced a pilot as Wiley Post would ever start out in the face of it."

The tail end of their flight, once over the mountains, later unfolded as reports came in to Barrow.

Some Natives tending a reindeer herd, three times detected the sound of a plane flying about as though lost over the tundra. Once

University of Alaska Fairbanks, John Neville Collection, UAF-1976-43-14

Barrow leader Charles "Charlie" Brower, seen here with a priest onboard a U.S. Coast Guard cutter, said he questioned whether Wiley Post and Will Rogers had heard about the storm.

Natives tending a reindeer herd about 90 miles away from Barrow heard an engine through the storm and briefly spotted a plane.

they even caught a glimpse of it, but not long enough to wave any signals. Since their camp was some 90 miles from Barrow, it is certain that the plane had been groping its way long before it got anywhere near Barrow.

Some of the territory covered was indicated by the report of a trader, Gus Maski, who was crossing Smith's Bay that same afternoon. He heard the plane but was unable to see it. A similar report came from a Native who had heard the plane above Point Tangent. From there, it was believed, they must have veered off west across country, since nothing more was heard of them until they got close to Okpeha's camp near the small lagoon at Walakpa.

Why did they crash?

Brower said that not only was there no gas in the tanks, but there was no sign of any on the surface of the landlocked lagoon. The evidence of the sudden sputtering of the motor that Okpeha mentioned, convinced Brower that the plane was entirely out of gas when it landed on the lagoon the first time.

According to Dr. Henry M. Greist, the Barrow physician who

inspected the bodies immediately following their removal from the overturned plane, investigations showed Post had made a mistake in handling the plane. Each wing had a gasoline tank. When one was emptied, the pilot had to turn on the other one by hand, and some people believe Post was too late in turning the hand control to switch tanks. Another theory was that Post made the mistake of taxiing down the lagoon for takeoff and his pontoons hit a submerged sandbar, catapulting the plane into the air and causing it to crash.

The opinion of the Accident Board of the Bureau of Air Commerce, as reported on Sept. 21, was that the probable cause of the accident was due to the loss of control after sudden engine failure, due to the extreme nose-heaviness of the aircraft.

Whatever the cause of the accident, Will Rogers and Wiley Post were dead and a black Friday broke over the village of Barrow.

Courtesy U.S. Coast Guard

A memorial to honor aviator Wiley Post and humorist Will Rogers was erected in Barrow.

"It is doubtful if a person in Barrow slept that night," reported Sgt. Stanley Morgan of the U.S. Signal Corps. "All sat around the hospital (where the bodies had been taken), with bowed heads and little or no talking. The chill spread over Alaska."

"Thursday, everybody in this country was smiling at Will's jokes," Rex Beach wrote. "Today there are no smiles here. This is the blackest day Alaska has known."

Col. Charles Lindbergh was at North Haven, Maine, when the Associated Press called and told him what had happened. Aware of the difficulties in ground and water transportation in Alaska, he suggested that a plane be sent, and soon word came to Joe Crosson in Fairbanks to retrieve the bodies of the two men he had laughed and joked with just a few days before.

With their bodies strapped to cots, Crosson flew from Point Barrow to Fairbanks, and with scarcely any rest, continued down the coast to Seattle. There he turned the job over to a Pan American Lines pilot, who flew to Los Angeles, where Rogers' body was taken out, and then flew on to Oklahoma City, where the funeral services were held for Post.

The "black fog" that had descended upon Alaska spread to the rest of the United States as the funeral journey proceeded.

Irish-born American tenor John McCormack expressed the mood of the country – and much of the world – when he said, "A smile has disappeared from the lips of America and her eyes are suffused with tears."

A memorial to both men sits in Barrow. Its inscription reads: "Will Rogers and Wiley Post, 'America's ambassadors of good will,' ended life's flight here August 15, 1935."

The stone used for the tribute was taken from the same quarry that supplied material for Oklahoma's memorial to Will Rogers at Claremore, Oklahoma.

31

OTHER NEWS AROUND ALASKA

ANCHORAGE 1935 – First Fur Rendezvous Celebrated

Anchorage Museum of History and Art, General Photograph File, AMRC-b02-1-10

Anchorage held its first Fur Rendezvous in 1935. Events included the blanket toss, an activity that was used long ago to propel hunters into the air to spot seals.

The name Fur Rendezvous came from swap meets where fur trappers gathered to sell their winter harvests. In early Anchorage, these usually took place in mid-February.

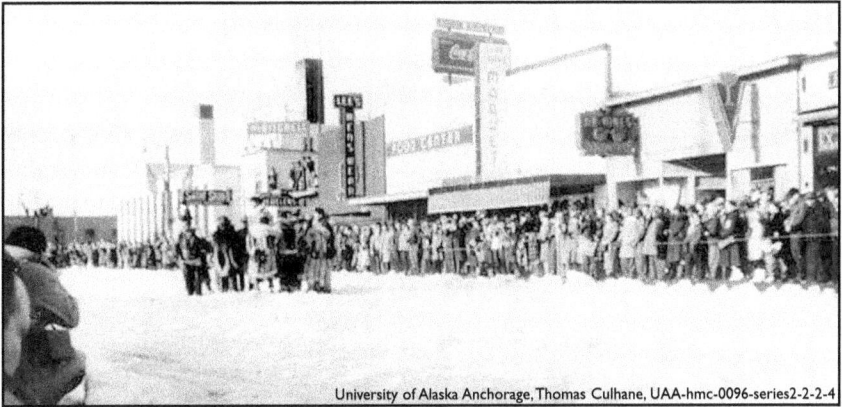

University of Alaska Anchorage, Thomas Culhane, UAA-hmc-0096-series2-2-2-4

Above: The Fur Rendezvous
parade followed Fourth Avenue in Anchorage.

In 1935, Anchorage had a population of around 3,000. Winter was a dark, lonely time, and the residents felt quite isolated. To bring the community together and lift spirits, resident Vern Johnson organized a three-day sports tournament called the Winter Sports Carnival. Its timing coincided with the fur-trading season, which brought increased activity.

As the fur trade was then the second-largest industry in Alaska, folding it into the event seemed natural. It was renamed the Winter Sports Tournament and Fur Rendezvous from 1937, and later the 10-day event was shortened to Fur Rendezvous.

Below: Dog teams delighted spectators along Fourth Avenue during Fur Rendezvous.

Anchorage Museum of History and Art, General Photograph File, AMRC-b01-2-45

BRISTOL BAY 1935 – Salmon was King

Above: As fishing boats started converting to gas engines, sailing vessels, similar to the one pictured here, still plied the waters of Bristol Bay.

Salmon packs peaked at 8,437,603 cases in 1935, and Fortune magazine published a long report on Pacific Ocean fish that found Alaska's canned salmon shipments were worth more than all the state's gold, silver, copper, furs and other fish combined.

Below: Fishermen unloaded salmon from a tender at a Bristol Bay cannery.

FAIRBANKS 1935 – Ice Carnival Created

Above: The Fairbanks Ice Carnival queen, decked out in a fur-trimmed parka and mukluks, was crowned near a throne made from blocks of ice as her court watched.

Below: The newly formed University of Alaska Polar Bear hockey team took on the Dawson, Yukon Territory, team at the first Ice Carnival in Fairbanks.

JUNEAU 1935 – Labor Strike Ends in Violence

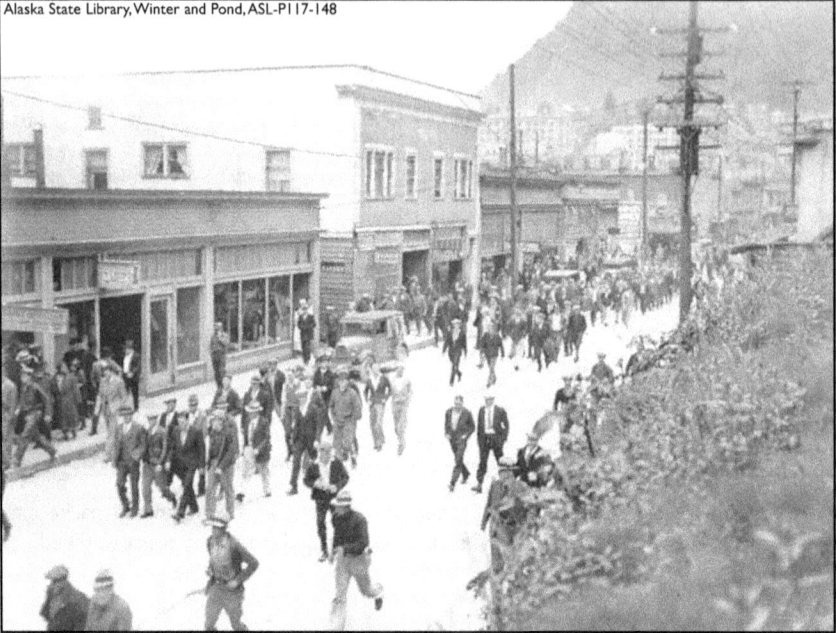

Alaska State Library, Winter and Pond, ASL-PI 17-148

On May 22, 1935, 900 Alaska-Juneau Gold Mine Company workers walked off the job to protest wages and working conditions.

Violence broke out after a new miners association, backed by the company, formed and marched to the A-J employment office on June 24.

Armed with clubs, tear gas and fire hoses, deputies soon had the situation under control – sending five people with serious head wounds to the hospital.

Although a grand jury indicted 33 miners, all were found not guilty.

The mine reopened July 5 with members of the new company-backed association. But one year later, the National Labor Relations Board ruled "the company had violated labor laws by fronting the association and ordered the company to recognize the union, rehire and pay back wages to 29 former strikers and give preferential treatment to another 100 strikers unemployed since the walkout," according to an article written by Cathy Brown about Juneau history at juneaualaska.com/history.

Right: Men crowded in front of the Alaska-Juneau Gold Mining Company offices, some wielding sticks, during a labor strike on June 24, 1935.

Alaska State Library, Winter and Pond, ASL-P117-147

Below: An injured man was carried to safety during the labor strike in Juneau in 1935.

Alaska State Library, Winter and Pond, ASL-P117-152

KETCHIKAN 1935 — *Alaska Sportsman* Born

Alaska State Library, Skinner Foundation, ASL-P44-01-011

Emery Tobin, who resided in Ketchikan – shown above in the 1930s – was a newsman.

In 1935, he and several others – including popular local artist Bill Gabler and well-known resident Ray Roady – formed a corporation to publish a magazine that focused on stories about hunting, fishing and adventure in Alaska, plus editorials that addressed Alaska's political challenges.

The magazine, called the *Alaska Sportsman*, soon found an audience nationwide.

There was a lapse between the first issue and the second, but from that time on, Alaska Magazine – the name changed when Tobin sold it in 1966 – has been published monthly.

NOME 1934 – Fire Destroys Downtown Businesses

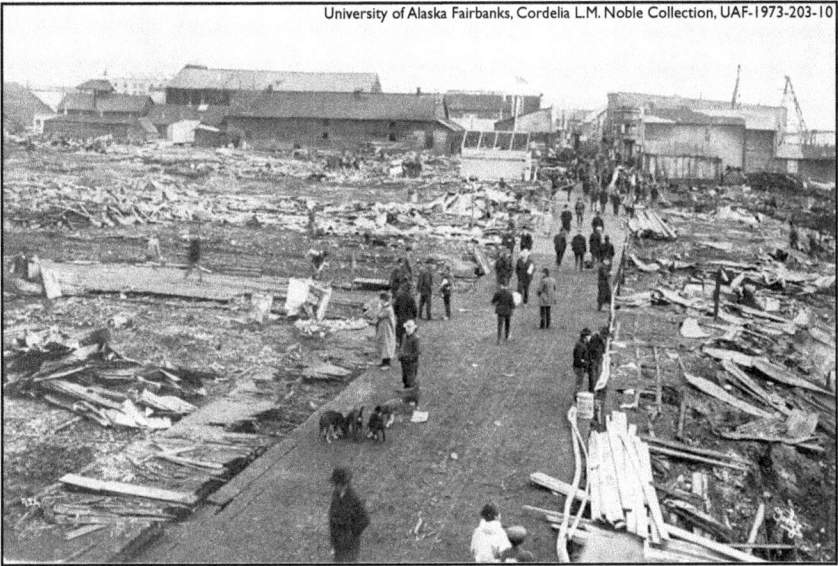

University of Alaska Fairbanks, Cordelia L.M. Noble Collection, UAF-1973-203-10

Above: Fire swept through Nome in 1934 and wiped out most of the downtown area – much like the fire that destroyed Nome's business district in 1905, shown here.

Below: Residents had rebuilt much of the downtown area by 1937.

University of Alaska Anchorage, Glenn H. Bowersox Collection, UAA-hmc-0731-154

PALMER 1936 – First Fair in the Valley

University of Alaska Anchorage, Almer J. Peterson, UAA-hmc-0413-series2-2-26a

Three 4-H Club boys showed off their horses at the first Palmer Fair in 1936. Held on school grounds, the event coincided with the opening of the Knik River Bridge, which linked Anchorage and the Valley by road for the first time.

SEWARD 1935 – Fire Swept Through Seward

Seward Community Library, Sylvia Sexton Collection, SCL-1-564

Residents battled a fire in downtown Seward in August 1935.

UGASHIK 1935 – Schooner Stalled on Sandbar

University of Alaska Anchorage, Glenn H. Bowersox, UAA-hmc-0731-136

The *Boxer* found itself high and dry on a sandbar near Ugashik Bay in 1935. A comment scribbled on the back of the photograph read: "The sand spit we were on was the only visible land for 10 miles around."

VALDEZ 1932 – Aviator Reeve Arrived in Alaska

University of Alaska Anchorage, Glenn H. Bowersox, UAA-hmc-0731-136

In January 1932, aviator Robert Reeve stowed away in the chain locker of a steamship and landed in Alaska with $2 in his pocket. Within a couple of years, he'd built this hangar in Valdez and was starting to make a name for himself in Alaska aviation

From the left are Al Palmenter, Robert "Bob" Reeve and Owen Meals. Reeve would eventually start Reeve Aleutian Airways.

Phyllis Downing Carlson, who arrived in Cordova, Alaska, in 1914 at the age of 5, lived and loved the history about which she wrote.

ABOUT THE AUTHORS

ABOUT THE AUTHORS

This book contains a collection of Alaska history stories written by my aunt, Phyllis Downing Carlson, as well as stories written by me that came from tidbits found among the notes and rare books I inherited when she died in 1993.

Born in 1909, Aunt Phil moved to Alaska in 1914 and lived the history so richly described in her work. She grew up in Cordova, where her father worked on building the railroad to the Kennecott copper mines; he then served as the conductor aboard the Copper River and Northwestern Railway. Phyllis graduated with a class of seven from Cordova High School in 1928, then studied journalism at the University of Washington and earned a teacher's certificate from Central College of Education in Ellensburg, Washington.

Aunt Phil landed her first job, which paid a whopping $150 a month, at Cooper Landing on the Kenai Peninsula. The new teacher kept the Yukon stove stoked in the little log schoolhouse and worked around cases of milk and staples stored for the winter.

After three years in the isolated community of 30, a widowed father of three of her pupils put an end to her single days. Carl Carlson moved her to the village of Tyonek, across Cook Inlet from Anchorage, and Phil again taught school in 1935 while Carl ran the village sawmill and served as postmaster.

The young bride met Tyonek Chief Simeon Chickalusion, who spoke English, Russian and his Native tongue. She later wrote an article, titled "The Tribe That Kept Its Head," about the chief and residents of Tyonek that ranked as one of the best articles submitted in a 1967 Writer's Digest contest. Years later, the village invited her back to a potlatch to share stories of the chief with the village young people.

The Carlsons moved to Anchorage in 1939, where Carl helped build Fort Richardson. The couple pitched a tent at Fifth Avenue and Denali Street and started framing a house over the tent. When they completed their home, they took down the tent and dragged it out the front door.

As a child, Alaska historian Phyllis Downing Carlson skipped down the dirt streets in Cordova, pictured here in 1919.

Phyllis Downing Carlson, who grew up in Cordova, taught school in the Native village of Tyonek in 1935. The village looked much like this photograph taken in 1898. She befriended Chief Simeon Chickalusion and was invited back to a potlatch when the village relocated after the village flooded during the 1960s.

ABOUT THE AUTHORS

After World War II, the couple moved to Cordova, where Aunt Phil honed her journalism skills. She produced her own radio show, "Woman to Woman," and conducted countless interviews that eventually led her to research Cordova's history through the local newspaper's archives.

"Oh, I had a wonderful time," she later recalled. "They had a real storehouse."

Her popular radio show led to the compilation of entertaining articles about Alaska, and for more than 40 years, Aunt Phil researched and wrote award-winning pieces as she moved about the state. Her stories appeared in a multitude of publications, including *Alaskana, Alaska Journal, Alaska Sportsman, The Anchorage Times* and *Our Alaska.*

She settled back in Anchorage from Kodiak after the Good Friday earthquake of 1964, and Phil spent so much time researching and talking with librarians at the Z.J. Loussac Public Library, they hired her. People said she didn't need to use the card catalog, because she knew the location of every volume.

"I don't remember faces," she said. "But I remember what I looked up for people."

The Alaska Press Women chose Aunt Phil for its Woman of Achievement Award in 1988. The organization cited her as an authority on Alaska history, recognized throughout the state by writers, researchers and politicians alike.

As a retiree, she served on a variety of boards, including the Anchorage Bicentennial Commission, Historical Landmarks Preservation Commission, State Historical Society and Alaska Press Women.

When she passed away in 1993, her treasured tales landed in my hands. As providence would have it, I, too, am a writer and lover of Alaska history. And since Aunt Phil was one of my favorite relatives, I feel privileged to perpetuate her work.

My Alaska roots stem from both sides of my family. My father, Richard Allie Downing – Aunt Phil's younger brother – was born in Cordova in 1916. Not only was his father a part of the railroad history there, but his grandfather, John Couch Downing, had witnessed the staking of gold claims around the area many years before when he sailed as the captain of the *Excelsior* and the *Portland*, both famous steamships that carried news of the riches found in the Klondike back to San Francisco and Seattle in July 1897.

My mother's grandfather, Robert Burns Mathison, arrived in Hope from Texas in 1898 and helped establish that little mining town. He pulled a small fortune out of Resurrection Creek and Chickaloon River and built a sawmill and mercantile. His son, Robert Lewis Mathison, married my grandmother, Inez Lee Brown, who traveled to the small community to work for her uncle, Charlie Shields, after being widowed in Kansas.

From that union came my mother, Hazel Isobel, and her identical twin, Hope Alisabeth, born at the Anchorage railroad hospital in 1920. The twins spent summers in Hope and winters in Seward, where they graduated high school in 1938.

My parents met at the University of Alaska Fairbanks, married in 1941, and settled in Fairbanks to raise their family. I was the fourth of their children born at old St. Joseph's Hospital, in 1951, following brothers Richard Ellsworth and Michael Woodrow and sister Meredith Lee.

I grew up between that gold-rush town and Juneau, where we moved after my father became the first commissioner of public works when Alaska became a state in 1959. That's where my younger sister, Deborah Lynn, was born in 1965 – shortly after my mother christened the *Taku*, the Alaska Marine Highway System's second ferry.

In 1973, I married and then spent 22 years in King Salmon with my fisheries biologist husband, Donald Bill. I worked for Bristol Bay Telephone Cooperative Inc. and raised two children, Kimberly and Ryan, and a foster daughter, Amie Morgan.

When the children graduated from Bristol Bay High School, and Don retired from the Alaska Department of Fish and Game, we moved to Anchorage. I went back to school in 1999, at the tender age of 48, and learned that I had a passion for writing. I earned a bachelor's degree in journalism in May 2003 from the University of Alaska Anchorage and have spent the past few years writing my own award-winning articles for various Alaska newspapers and magazines while working on this labor of love.

Condensed versions of articles found in *Aunt Phil's Trunk* appeared in *The Anchorage Chronicle*, a weekly newspaper published by Alaska Newspapers Inc., from July 2002 until the paper closed its doors on Dec. 31, 2004. The *Senior Voice*, a monthly Alaska newspaper, picked up the column in February 2005 and it continues to appear in that publication.

I truly hope you enjoy this volume packed with Aunt Phil's articles and other stories that came from research jotted down in piles of notebooks, countless lined tablets and in the margins of rare books.

– Laurel Downing Bill

Left, Robert L. Mathison, maternal grandfather of Laurel Downing Bill, and his brother, Charles, walk away from the Pacific Coast Trading Company and U.S. Mineral Surveyor and Assaying Office in Seward around 1906. The brothers, who mined with their father, Robert Burns Mathison, prospected around the gold-rush town of Hope.

Seward Community Library, SCL-1-798

BIBLIOGRAPHY

Adney, Tappan. The Klondike Stampede of 1897-1899. New York, NY: 1900.

Alexan, Nickafor. Recorded and transcribed history of Tyonek.

Alexander, H. The Mythology of All Races. New York, NY: 1964.

Allan, A.A. Gold, Men and Dogs. New York, NY: 1931.

Allen, Lt. Henry T. Report of an Expedition to the Copper, Tanana and Koyukuk Rivers in the Territory of Alaska in the Year 1885.

Ameigh, George C. Jr. and Yule M. Chaffin, Alaska's Kodiak Island. Author: 1962.

Andrews, Clarence L. The Story of Alaska. Caldwell, ID: Caxton Printers Ltd., 1947.

Archer, S.A. A Heroine of the North. London, England: 1929.

Atwood, Evangeline. Frontier Politics. The Western Historical Quarterly, April 1980.

Bagoy, John P. Legends & Legacies. John P. Bagoy: 2001

Bailey, Thomas A. Notes and Documents: The Russian Fleet Myth Re-examined. Mississippi Valley Historical Review, 1951.

Bancroft, Hubert Howe. The History of Alaska 1730-1885. San Francisco, CA: A.L. Bancroft & Company, 1886.

Barry, Mary J. A History of Mining on the Kenai Peninsula, Alaska. Anchorage, AK: MJP BARRY, 1997.

Beach, Rex. Personal Exposures. Harper & Brothers, New York, NY: 1940

Beach, Rex. The Iron Trail. Hard Press, 2006.

Becker, Ethel A. Klondike '98. Portland, OR: 1949.

Berton, Laura B. I Married the Klondike. Little Brown, 1954.

Berton, Pierre. Klondike. Toronto, Canada: McClelland & Stewart Ltd., 1962.

Berton, Pierre. The Klondike Fever. Alfred A. Knopf, New York, NY: 1969.

Blower, James. Gold Rush. American Heritage Press, 1971.

Brooks, Alfred. Blazing Alaska Trails. University of Alaska and Arctic Institute of America, 1953.

Carberry, Michael and Lane, Donna. Pattern of the Past. The
     Municipality of Anchorage, Community Planning Department: 1986.
Cashen, William. Founding of Fairbanks. University of Alaska
     Alumni, Summer, 1968.
Chaffin, Yule M. From Koniag to King Crab. Utah: Desert News Press,
     1967.
Chase, Will. Sourdough Pot. Kansas City, MO: 1923.
Chooutla Indian School. Northern Lights. Carcross, Yukon Territory,
     Canada: 1913.
Clifford, Howard. Rails North, the Railroads of Alaska and the Yukon.
     Superior Publishing Company, Seattle, WA: 1981
Coates, Ken, and Bill Morrison. The Sinking of the Princess Sophia:
Taking the North Down With Her. Fairbanks: University of Alaska
     Press, 1991.
Colby, Merle. A Guide to Alaska. New York, NY: MacMillian
     Company, 1954.
Couch, James S. Philately Below Zero. American Philatelic Society,
     State College, PA: 1853.
Crosby, Alfred W. America's Forgotten Pandemic. Cambridge
     University Press, NY: 1989.
Dall, William H. Alaska and Its Resources. Boston, MA: Lee and
     Shepard, 1870.
Davis, Mary Lee. Sourdough Gold. Boston, MA: 1933.
Dean, John W. Warren G. Harding. Times Books, NY: 2004
Delahaye, Tom. The Bilateral Effect of the Visit of the Russian Fleet in
     1863. Loyola University, New Orleans, LA: 1984.
Donaldson, Jordan and Edwin Pratt. Europe and the American Civil
     War. Boston, MA: Houghton Mifflin Company, 1931.
Drago, Harry Sinclair. The Great Range Wars: Violence on the
     Grasslands. University of Nebraska Press, 1985.
Farrar. Annexation of Russian America to the United States.
     Washington, DC: 1937.
Faulk, Odie B. Tombstone, Myth and Reality. New York, NY: 1972.
Fitch, Edwin M. The Alaska Railroad. New York, NY: Frederich A.
     Praeger Publishers, 1967.

Gideon, Kenneth. Wander Boy, Alaska 1913 to 1918. East Publishing Co., Fairfax, VA: 1967

Goddard. Indians of the Northwest Coast. New York, NY: 1945.

Golder, F. A. The Russian Fleet and the Civil War. American Historical Review, 1915

Griest, Henry W. Seventeen Years with the Eskimo, manuscript. University of Connecticut.

Griggs, Robert F. The Valley of Ten Thousand Smokes. Washington, DC: The National Geographic Society, 1935.

Hamilton, W.R. Yukon Story. Vancouver, Canada: Mitchell Press, 1964.

Harris, A.C. Alaska and the Klondike Goldfields. Chicago, IL: Monroe Book Company 1897.

Higginson, Ella. Alaska. New York, NY: MacMillan Company, 1908.

Hubbard, Father Bernard. Alaska Odyssey. Robert Hale Ltd., London, England: 1952

Hubbard, Father Bernard. Cradle of the Storms. Dodd Mead, New York, NY: 1935.

Huntington, James. On the Edge of Nowhere. Crown ublishers, 1966.

Ingersoll, Ernest. Gold Fields of the Klondike. New York, NY: 1897.

Janson, Lone. The Copper Spike. Alaska Northwest Books, 1975.

Kennedy, Kay. The Wien Brothers' Story. Wien Air Alaska. 1967.

Kitchener, L.D. Flag Over The North. Superior Publishing Company, 1954.

Kirk, R.C. Twelve Months in the Klondike. William Hernemann, 1899.

Kolata, Gina. The Story of the Great Influenza Pandemic of 1918 and the Search for the Virus That Caused It. Farrar, Straus and Giroux, NY: 1999.

Kushner, Howard L. The Russian Fleet and the American Civil War: Another View. Historian, 1972.

Laguna, Frederica de. Archaeology of Cook Inlet, Alaska. University of Pennsylvania Press, 1934.

Laserson, Max M. The American Impact on Russia: 1784-1917. New York, NY: Collier Books, 1950.

Lathrop, Thornton K. William Henry Seward. American Statesman Series.

Lawing, Nellie Neal. Alaska Nellie. Chieftain Press, Seattle, WA: 1940.

Leonard, John W. Gold Fields of the Klondike. Chicago, IL: A.N. Marquis and Company, 1897.

Lethcoe, Jim and Nancy. Valdez Gold Rush Trails of 1898-99. Todd Publications, 1997.

Lively, Brigitte. Matanuska Colony, Fifty Years. Matanuska Impressions Printing, Palmer, AK: 1985.

Lockley, Fred Alaska's First Free Mail Delivery in 1900.

Lung, Edward B. Black Sand and Gold. New York, NY: 1956.

Lung, Edward B. Trails to North Star Gold. Portland, OR: 1969.

Lunn, Arnold. Century of Mountaineering. George Allen and Unwin, Ltd. London, England: 1957.

MacDonald, Ian, and Betty O'Keefe. The Final Voyage of the Princess Sophia: Did They All Have to Die? Surrey: Heritage House Publishing Co.: 1998.

Marshall, Robert. Arctic Village. University of Alaska Press, 1991.

Mathews, Richard. The Yukon. New York, NY: Holt, Rinehart and Winston, 1958.

McLain, John Scudder. Alaska and the Yukon. New York, NY: McClure, Phillips and Company, 1905.

McMorris, Ian, Noyce, Wilfred, editors. World Atlas of Mountaineering. Thomas Nelson and Son, Ltd. London, England: 1969.

Michael, Henry. Lieutenant Zagoskin's Travels in Russian America, 1842-1844.

Miller, Orlando W. The Frontier in Alaska and the Matanuska Colony. Yale University Press, New Haven, CT: 1975.

Morgan, Lael. Good Time Girls. Seattle, WA: Epicenter Press Inc., 1998.

Morgan, Murray. One Man's Gold Rush. Seattle, WA: 1967.

Naske, Claus M. and Rowinski, Ludwig J. Anchorage, A Pictorial History. Donning Company, Norfolk, VA: 1981

Naske, Claus M. and Slotnick, Herman E. Alaska, A History of the 49th State. Grand Rapids, MI: William E. Eerdmans Publishing Company, 1979.

O'Conner, Richard. High Jinks on the Klondike. New York, NY: Bobbs-Merrill Company, New York, NY: 1954.

Ogilvie, William. Early Days on the Yukon. New York, NY: John Lane Company, 1913.

Osgood, Cornelius. Contributions to the Ethnography of the Kutchin. New Haven, CT: 1936.

Osgood, Cornelius. Ethnology of the Tanaina. New Haven, CT: Yale University Press, 1937.

Osgood, Cornelius. Ingalik Mental Culture. New Haven, CT: Yale University, Press, 1959.

Oswalt, M. Alaskan Eskimos. San Francisco, CA: 1967.

Page, Dorothy. Polar Pilot-The Carl Ben Eielson Story. Vero Media Inc., Moorhead, MN: 1992.

Pearson, Grant. My Life of High Adventure. Englewood Cliffs, NJ: Prentice-Hall, 1962.

Petroff, Ivan. 10th Census Report, 1880. Washington, DC.

Petroff, Ivan. Report on the Population, Industries, and Resources of Alaska. Washington, DC: U.S. Printing Office, 1884.

Pierce, Richard A. Russian America: A Biographical Dictionary. Fairbanks, AK: The Limestone Press, 1990.

Pilgrim Shaw, Mariette. Alaska, Its History, Resources, Geography, and Government. Caldwell, ID: Caxton Printers, 1939.

Remington, Charles H. A Golden Cross on the Trails from the Valdez Glacier.

Richard, T.A. Through the Yukon and Alaska. San Francisco, CA: 1909.

Roppel, Pat. An Historical Guide to Revillagigedo and Gravina Islands, 1995.

Salisbury, Gay and Laney. The Cruelest Miles. W.W. Norton & Company, NY: 2003.

Schaller, George B. When the Earth Exploded. Alaska Book, Ferguson Press, Chicago, IL: 1960.

Seton-Karr. Shores and Alps of Alaska. Samson Low, Marston, Seane and Rivington. London, England: 1887.

Service, Robert W. Harper of Heaven. Dodd, Mead, 1948.

Service, Robert W. Ploughman of the Moon. Dodd, Mead, 1945.

Seton-Watson, Hugh. The Russian Empire: 1801-1917. Oxford: The Clarendon Press, 1967.

Seward, Frederick W. Reminiscences of a War-time Statesman, Seward at Washington as Senator and Secretary of War, and William H. Seward, an Autobiography ... Selections from Letters.

Sherwonit, Bill. To the Top of Denali: Climbing Adventures on North America's Highest Peak.

Sherwood, Morgan. Alaska and Its History. Seattle, WA: University of Washington Press, 1967.

Sherwood, Morgan. Exploration of Alaska, 1865-1900. New Haven, CT: Yale University Press, 1965.

Sinclair Drago, Harry. "The Great Range Wars: Violence on the Grasslands." University of Nebraska Press, 1985.

Sovereign, A.H. In Journeyings Often.

Spencer, R. North Alaskan Eskimo. Washington, DC: Smithsonian Press, 1969.

Stauter, J.J. Genius of Seward. Chicago, IL: J.G. Ferguson Company, 1960.

Stevens, Robert W. Alaskan Aviation History, Volume 1 and 2. Polynyas Press, Des Moines, WA: 1990.

Stone, Kirk H. The Matanuska Valley Colony,. U.S. Department of the Interior, Bureau of Land Management, Washington, D.C.: 1950.

Stuck, Hudson. Episcopal Missions in Alaska. New York, NY: Domestic and Foreign Missionary Society, 1920.

Stuck, Hudson. The Ascent of Denali. Brompton Book Corp., 1989.

Stuck, Hudson. Voyages on the Yukon and its Tributaries. 1917.

Stumer, Harold M. This was Klondike Fever. Seattle, WA: Superior Publishing Company, 1978.

Swineford, Alfred P. Report of the Governor of Alaska. Sitka: 1886.

Tollemache, Hon. Stratford. Reminiscences of the Yukon. Toronto, Canada: 1912.

Tower, Elizabeth. Anchorage. Epicenter Press Inc., Canada: 1999

Underhill, R. Red Man's Religion. Chicago, IL: 1965.

Ungermann, Kenneth A. The Race to Nome. Harper & Row, NY: 1963.

U.S. Department of the Interior, Alaska Resources Library, Seventeen Years with the Eskimo manuscript, Henry W. Griest

U.S. Department of the Interior, Bureau of Land Management. Iditarod Gold Rush Trail Seward-Nome.

U.S. Revenue Cutter Service. Report of the Operations of the U.S. Revenue Steamer Nunivak on the Yukon River Station, Alaska, 1899-1901.

U.S. War Department Adjutant Office. Reports of Exploration in Territory of Alaska. Washington, DC: 1899.

Valdez Museum and Historical Archive

Walden, Arthur T. A Dog Puncher on the Yukon. Boston, MA: 1928.

Waters, Frank. The Earp Brothers of Tombstone. New York, NY: 1960.

Wickersham, Hon. James. Old Yukon. Washington, DC: Washington Law Book Company, 1938.

Wickersham, James. Personal diaries. Alaska State Library.

Williams, Gerald O. 50 Years of History. Alaska State Troopers, 1991.

Williams, Howell. Landscapes of Alaska. University of California Press, 1958.

Williams, William. Mountain Climbing. Climbing Mt. St. Elias; Karr, Mark, Mt. St. Elias and Its Glaciers. Charles Schibners & Son, 1897.

Winslow, Kathryn. Big Pan-Out. New York, NY: 1951.

Wold, Jo Anne. Fairbanks The $200 Million Gold Rush Town. Wold Press, 1971.

Woldman, Albert A. Lincoln and the Russians. Cleveland, OH: The World Publishing Company, 1952.

Whymper, Frederick. Travels and Adventures in the Territory of Alaska. London, England: 1868.

Periodicals and Newspapers

Alaska, May 1971
Alaska Call, May 1959
Alaska Call, March 1960
Alaska Life, July 1941
Alaska Life, March 1943
Alaska Life, August 1944
Alaska Life, November 1945
Alaska Life, February 1946
Alaska Life, April 1946
Alaska Life, January 1947
Alaska Living, October 1968
Alaska Review, Fall 1965
Alaska Sportsman, February 1936
Alaska Sportsman, July 1937
Alaska Sportsman, May 1938
Alaska Sportsman, October 1939
Alaska Sportsman, May 1942
Alaska Sportsman, May 1951
Alaska Sportsman, January 1953
Alaska Sportsman, January 1956
Alaska Sportsman, December 1958
Alaska Sportsman, February 1959
Alaska Sportsman, April 1963
Alaska Sportsman, July 1963
Alaska Sportsman, October 1965
Alaska Yukon Magazine, 1909
American Heritage, December 1960
Anchorage Daily Times Feb. 3, 1921
Anchorage Daily Times April 4, 1923
Anchorage Daily Times May 27, 1923
Anchorage Daily Times, July 2, 1964
Anchorage Daily Times, July 29, 1964
Anchorage Daily Times, August 5, 1965
Anchorage Daily Times, June 15, 1967
Cook Inlet Pioneer June 1915
Cook Inlet Pioneer July 12, 1915
Cook Inlet Pioneer September 1915
Dawson Daily News, October 26, 1918
Fairbanks Daily News Miner, May 9, 1903
Fairbanks Daily News Miner July 1923

Island Times, January 1971
Journal of the West, Vol. 5, 1966
Heritage of Alaska (The Flying North)
Juneau Daily Empire, April 13, 1917
Ketchikan's Stories in the News, July 2003
Klondike News, April 1898
Kodiak Daily Mirror, June 1971
Los Angeles Times, May 1, 1900
National Geographic, February 1948
National Geographic, June 1963
New York Sun, 1896
Nome News, various
Orphanage Newsletter (Wood Island), 1905
Pacific Northern Quarterly, January 1968
Pathfinder, September 1920
Pathfinder, October 1922
The Cordova Times, May 3, 1926
The Cordova Times, May 7, 1926
The Cordova Times, May 10, 1926
The New York Times Magazine, January 1930
The Northern Light, December 2007
The San Francisco Coast Seamen's Journal, February 21, 1894
True West, December 1972
Tundra Times, June 17, 1963
Seward Daily Gateway, 1906
The Seward Weekly Gateway, 1915
Sitka Alaskan, 1890
Yukon Press, March 17, 1899

Personal Communication
Bruce D. Merrell, Alaska bibliographer, ZJ Loussac Public Library
John P. Bagoy, Anchorage historian

Journals
Library and Archives Canada. Department of Marine Fonds. RG 42. Series B-4. Volume 355.
Library and Archives Canada. Government of Canada. Sessional Papers, 21-24, Volume LVI, No. 7, 1920.

Web sites
www.ankn.uaf.edu
Alaska History and Cultural Studies
Public Broadcasting System
The Frederick A. Cook Society at www.cookpolar.org
U.S. Postal Museum at www.postalmuseum.si.edu/gold

INDEX

automobile, 120–129, 130–131

aviation, 187–249. see also pilots

streetcar, 136–139

Troy, John Weir, 282–287

U

Ugashik Bay, 313

United States purchase of Alaska, 14

University of Alaska, 286–287

V

Valdez-Fairbanks Trail, 120–129

W

Wickersham, Judge James, 24, 33

Wien, Noel, 197, 233–239

Wien, Ralph, 237–239

Wilson, President Woodrow, 24–25, 32–33, 60, 83

World War I, 60, 64–66

PREVIEW OTHER VOLUMES
AUNT PHIL'S TRUNK

PREVIEW OF VOLUME ONE

Aunt Phil's Trunk Volume One, released in 2006, features the early days in Alaska's past when Native people settled the land, Russians explored and exploited the fur trade and prospectors flooded into the country in search of gold.

Alaska State Library, Place File, ASL-P01-4184

Rock carvings dot landscape

Alaska's petroglyphs, Greek for rock carving, are among many enigmas of science. Because their true meanings are elusive, they remain a mysterious link to a people who inhabited Alaska a long time ago.

Massacre at Nulato

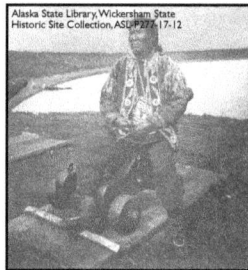
Alaska State Library, Wickersham State Historic Site Collection, ASL-P277-17-12

Russians had traded peacefully with the Natives of Nulato, but one day in 1851 that all changed when the Koyukon Indians came to town. Red Shirt, seen here, may have led the raid.

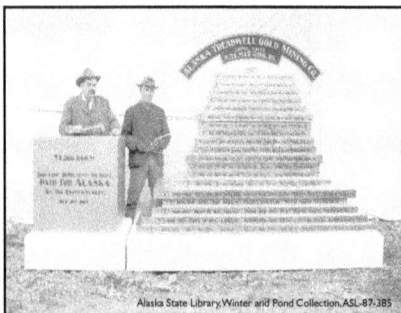
Alaska State Library, Winter and Pond Collection, ASL-87-385

Gold found near Juneau

The stack on the right shows around $22 million in gold dug out near Juneau between 1885-1904. The cube on the left represents what America paid Russia for Alaska in 1867, $7.2 million.

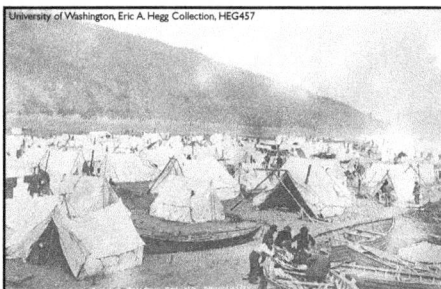

University of Washington, Eric A. Hegg Collection, HEG457

Tent cities sprout up

Following discoveries of gold in the Klondike region, tent cities, such as Dawson seen here, sprang up on the boggy flats in the wilderness.

Gold seekers head north

Thousands of prospectors streamed north and climbed the Chilkoot Trail, seen here, in the hopes of reaching their fortunes of gold.

University off Washington, Alaska and Western Canada Collection, AWC442

Flame of the Yukon

Kathleen Eloisa Rockwell, also known as Klondike Kate, whirled her way across dancehall stages in the Yukon, delighting her audiences with her moves and fancy costumes. She and other dancehall beauties helped lonely miners cope in the wilderness.

University of Alaska Fairbanks, Barrett Willoughby Collection, UAF-1972-116-335

Nuggets in Nome

By July 1, 1900, Nome was a busy frontier town with a population of around 20,000. It also boasted more than 60 saloons, dozens of criminals, a few hundred prostitutes and dishonest officials.

University of Washington, Eric A. Hegg Collection, HEG270

University of Washington, Alaska Western Canada Collection, AWC1134

Alaska Natives and the rush for gold

Some Alaska Natives saw opportunity in the rush for gold, as in this photo of Metlakatla Indians transporting gear, food and tools for pay.

Anchorage Museum of History and Art, Ickes Collection, AMRC-b75-175-158

Richest Native woman

While the various gold rushes to Alaska did not overwhelmingly benefit most Natives, one baby girl born in 1865 would become the richest Native woman in the North and grow famous because of reindeer. Known as Reindeer Mary, she is seen here sitting next to a corral fence where she kept her reindeer in 1938 near Unalakleet.

PREVIEW OF VOLUME TWO

Aunt Phil's Trunk Volume Two, released in 2007, features entertaining stories that include the birth of Fairbanks, the lawless years following the Klondike Gold Rush and how the Iditarod Trail was blazed. This volume, also filled with more than 350 historical photographs that showcase life in Alaska from 1900 to 1912, will keep you spellbound!

University of Washington, Alaska Western Canada Collection, AWC I 134

Fairbanks springs up on the tundra

After Felix Pedro discovered gold in the Interior in 1902, hordes of prospectors rushed into Alaska's interior. One savvy merchant, who set up his trading store along the banks of the Chena River, helped put the town of Fairbanks – pictured above – on the map.

And all the gold that came out of the region was just too tempting for outlaws to resist. One in particular, the Blue Parka bandit, proved daring and bold – until he robbed an Episcopal preacher!

Aunt Phil File photo

Alaska's first law officer

Alaska's first law officer in the Interior knew a thing or two about the criminal element. Frank Canton, appointed deputy marshal for Circle in February 1898, had served with distinction as a peace officer in Wyoming and Oklahoma Territory. He'd also escaped from prison while serving time for a litany of offenses, including murder.

Tombstone temporarily transplanted in Alaska

NOAA photo

Many of those hardy gunslingers and prospectors who made Tombstone a household word in the late 1800s, landed in Alaska and the Yukon after the demise of the Arizona city. Among them were lawman and gunslinger Wyatt Earp, pictured on the left, and John Clum, right, who set up Alaska's postal system in the late 1890s.

NOAA photo

Gold discovered in the Iditarod region

Anchorage Museum at Rasmuson Center, John Urban Collection, AMRC-b64-1-171

On Christmas Day 1908, two men discovered gold along the Haiditarod River, a tributary of the Innoko. Soon a new settlement called Iditarod became the largest town in Alaska, boasting more than 4,000 people and sporting newspapers, hotels, electricity and telephone service. Soon teams of men and dogs had blazed a trail from Seward to Nome to haul gold and supplies.

University of Alaska Fairbanks Museum Classification UA91-017-001

Cordova's Sourdough preacher painter

Paul Eustace Ziegler's work aptly captures the epic struggle of sourdough days, portraying that historic period when pioneer men and women conquered a rugged wilderness and opened the Alaska Frontier.

Massive volcanic eruption 1912

June 6, 1912, the earth exploded. People living within several hundred miles in Southwest Alaska were given a taste of what hellfire and brimstone of Biblical teachings might be like when a volcano erupted.

University of Alaska Fairbanks, Amelia Elkinton Collection, UAF-1974-175-399

PREVIEW OF VOLUME FOUR

Aunt Phil's Trunk Volume Four, released in 2009, shares the highs and lows during the World War II years in Alaska's history. Follow the GIs north as they build the Alaska-Canada Highway, drive the Japanese from the Aleutian Chain and turn Anchorage into a metropolis. This volume also shines a spotlight on the Cold War, the Natives' struggle for equality and the march toward statehood. Just as with Volumes two and three, this book has more than 350 historical photographs that complement the entertaining stories from 1935 to 1960.

University of Alaska Fairbanks, Kay J. Kennedy Aviation Collection, UAF-1991-98-851

Secret mission with Russia

America and the Soviet Union had a secret pact during World War II. Soviet pilots landed at Ladd Field in Fairbanks on Sept. 24, 1942, to begin training for their missions between Alaska and Russia.

Alcan Highway built in record time

Thousands of GIs with the U.S. Army Corp of Engineers, along with more than 6,000 civilians, laid 1,400 miles of primitive road through the wilderness of Canada and Alaska in record time. Built in less than nine months, the rough trail and its 133 bridges were a great accomplishment, especially considering the extreme temperatures and conditions.

Alaska State Library, Alaska Highway Construction, ASL-P193-044

Japanese bomb Aleutians

Dutch Harbor families awoke early on June 3, 1942, unaware that their world was about to explode. But soon the drone of Japanese Zeros cracked the silence of the dawn. By 5:45 a.m., more than a dozen bombers and fighters were screaming over their town.

Alaska State Library, Aleutian/Pribilof Project Collection, ASL-P233-v150

Japanese ousted from Attu

On May 11, 1943, U.S. troops headed for Attu Island in the military's first-ever amphibious landing. A campaign that was expected to last a few days, stretched into weeks, and it wasn't until May 29 that the American pincers finally closed. Before the battle was over, there would be 549 American and 2,351 Japanese dead.

PREVIEW OF VOLUME FIVE

Aunt Phil's Trunk Volume Five is scheduled to be released between 2014-2015. The final book in the *Aunt Phil's Trunk* series will take readers on a journey through the headlines of Alaska's history between 1960 and 2000, including the Good Friday earthquake of 1964, the construction of the Trans-Alaska Oil Pipeline and historic government decisions that profoundly impacted Alaska's Native people.

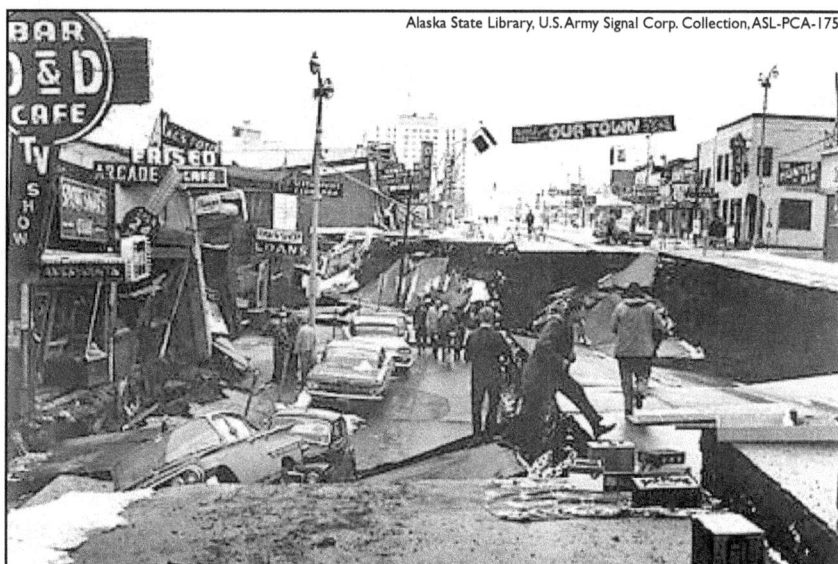

Alaska State Library, U.S. Army Signal Corp. Collection, ASL-PCA-175

Earthquake!

The Great Alaska Earthquake struck on Good Friday, March 27, 1964, at 5:36 p.m. It registered 8.6 on the Richter Scale, although scientists now favor a different magnitude scale for large quakes that shows it as 9.2. It devastated much of Alaska, including downtown Anchorage.

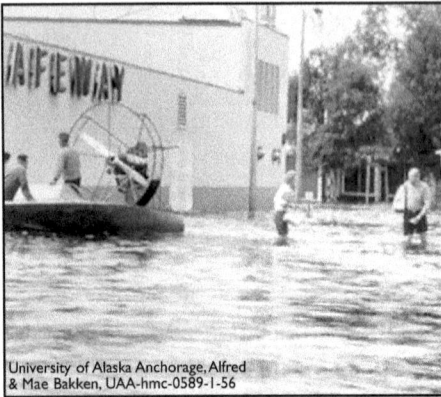
University of Alaska Anchorage, Alfred & Mae Bakken, UAA-hmc-0589-1-56

Flood!

Water spilled over the banks of the Chena River and rushed into downtown Fairbanks on Aug. 20, 1967. Flood waters filled the city's streets, submerged cars and sent debris throughout the area.

Oil Discovered!

Following a massive oil discovery on Alaska's North Slope in the late 1960s, Trans-Alaska Oil Pipeline workers began laying 800 miles of pipe in March 1975. The $8 billion project crossed three mountain ranges and 800 waterways.

Alaska State Library, Trans-Alaska Pipeline Construction, ASL-P002-6-14

Courtesy of NOAA

Serial Killers and Mass Murderers!

Citizens across Alaska were stunned when six mass murderers wielded their deadly will in less than five years. By 1984, residents were wondering if a sense of safety and peace would ever return to the Last Frontier..

School Curriculum Now Available

More books from
Aunt Phil's Trunk!

Aunt Phil's Trunk of Trivia $9.95

If you love Alaska trivia and you love solving easy to medium puzzles of all kinds from word searches to crosswords to sudokus, then these books are for you. While you challenge your mind, you'll expand your knowledge of Alaska history because each puzzle involves a bit of Alaska lore.

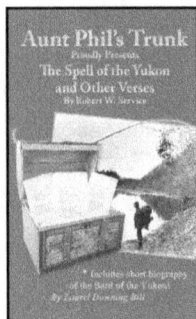

The Spell of the Yukon $14.95

This recreation of Robert Service's first published works (in 1907) is sure to please any Alaska history buff. It includes classics like "The Shooting of Dan McGrew" and "The Cremation of Sam McGee," along with a short biography about the bard, who was known as the Voice of the Yukon.

*** Curriculum Available! ***

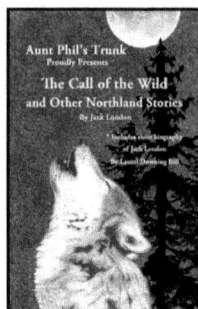

The Call of the Wild $19.95
and Other Northland Stories

Written after Jack London returned from the Klondike, this tale of adventure in the frigid north introduced the rest of the world to Alaska in the early 1900s. Several more stories that London wrote about the northland also are included in this collection. Alaska Author Laurel Downing Bill wrote a short biography about London in the back of the book.

*** Curriculum Available! ***

Sourdough Cookery $14.95

More than 100 heart-healthy recipes, including mouth-watering cakes, cookies, breads and more. And if you order through www.auntphilstrunk.com, you will receive a FREE packet of sourdough starter from the 1896 gold fields of Hope, Alaska!

Alaska Children's Books

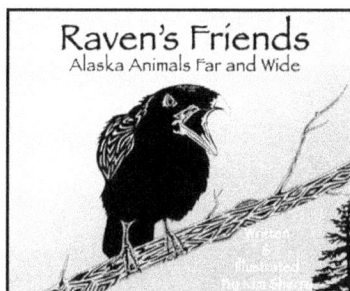

Raven's Friends $9.95
Alaska Animals Far and Wide

Raven's Friends, Alaska Animals Far and Wide, released June 2012, is written and illustrated by Kim Sherry. Children ages 3-8 will love this book as they follow its narrator, Raven, through 32 pages filled with colorful illustrations and poems that share facts about animals that call Alaska home.

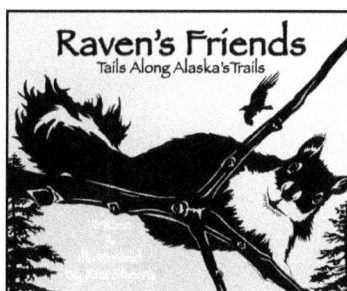

Raven's Friends $9.95
Tails Along Alaska Trails

Raven's Friends, Tails Along Alaska Trails, released June 2013, is written and illustrated by Kim Sherry. Children ages 3-8 will love this book as they learn new things about animals that travel along Alaska trails. These 32 pages are filled with colorful illustrations and poems.

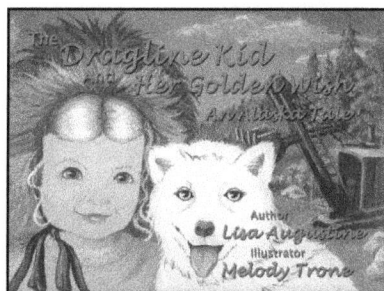

The Dragline Kid $9.95

The Dragline Kid and Her Golden Wish, released July 2014, is written by Alaska author Lisa Augustine and illustrated by artist Melody Trone. Children ages 3-8 will delight in this story of a little girl who dreams of finding a gold nugget in Alaska's wilderness.

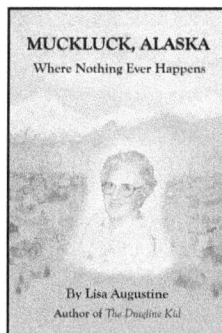

Muckluck, Alaska $14.95

From Grannie Annie, to Olav the town marshal, to Mrs. Eversall and her cow "Bossy," these pages are filled to the brim with humorous and poignant fictional stories set in 1930-1940s Alaska.

NEW in 2018!

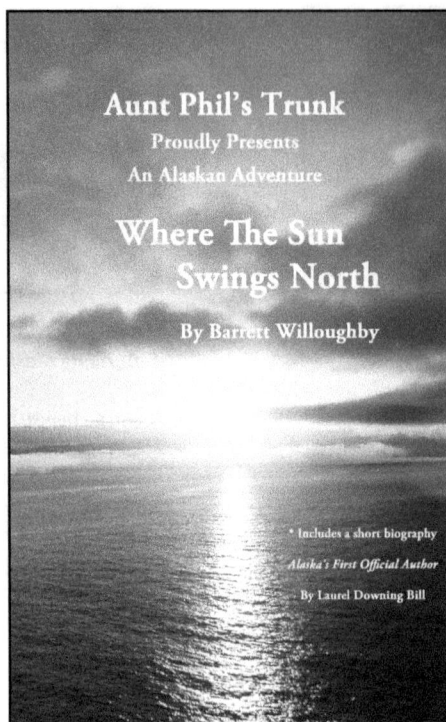

Aunt Phil's Trunk
Proudly Presents
An Alaskan Adventure

Where The Sun
Swings North

By Barrett Willoughby

* Includes a short biography
Alaska's First Official Author

By Laurel Downing Bill

$19.95

Published in 1922, Where The Sun Swings North is the first novel written by Florence Barrett Willoughby, who many call Alaska's first official author.

This tale of adventure is a fictionalized account of her family's real-life experience when stranded on Middleton Island in the Gulf of Alaska for 10 months in 1896-1897 when Willoughby was 10 years old. They may have had few provisions, but they had an intense will to live.

The cast of characters in this story includes a heroine and her Irish husband, a younger lady pure of heart, a drunkard and a diabolical trader who wants the Irishman's wife for his own. Add to this group the elements of Alaska's wild land and unpredictable weather and you've got a tale of adventure you won't soon forget.

***** Includes short biography of Barrett Willoughby
compiled by Alaska author Laurel Downing Bill *****

www.ingramcontent.com/pod-product-compliance
Lightning Source LLC
Chambersburg PA
CBHW060243100426
42742CB00011B/1624